The Way We Really Are

Also by Stephanie Coontz

The Way We Never Were: American Families and the Nostalgia Trap

The Social Origins of Private Life:
A History of American Families, 1600–1900

The
Way
We
Really
Are

Coming to Terms with America's Changing Families

Stephanie Coontz

BasicBooks

A Division of HarperCollins*Publishers*

Published by BasicBooks,
A Division of HarperCollins Publishers, Inc.

Designed by Elliott Beard

Library of Congress Cataloging-in-Publication Data

Coontz, Stephanie.
    The way we really are : coming to terms with America's changing
families / by Stephanie Coontz.
      p. ˙cm.
    Includes bibliographical references and index.
    ISBN 0-465-07787-0
    1. Family—United States.   2. United States—Social
conditions—1980– . I. Title.
HQ535.C644   1997
306.85'0973—dc21   96-45068
                                                              CIP

97 98 99 00 ◆/RRD 9 8 7 6 5 4 3 2 1

Contents

The Way We Really Are

Introduction

Five years ago I wrote a book called *The Way We Never Were: American Families and the Nostalgia Trap*. As a family historian bothered by widespread misconceptions in the popular press about "traditional" families, I hoped to get people to look more realistically at the strengths, weaknesses, and surprising variability of family life in the past.

My book went to press just as Dan Quayle issued his famous condemnation of Murphy Brown, the fictional television character who decided to bear her child out of wedlock. The ensuing polemics over whether Murphy Brown was setting a bad example for our nation's youth were followed by an all-out war over family values as the 1992 election approached. Since much of the discussion focused on the contrast between today's families and "the way things used to be," I began to get calls from congressional committees, reporters, and television producers asking me for a historical perspective on these issues. Soon I found myself in the thick of a national debate over what was happening to the American family.

Getting dragged into this debate was a heady but humbling experience. For about four months, I averaged three radio talk shows a day, as well as several television appearances a month. I was quoted by *Newsweek* and misquoted by the *National Enquirer*. As new issues came up, such as controversies over "fatherlessness" in 1993 and 1994 and proposals to repeal no-fault divorce in 1995 and 1996, I appeared on *Oprah, Crossfire, CNN Talkback Live,* and other national television shows. I also went on an extensive lecture tour, where I had the opportunity to meet people from every type of background who were struggling with today's family issues.

It was an extraordinary learning experience. I worked my way through eighteen-page handwritten letters and struggled to learn e-mail so I could answer more time-pressed souls who sent me instantaneous feedback after television interviews. I also had the opportunity for additional dialogue in PTA forums, high school classes, church seminars, and drug and alcohol

1

rehabilitation workshops across the country. At conferences on early child-hood education I heard the experiences of child care workers and the parents who use their services. Attorneys and judges who deal with divorce, mediation, and custody explained the dilemmas they face in their work. Displaced union workers, mostly male, talked about their economic and personal struggles. Displaced homemakers, all female, told me about their lives. People shared their family stories with me and raised heartfelt anxieties or perceptive questions that pushed my research in new directions and refocused my thinking.

This book comes directly out of such exchanges. It addresses the questions I have been asked by people from all kinds of families, both "traditional" and "new," about how their own families are changing, how to understand the very different experiences their neighbors may be going through, and what to make of the contradictory proclamations they hear from political pundits. Writing this book has given me a chance to translate into accessible terms some of the helpful new research on family forms, functions, and trends that has emerged in scholarly journals since 1992. But it has also forced me to respond to a more challenging task set me by many of my readers and audiences. For people consistently tell me that, although they may enjoy hearing what is fact and what is fiction in American family history, they also want to know what history and sociology have to teach them, not just about where we've been *before* or where we've *never* been, but about where to go from here.

In my last book, I demonstrated the tremendous variety of family types that have worked—and not worked—in American history. When families succeeded, it was often for reasons quite different than stereotypes about the past suggest—because they were flexible in their living arrangements, for example, or could call on people and institutions beyond the family for assistance or support. And when families failed, the results were often devastating. There never was a golden age of family life, a time when all families were capable of meeting the needs of their members and protecting them from poverty, violence, or sexual exploitation.

The "traditional" sexual double standard, for example, may have led more middle-class girls to delay sex at the end of the nineteenth century than today, but it also created higher proportions of young female prostitutes. Respect for elders may have received more lip service in the past, but elders were until very recently the segment of the population most likely to be destitute.[1]

Yet knowing there was no golden age in history does not satisfy most people. Okay, they say, so the past wasn't great, and people have been lamenting the "breakdown of the family" or the "crisis of modern youth" since colonial days. It may be entertaining to know that John Watson, the most famous child psychiatrist of the early twentieth century, predicted in 1928 that marriage would be dead by 1977, and that in 1977, noted sociologist Amitai Etzioni announced that "by mid-1990 not one American family will be left."[2] But even a stopped clock is right twice a day. What if these fears are finally coming true? Am I claiming that the more things change, the more they remain the same? Do I think people are crazy to feel anxious about recent trends in family life?

"Perhaps it's good to have our illusions about the past shattered," people often say, "but once we reject the lies and the myths, what do we put in their place?" Are the only lessons from history negative? Isn't there anything positive families can learn from history and sociology?

These are the questions that drove me to write this book. I believe that history and social science do have concrete applications and positive lessons for people who are concerned about what is happening to today's families. In fact, I think that learning history can be as useful to people in sorting through many family issues as undergoing counseling, and a lot *more* useful than trying to apply today's political rhetoric to the problems of daily life.

This book is for the wide range of families and individuals in America who are worried about what is happening with family life but don't think there are easy answers that can be applied to every situation. I hope the information I provide will be useful not just for "new" families—single parents, stepfamilies, and dual-earner couples—but also for those who have tried, often at considerable sacrifice, to maintain a male breadwinner family where the wife cuts back on paid employment during the child-raising years. I write as well to people who live in single-person or nonfamily households but understand that, however the census labels them, they remain family members—daughters, sons, aunts, uncles, cousins, siblings, or grandparents—and that their family commitments are not wiped out by their lack of coresidence.

Most discussions of family issues assume too sharp and permanent a division between different family forms. Too little attention has been paid to the links between "traditional" and "nontraditional" families, the fluidity of those categories, and the many transitions people make in their lives, as they or their relatives move through several different types of families and households. I hope this book will help people to understand the shifting interactions within and among families, as well as to realistically consider what changes they might face in their own family lives and how they can best handle those changes.

Because so much of this book comes out of discussions I have had over the past few years, I often reproduce a conversation I had at a public meeting, quote letters I have received or remarks recorded on talk shows, or share with you some of the stories I have been told and experiences I have had. But I do not generalize from such personal anecdotes and quotes without other evidence. As helpful as interviews with families and focus groups can be, their stories do not necessarily represent anything more than the experience of a certain individual or a particular group.

All such experiences, whether typical or not, are important to consider. But I use people's personal stories only when they illustrate broader trends or typical patterns that I can demonstrate with historical and statistical evidence. My notes allow you to check the evidence for my claims and see whether the cases I discuss accord with research on general trends, either for the nation as a whole or for any particular segment of the population.

I offer this book now because the oversimplified debate that emerged during the 1992 election campaign has turned over the past few years into an equally oversimplified consensus—all without ever actually touching the solid ground of people's daily lives. The evolution of an artificial debate into an equally artificial consensus tells us more about the career moves of politicians and self-appointed family experts than it does about what Americans have truly been thinking and doing about family life. It is time to get beyond the rhetoric and the sound bites to see what has actually been happening.

When the family values debate first emerged in 1992, one group said flatly, "it's the economy," ignoring the moral and spiritual uneasiness felt by many Americans who were not in financial distress. Another group answered equally positively, "it's moral breakdown," dismissing the effects of job insecurity, poverty, community decay, or the lack of support systems for dual-earner families. The first group accused opponents of "blaming the victim"; the second said people who didn't agree with them were afraid to demand "personal responsibility." "Value diversity," urged the first school of thought. "Reaffirm bedrock values" implored the other. No one explained what these slogans meant in real situations, with real people. Yet that is exactly what people were crying out to hear.

Also lacking in the debate was a serious discussion of the *links* between economic and moral issues in families, communities, and work settings. While most Americans rejected moralistic invective against single mothers and working women, they did not want their serious concerns about family change to be ignored. Their desire for a more balanced appraisal of the problems facing families showed up in the way poll results shifted from day to day, often varying according to the pollsters' choice of a single word or phrase. Even individuals who agreed with a particular side's code phrase tended to modify it out of all recognition when it came to dealing with the messy complications of special circumstances and individual differences.[3]

As well they should. It is not inconsistent to take account of *context*. It is actually a far more sophisticated way of thinking than that of ideologues who try to squash all our complicated interpersonal arrangements and family situations into oversimplified "trends" that can be summed up in catchphrases.

For a short time during the 1992 election, it looked as if politicians would have to respond to people's desire to get beyond the slogans. But the opportunity for more in-depth discussion was lost around the time of the Republican National Convention that summer, when a radical right-wing section of the party grabbed the spotlight, alienating millions of Americans with slurs against single parents, "careerist" mothers, and nontraditional families. Faced with the extremism of people such as Pat Robertson, who accused feminists of leading "a socialist, anti-family political movement that encourages women to leave their husbands, kill their children, practice witchcraft, destroy capitalism, and become lesbians," many voters felt compelled to repudiate this misuse of their anxiety about family change. Coming into the homestretch of the campaign, 95 percent of voters told pollsters that family forms and values were not the main problems facing America. Feeling the need to choose between slogans, a majority went with the Clinton team's insistence that "it's the economy, stupid."[4]

Clinton won the presidency in 1992 because he promised to respond to people's concerns about the decay of our communities, the loss of stable jobs offering decent benefits, the fall in real wages and rise in work hours of most families, and the declining educational prospects for youth. That did not mean the people who voted for him were unconcerned with moral or ethical issues: The economy itself was a moral issue for most families, raising hard questions about the meaning of long-term commitments (for companies as well as individuals) in a free market society and about the impact of too much choice in leisure decisions, too little choice in work ones.

But once in office Democrats quickly retreated from economic issues that raised larger moral questions, such as what we want our urban centers to be like in the twenty-first century, how we might build coherent communities in the suburbs, what our goals should be for government investment and tax subsidies, and how job structures or work policies could be reorganized to make them compatible with family life. Meanwhile, Republicans moderated their family values rhetoric. The way was paved for politicians to revive the family values issue as a *substitute* for the economy issue rather than as an integral part of it.

Within months of the 1992 presidential election, both liberal and conservative commentators were proclaiming a new "bipartisan consensus" that "Dan Quayle was right." New think tanks were formed and old ones reorganized to proclaim "The Controversial Truth: Two-Parents Are Better." President Clinton declared that "there were a lot of very good things" in Quayle's Murphy Brown speech after all. By 1994, the *LA Times* reported, candidates of both parties were "lining up" to join the family values bandwagon. In 1996, Dan Quayle felt able to report that "America has truly reached a new consensus" to "support the unified model of father, mother, and child."[5]

The "new consensus" blamed all of America's social and economic ills on people who failed to maintain this "unified model." In a computer search of newspapers from March 1993 through January 1995, I found 263 articles attributing more than twenty distinct "crises"—teenage drug use, urban violence, unemployment, America's declining international competitiveness, federal budget deficits, even individual "narcissism"—to the "collapse of family values" or abandonment of "the two-parent paradigm." As the American Enterprise Institute put it, "The drug crisis, the education crisis, and the problems of teen pregnancy and juvenile crime" can all be traced "to one source: broken families." One architect of the new consensus declared: "It ain't 'the economy, stupid' anymore."[6]

By the 1996 election, the dominance of this new consensus had the ironic effect of marginalizing serious debate over family issues. Republicans talked vaguely about a tax cut to allow more mothers to stay home with their children, ignoring the fact that such a cut would replace only an insignificant fraction of the average working woman's contribution to family income. Democrats touted curfews and school uniforms, ignoring the fact that the biggest worry for most working parents is what their kids are doing and wearing between the time when school gets out and parents get home.

Meanwhile, the "bipartisan consensus" has produced a flourishing cottage industry of "pro-family" experts and consultants, churning out reports, position papers, and news releases on the need for families to stay together and for parents to take better care of their kids. But the platitudes of the new consensus do not get at the everyday issues facing families any better than did the polarization of the earlier debate. Today's interpretation of what constitutes a "values" question, for example, is even more narrow than the truncated definition of what counts as an economic issue. If "family values" are what we need to confront our most urgent social ills, what precisely does this phrase mean? Robert Knight of the Washington, D.C.-based Family Research Council says, "It's a shorthand term for the channeling of sexuality into marriage and all that comes of that: family structure; parental responsibility for children's education, welfare, and moral and spiritual well-being." A leader of the New York-based Institute for American Values puts it this way: "Family values are how we live and what we believe regarding sexuality, marriage and parenthood."[7]

Obviously, how we live and what we believe about such issues are very important, but by this definition Mafiosa families could place high on the list of leading moral exemplars. After all, who believes more firmly in (female) premarital virginity, marital permanence, and taking care of one's own?

The reduction of morality to questions of sexuality, marriage, and parenthood leads to some serious instances of moral blindness. Thus Focus on the Family founder James Dobson claims that no youthful generation "in the history of Western nations" has "been bombarded with more evil and dangerous ideology" than today's. Similarly, author Gertrude Himmelfarb argues that the main source of hope for our immoral age lies in a crusade to revive shame and stigma as responses to divorce or unwed motherhood, along with an effort to substitute private charity for public support of needy children. "If shame, cleanliness and charity are rediscovered, can that other Victorian virtue, chastity, be far behind?"[8]

This kind of simplistic moralizing does not take us very far, no matter how many collections of traditional fairy tales and moral aphorisms hit the best-seller lists. As a writer in the *Christian Century* has put it, a *Book of Virtues* in which hard work is rewarded by elves, saints, and fairies does not give people many guidelines for coping with the perverse incentives of the modern market. Is sex education, however explicit, worse than indoctrination with Nazi and fascist ideology? Is letting young people see R-rated movies worse than taking them to watch lynchings, as was commonly done in the South up through the 1930s? We cannot help contemporary families if we accept a one-dimensional analysis of where their problems originate, insist there is only one blueprint for how all families should look and act, or offer feel-good homilies about cleanliness, chastity, and charity in place of concrete reforms to relieve the stresses on working parents and offer positive alternatives to youth.[9]

What I would like to do in this book, then, is to complicate an issue that the consensus proclaimers argue is so self-evident only a fool or a knave would disagree. In the abstract, of course, they're right. At the general level, everyone can agree that two good parents are better than one, that values are important, that kids have suffered from the me-first, winner-take-all individualism of contemporary culture, and that many parents, married or not, are having trouble meeting (or even identifying) their obligations to kids. At the general level, we all agree that people should value their families.

The problem is that most of us don't live at the general level. We live in a complicated real world where similar-sounding problems have radically different causes for different groups or individuals and therefore require very different solutions; where families sometimes have to choose a lesser evil rather than a positive good; where sweeping pronouncements about the "correct" family structure or value sometimes harm people more than they help.

I recently heard an expert on neurodevelopment describe the mistakes that occur when teachers or physicians make global diagnoses of learning disorders and create cookie-cutter treatments for them, assuming that kids with similar symptoms must have the same disease. In fact, he explained, neurodevelopmental diversity among children is so widespread that the use of "undifferentiated" diagnoses prevents professionals from accurately assessing a child's individual strengths and weaknesses. Medical researchers, he said, need more "multifactorial" explanations, individualized assessments, and personalized treatment plans. They must also stop assuming that "nonstandard" learning patterns are necessarily abnormal or inferior.

Hearing this critique of medical overgeneralization made me realize why many of the pronouncements of the new family think tanks sound like the classic pitch of the medicine con man. Both pretend that one can prescribe on the basis of one-size-fits-all diagnoses rather than careful case-by-case examination. Political demagogues are the worst practitioners of today's quack family medicine, with their gross oversimplifications about what makes for a "good" or a "bad" family. But self-appointed psychological gurus run a close second, with their equally one-dimensional generalizations about at-risk kids and dysfunctional families. Both groups ignore the variability within and among families, as well as the different resources and challenges with which different families must cope. The fact is that there is no single political formula or "good values" patent medicine we can prescribe to produce a healthy marriage, an effective parent, or a "normal" child.

The problems facing inner-city families who don't have access to jobs, parks, libraries, or safe streets are different from those facing working parents who are saddled with overtime and can't take parental leave or sick days to care for their kids. The solutions to those problems have to be different too. Sometimes kids who have had *too much* luxury and indulgence act like kids who've had *too little,* but both the reasons and the treatments for their seemingly superficial behaviors are quite distinct. The issues in two-parent families where one parent is an alcoholic are not necessarily easier or harder, yet are certainly not the same, as those in families headed by a parent who has left an alcoholic spouse. The consequences of divorce are different for a family where two parents split up after years of discord than they are for one where a man dumps his homemaker wife for a younger, trimmer model and transfers his paternal energy to a new set of children.

"All I hear is how complicated everything is," complained a spokesman for the Institute for American Values when I tried to make these points in an exchange we had at the offices of *Mirabella* magazine: "Let's get beyond how complicated everything is and have some analysis."[10] But an analysis based on oversimplification is only helpful to patent medicine hucksters, not to real people. Most Americans are perfectly capable of understanding the complexity and diversity of family life. They deal with it every day.

Indeed, the most encouraging thing I have learned from my experiences over the past few years is how hungry people are to get beyond the sweeping overgeneralizations they hear from politicians, pundits, and the mass media. There's an on-the-ground consensus that is quite different from the one up in the rarefied atmosphere occupied by the politicians and the think tanks. It's about getting down to cases. What is really going on and what does it mean for my family? How does this apply to my divorced sister who doesn't have health insurance and needs food stamps? Or to my homemaker cousin and her hardworking husband? How do the issues facing families in our community differ from those in other cities, suburbs, or farms? Where can we actually find agreement about what families need without pretending every family can work in exactly the same way?

Those are the questions I try to address in this book. I want to show that developing a grounding in history and sociology gives you something more than an extra edge in playing Trivial Pursuit. Although accurate social-historical analysis is no substitute for the hard work of building family support systems and negotiating family relationships, it does help us to depersonalize and defuse family conflicts, as well as to resist pat answers or quick-fix gimmicks. At both the social and the personal level, it encourages us to focus on constructive solutions rather than destructive labeling, so that we can learn how to minimize the distinctive vulnerabilities and build on the special strengths that can be found in almost any family.

1

Getting Past the Sound Bites: How History and Sociology Can Help Today's Families

When lecture audiences first urged me to talk about how family history and sociology were relevant to comtemporary life, I wasn't sure I wanted to abandon the safety of my historical observation post. But my experiences in recent years have convinced me that people are eager to learn whether historians and social scientists can help them improve their grasp of family issues. And I've come to believe that it's our responsibility to try.

I don't want to make false promises about what history and sociology offer. I can't give you five tips to make your relationship last. I don't have a list of ten things you can say to get your kids to do what *you* want and make them think it's what *they* want. Nor can I give kids many useful pointers on how to raise their parents.

But a historical perspective can help us place our personal relationships into a larger social context, so we can distinguish individual idiosyncracies or problems from broader dilemmas posed by the times in which we live. Understanding the historical background and the current socioeconomic setting of family changes helps turn down the heat on discussion of many family issues. It can alleviate some of the anxieties of modern parents and temper the recriminations that go back and forth between men and women. Seeing the larger picture won't make family dilemmas go away, but it can reduce the insecurity, personal bitterness, or sense of betrayal that all of us, at one time or another, bring to these issues. Sometimes it helps to know that the tension originates in the situation, not the psyche.

Putting Teen–Parent Conflicts in Perspective

Consider the question of what's happening to American youth. It's extremely difficult for parents today to look at a specific problem they may have with their teenager, whether that is sneaking out at night or experimenting with alcohol and drugs, without seeing it as a sign of the crisis we are told grips modern youth. Parents tell me they are terrified by headlines about the "epidemic" of teen suicide and by chilling television stories about kids too young to drive a car but old enough to carry an AK-47.

Concerns over adolescent behavior are not entirely new. "Let's Face It," a *Newsweek* cover story of September 6, 1954, declared: "Our Teenagers Are Out of Control." The 1955 film, *Blackboard Jungle,* claimed that teens were "savage" animals because "gang leaders have taken the place of parents." Still, there *are* new structural and historical changes in American life that have recently complicated the transition from early adolescence to young adulthood, making youth–adult relations seem more adversarial.

It doesn't help us understand these changes, however, when people exaggerate the problems of today's teens or turn their normal ups and downs into pathologies. Most teens do not get involved in violence, either as criminals or victims. While teen suicide rates have indeed been increasing, any growth from a low starting point can sound dramatic if presented as a percentage. For example, a 1995 report from the Centers for Disease Control stated that suicides among 10- to 14-year-old youths had "soared" between 1980 and 1992. What this meant in real figures, points out researcher Mike Males, was that 1 in 60,000 youths in this age group killed themselves in 1992, compared to 1 in 125,000 in 1980. The actual death rate among teens from firearms and poisoning has scarcely changed since the 1950s, but the proportion attributed to suicide has risen dramatically, while the proportion attributed to accident has declined.[1]

Furthermore, many "teen" suicide figures are overstated because they come from a database that includes people aged 15 to 24. Suicide rates for actual teenagers, aged 13 to 19, are among the lowest of any age group. In fact, notes Kirk Astroth, "teens as a whole are *less likely* to commit suicide than any other age group *except* preteens. . . . Occupational surveys consistently show that parents and teachers are *twice* as likely, counselors and psychologists are *four* times as likely, and school administrators are *six* times as likely to commit suicide as are high school students."[2] (When I read this statistic to a teenage acquaintance of mine, he told me dourly, "Yeah, but they'll just say we drove them to it.")

It's not that we have more bad parents or more bad kids today than we used to. It's not that families have lost interest in their kids. And there is no evidence that the majority of today's teenagers are more destructive or irresponsible than in the past. However, relations between adults and teens are especially strained today, not because youths have lost their childhood, as is usually suggested, but because they are not being adequately prepared for the new requirements of adulthood. In some ways, childhood has actually been prolonged, if it is measured by dependence on parents and segregation from adult activities. What many young people have lost are clear paths for gaining experience doing responsible, socially necessary work, either in or out of the home, and for moving away from parental supervision without losing contact with adults.

The most common dilemma facing adolescents, and the one that probably causes the most conflicts with adults, is their "rolelessness" in modern society. A rare piece of hard data in all the speculation about what makes adolescents tick is that young people do better on almost every level when they have meaningful involvement in useful and necessary tasks. This effect exists independently of their relationships with parents and friends. Teens also benefit from taking responsibility for younger or less-fortunate children. As one author observes, teens "need some experience of being older, bigger, stronger, or wiser."[3]

But today's adolescents have very few opportunities to do socially necessary work. The issue of rolelessness has been building for eighty years, ever since the abolition of child labor, the extension of schooling, and the decline in farm work that used to occupy many youths in the summer. The problem has accelerated recently, as many of the paths that once led teenagers toward mastery of productive and social roles have turned into dead ends. Instead of having a variety of routes to adulthood, as was true for most of American history, most youngsters are now expected to stay in high school until age 17 or 18.

High schools were originally designed for the most privileged sector of the population. Even now they tend to serve well only that half of the high school population that goes on to college. Non-college-bound students often tell me they feel like second-class citizens, not really of interest to the school. And in recent decades a high school degree has lost considerable value as a ticket to a stable job. Even partial college work confers fewer advantages than in the past. Because of these and other trends, researcher

Laurence Steinberg claims, adolescence "has become a social and economic holding period."[4]

Parents are expected to do the holding. In 1968, two researchers commented that most teen–parent conflicts stemmed from the fact that "readiness for adulthood comes about two years *later* than the adolescent claims and about two years *before* the parent will admit."[5] There is some evidence that the level of miscalculation has widened for *both* parents and kids.

From the point of view of parents, it is more necessary than ever for kids to stay in school rather than seek full-time work, and to delay marriage or pregnancy. After all, the age at which youths can support themselves, let alone a *family*, has reached a new high in the past two decades. From the kids' point of view, though, this waiting period seems almost unbearable. They not only know a lot more than their folks about modern technology but they feel that they also know more about the facts of life than yesterday's teens. Understandably, they strain at the leash.

The strain is accentuated by the fact that while the age of economic maturation has been rising, the age of physical maturation has been falling. The average age of puberty for girls, for instance, was 16 in 1820, 14 in 1900, and 13 in 1940. Today it is 12, and may still be dropping. For boys, the pace and timing of pubertal development is the most important factor in determining the age at which they first have sex; the influence of parents, friends, income, and race is secondary. Although parents and friends continue to exert considerable influence on the age at which girls begin to have sex, there are obvious limits to how long parents can hold their teenagers back.[6]

And even as the job market offers fewer and fewer ways for teens to assert their independence and show that they are more grown up than younger kids, consumer markets and the media offer more and more. Steinberg points out that while teens "have less autonomy to pursue societally-valued *adult* activities" than in the past, they "have more autonomy than did their counterparts previously in matters of leisure, discretionary consumption, and grooming." As a result, adolescents "find it easier to purchase illicit drugs than to obtain legitimate employment."[7]

Another problem for parent–child relations is society's expectation that teens abide by rules and habits that grown-ups have abandoned, and that parents ought to be able to *make* them do so. In preindustrial societies most kids were integrated into almost all adult activities, and right up until the twentieth century there were few separate standards or different laws for teens and adults. For centuries, youth and adults played the same games by the same rules, both literally and figuratively. From "blind man's bluff" to "follow the leader," games we now leave to children were once played by adults as well. There were few special rules or restrictions that applied solely to teens. *All* premarital sex was supposedly out of line in the nineteenth century; teen sex was not singled out as a special problem. In fact, as late as 1886, the "age of consent" for girls was only 10 in more than half the states in the union.[8] However, girls or women who *did* consent to premarital sex were ostracized, regardless of their age.

Today's adults have moved on to new amusements and freedoms, but we want teens to play the old games by the old rules. There may be some good reasons for this, but any segregated group soon develops its own institutions, rules, and value systems, and young people are no exception.

Sports is virtually the only adult-approved and peer-admired realm where teens can demonstrate successive gains in competency, test their limits, and show themselves bigger, stronger, and better than younger children. But for teens who aren't good at sports, or those who reject it as busywork designed to keep them out of trouble, what's left? Music, clothes, drugs, alcohol—the choices differ. Many kids experiment and move on. Others get caught in the quagmire of seeking their identity through consumption. What we often call the youth culture is actually adult marketers seeking to commercially exploit youthful energy and rebellion. But sometimes consumerism seems the only way teens can show that they are growing up and experimenting with new social identities while adults try to keep them suspended in the children's world of school or summer camp.

Of course, many teens get a lot out of school and summer camp. But the dilemmas of rolelessness often put adolescents and their parents on a collision course. Young people feel that adults are plying them with make-work or asking them to put their lives on hold as they mature. They're pretty sure we didn't put *our* lives on hold at comparable levels of maturity, so they suspect us of hypocrisy. Often, they have a point.

On the other hand, while many parents recognize that risk taking among teenagers hasn't changed much since their own youth, they feel that there are more serious consequences for those behaviors than there used to be, given the presence of AIDS (acquired immune deficiency syndrome), high-tech weapons, and new potent drugs. So adults are not necessarily being hypocritical when they hold kids to higher standards than they met themselves. Many of us fear that the second chances and lucky breaks we got may not be available to the next generation.

Balancing the legitimate fears of adults against the legitimate aspirations of teens is not easy. But it helps for both teens and adults to realize that many of their conflicts are triggered by changes in social and economic arrangements, not just family ones. The best way I've found to personally confirm the sociological studies of rolelessness is to ask older men to talk about their life histories. Some of the most interesting discussions I've had over the past few years have been with men over age 60, whose memories extend beyond the transitional period of the 1960s and 1970s to what teen life was like in the 1930s, 1940s, or early 1950s.

The conversations usually start with comments on irresponsible behavior by today's teenage males. "I'd have had my hide tanned if I'd been caught doing that," someone always says, which generally leads to examples of how they got "whomped" or "taught a lesson." Soon, though, the subject switches to the things these upstanding men *didn't* get caught doing in their youth. And most of the time, it turns out the first lesson they learned by getting whomped was how not to get caught.

When they talk about what *really* set them on the right path, almost every older man I've talked with recalls his first job. "I was supporting myself when I was 17" (16, 18, 19, even 15), or "I was in the army with a job to do," the stories go: "What's the matter with today's kids?" And soon they provide their own answers. The typical job a teenager can get today provides neither the self-pride of economic independence nor the socializing benefits of working alongside adult mentors. Teens work in segregated jobs where the only adult who ever comes around is the boss, almost always in an adversarial role. Few jobs for youth allow them to start at the bottom and move up; the middle rungs of the job ladder have been sawed off. Marking time in dead-end jobs that teach no useful skills for the future, teens remain dependent on their parents for the basic necessities of life, simultaneously resenting that dependence and trying to manipulate it.

The stories older men tell about their first jobs are quite different from those told by today's teens. Even men who later became businessmen or highly educated professionals say that their first jobs were in construction, factory work, or some menial setting where they worked beside older men who were more skilled or highly paid. The senior men teased the youngsters, sending them out for a left-handed hammer or making them the butt of sometimes painful practical jokes, but they also showed kids the ropes and helped protect them from the foreman or boss. And they explained why "putting up with the crap" was worth it. After older men talk for a while about what these work experiences meant to them, they are almost always surprised to find themselves agreeing that the loss of nonparental male mentoring may be a bigger problem for boys today than the rise of single-mother homes.

Even allowing for nostalgia, such work relations seem to have been critical experiences for the socialization of many young men in the past. Such jobs integrated youths into adult society, teaching skills they would continue to use as they aged, instead of segregating them in a separate peer culture. As late as 1940, about 60 percent of employed adolescents aged 16–17 worked in traditional workplaces, such as farms, factories, or construction sites. The jobs they did there, or at least the skills they used, might last well into their adult lives. By 1980, only 14 percent worked in such settings.[9]

Girls, who were excluded from many such jobs, have lost less in this arena of life. Up through the 1960s an adolescent girl typically had more responsibilities at home, from washing dishes to taking care of siblings, than she does today. While such tasks may have prepared girls for adult roles as wives and mothers, they also held girls back from further education or preparation for future work outside the home. The change in work patterns for girls has thus made it *easier* for them to see that they have paths toward adult independence. On the other hand, it raises a different set of tensions between girls and their parents. The decline of the sexual double standard, without an equal decline in economic and social discrimination against women, leads parents to worry that their daughters may have too much opportunity, too early, to engage in sexual risk taking for which girls still pay a far higher price than boys.

Another issue facing teens of both sexes is their increasing exclusion from public space. People talk about how kids today are unsupervised, and they often are; but in one sense teens are under *more* surveillance than in the past. Almost anyone above the age of 40 can remember places where young people could establish real physical, as opposed to psychic, distance from adults. In the suburbs it was undeveloped or abandoned lots and overgrown woods, hidden from adult view, often with old buildings that you could deface without anyone caring. In the cities it was downtown areas where kids could hang out. Many of these places are now gone, and only some kids feel comfortable in the malls that have replaced them.

Much has been written about the gentrification of public space in America, the displacement of the poor or socially marginal from their older niches, followed by fear and indignation from respectable people suddenly forced to actually see the homeless doing what they always used to do. Over the years we have also seen what I think of as an "adultification" of public space. Kids are usually allowed there, as long as they're young enough to be in their parents' charge. But where in your town are teenagers welcome on their own?

Teens today have fewer opportunities than in the past for gradual initiation into productive activities, both at home and in public, and fewer places to demonstrate their autonomy in socially approved ways. At the same time, though, they have more access to certain so-called adult forms of consumption than ever before. This makes it hard for adults to avoid the extremes of overly controlling, lock-'em-up positions on the one hand and frequent breakdowns of supervision on the other. Some parents clearly underprotect their kids. We've all seen parents who are too stressed to monitor their kids effectively or who have had their limits overrun so many times that they have given up. Other parents, however, overprotect their kids, trying to personally compensate for the loss of wider adult contacts and of safe retreats. Both extremes drive kids away. But, in most cases, both are reactions to structural dilemmas facing parents and teens rather than abdications of parental responsibility.

What Social Science Tells Us About Male–Female Conflicts

The same kind of perspective can be useful in sorting through conflicts between modern couples. I vividly remember the first people who forced me to bring my historical and social analysis down to individual cases. Following one of my talks, a couple stood up and described a conflict they were having in their marriage. She complained about how unappreciative he was of the effort she took in making gourmet dinners and keeping the house clean. He said: "Hang on a minute. I never asked her to do any of those things. I can't help it if she has higher standards than I do. I don't *care* what we have for dinner. I don't *care* if the floor gets mopped twice a week." They wanted me to comment on their situation.

This is not fair, I thought, as I tried to wriggle out of doing so. I've just summed up the history of family diversity and changing gender roles since colonial times and they want me to settle a marital argument—over housework, of all things? I'm not a counselor; I don't know anything about mediating these issues. I tried to change the subject, but they wouldn't let up, and the audience was clearly on their side. You think family history is relevant, they seemed to be saying. Prove it.

Trapped, but unwilling to pretend I had therapeutic expertise, I cast about for something in my own research or training that might by any stretch of the imagination be helpful. The only thing that came to mind was a concept I had read about in an academic journal. "So," I said, feeling a bit silly, "perhaps the problem we have here lies in what social scientists would call your 'situated social power.'"[10]

It sounded very academic, even downright pompous, but the more we talked about it, the more I realized this *was* a useful concept for them. In plain English it means that various groups in society have unequal access to economic resources, political power, and social status, and these social differences limit how fair or equal a personal relationship between two individuals from different groups can really be. Such social imbalances affect personal behavior regardless of sincere intentions of both parties to "not let it make a difference."

Teachers, for example, have social power over students. I tell my students that I want them to speak their minds and express their disagree-ments with me. And I mean it. But often I don't even notice that they con-tinue to defer until someone finally gets angry at me for "dominating the discussion." Even after all these years, my initial reaction is usually indigna-tion. "I told you to speak up," I want to say; "it's not my fault if you hold back." Then I remind myself that in any situation of unequal power, it's the party with the most power who always assumes that other people can act totally free of outside constraints.

When a person with power pretends not to have it, people with less power feel doubly vulnerable. Although they continue to be unequal, they are now asked to put aside the psychological defenses they have constructed against that inequality, including a certain amount of self-protective guard-edness. So they clam up or get sore, which leaves the more powerful person feeling that his or her big-hearted gestures are being rebuffed. This tension arises between people of different races and classes, between employees and supervisors, and between men and women, as well as between my students and me.

With this awareness, I try to remember that my students are never go-ing to feel as free criticizing my work as I'm going to feel criticizing theirs. I have to adjust the structure of my class to facilitate discussion. I need to in-stitute protected spaces for criticism, such as providing anonymous evalua-tion forms for assessing my performance. But I also have to recognize that our power imbalance will always create tensions between us. I should nei-ther blame my students for that nor feel that I've failed to communicate my "authentic self" to them. None of us exists independently of the social rela-tions in which we operate.

Remembering how helpful this concept is to me in depersonalizing conflicts with students, I reminded the couple that men and women have different options in our society, outside and independent of their personal relationships. Research shows that men are happiest in a relationship when they don't have to do much housework and yet meals get made, clothes get ironed, and the house looks good. This doesn't mean they are chauvinist pigs. Who *wouldn't* be happier under those conditions?

But the wives of such men tend to be depressed. A wife may feel, espe-cially if she jeopardized her earning power by taking time off to raise chil-dren, that she can't give up the domestic services she performs, because if her husband *does* get dissatisfied, she has fewer options than he does in the work world, and will be far worse off after a divorce.

Consciously or not, the wife in this particular marriage seemed to be assessing the risk of not keeping a nice house or putting delicious meals on the table, and finding it too high to just relax and let the housework go. But she was also resenting her husband's unwillingness to help out. This very common pattern of seemingly voluntary sacrifice by the woman, followed by resentment for the man's failure to reciprocate, originates outside the individual relationship. The man was probably completely sincere about not caring if the work got done, but he was missing the point. His wife had looked around, seen what happened to wives who failed to please their husbands, and tried extra hard to make her husband happy. He could not understand her compulsion, and resented being asked to participate in what he saw as unnecessary work. Counseling and better communication might help, but would probably not totally remove the little kernel of fear in the wife's heart that stems from her perfectly reasonable assessment of the unequal social and economic options for men and women.

Similarly, two people trying to raise a child while they both work full-time are going to get stressed or angry. Part of the problem may be that the man isn't doing enough at home (on average, research shows, having a man in the house *adds* hours to a woman's workday).[11] Part of the problem may be that the woman is sabotaging her own stated desire to have the man do more—treating him as an unskilled assistant, refusing to relinquish her control over child-raising decisions, and keeping her domestic standards too high for him to meet. But another part of the problem will remain even if they are the most enlightened individuals in the world.

There's no nonstressful way to divide three full-time jobs between two individuals. Better communication can make the sacrifices more fair, or help clear away the side issues that get entangled with the stress, but the strains are a social problem existing outside the relationship. The solution does not lie in Martians learning to talk Venusian or Venusians being tolerant of the cultural oddities of Martians, as one pop psychologist describes the differences between men and women, but in changing the job structures and social support networks for family life. Until businesses and schools adjust their hours and policies to the realities of two-earner families, even the best-intentioned couples are going to have difficult times.

Improving communication or using the shortcuts offered by self-help books can alleviate some of the conflicts between men and women in this period of rapidly changing roles and expectations. But addressing communication problems alone ignores the differing social options and the patterned experiences of inequality that continually *re-create* such problems between men and women. So people move from one self-help book to another; they try out new encounter groups and memorize new techniques; they slip back and must start all over again. They are medicating the symptoms without solving the problem.

For example, the Venusian–Martian reference comes from best-selling author John Gray, who has found a strikingly effective analogy for getting men and women to realize that they bring different assumptions and experiences to relationships: Men and women, he says, come from different planets. They need to learn each other's culture and language. Gray tells women why men's periodic withdrawals from communication do not mean lack of interest in a relationship. Martians, he says, like to retreat to caves in times of stress, while Venusians tend to crowd around, offering each other support and empathy. He explains to men that women are often just asking for reassurance, not trying to control men's lives, when they pursue subjects past the male comfort zone.[12]

But Gray doesn't urge either sex to make any big changes, merely to take "tiny steps toward understanding the other." He offers women hints on how to ask their partners for help without antagonizing them or making them feel manipulated, but he doesn't demand that men share housework or that women accept the responsibilities that go with egalitarian relationships. For Gray, a healthy relationship exists "when both partners have permission to ask for what they want and need, and they both have permission to say no if they choose." This is certainly better than no one feeling free to ask, but it leaves a rather large set of issues unresolved.[13]

The problem is that many advice books refuse to ask hard questions about the division of household work and decision-making power. In a section called "scoring points with the opposite sex," for example, Gray's advice to women revolves around issues such as not criticizing men for their driving or choice of restaurants. Men, by contrast, are advised: "offer to make dinner," "occasionally offer to wash the dishes," "compliment her on how she looks," "give her four hugs a day," and "don't flick the remote control to different channels when she is watching TV with you."[14]

Now, most women will say that the book would be worth its weight in gold if their husbands would just follow that last tip, but the fact remains that the unequal bargaining power and social support systems for men and women are not addressed, *or even acknowledged,* in this kind of advice. In the long run, failure to address the roots of gender differences perpetuates the problem of communication, or merely replaces one set of misunderstandings with another. As therapist Betty Carter writes, communicating about feelings rather than addressing issues of power and daily behavior can lead to manipulation that eventually degenerates into mutual blame and psychological name-calling.[15] If we're going to think of men and women as being from different planets, they need more than guidebooks and language translations; we must make sure that the social, economic, and political treaties they operate under are fair to both parties.

It's not only women's dissatisfactions that are addressed by a historical and sociological perspective. Men often complain that feminists ignore male insecurities and burdens, and they have a point. Men *do* feel injured and alienated, despite their economic and political advantages over women of the same social group. But history and sociology can identify the sources of men's pain a lot more accurately than myths about the loss of some heroic age of male bonding when Australian aborigines, Chinese sun kings, and Greek warriors marched to their own drumbeat. Going "back to the woods" makes a nice weekend retreat, but it doesn't help men restructure their long-term relationships or identify the social, economic, and political changes they need to improve their family lives.[16]

Male pain is the other side of male power. Not all men, contrary to the rhetoric of masculinity, can be at the top of the pyramid. The contrast between rhetoric and reality is very painful for men whose race, class, health, or even height does not allow them to wield power, exercise authority, or just cut a figure imposing enough to qualify as a "real man." Even successful men pay a high price for their control and authority. The competitive, hierarchical environments men are encouraged to operate in cut them off from intimacy and penalize them for letting down their guard. The myth that male power is all individually achieved, not socially structured, means masculinity can be lost if it is not constantly proven in daily behavior.[17]

Structural analysis helps us get beyond the question of "who hurts more" to explore the different rewards and penalties that traditional gender roles impose on today's men and women. For girls, societal pressures descend heavily at about age 11 or 12, penalizing them for excelling and creating a sharp drop in their self-esteem. There is overwhelming evidence, for example, that girls are treated in ways that hinder their academic and intellectual development. But sometimes this discrimination takes the form of too easy praise and too little pressure to complete a task, leading boys to feel that "girls get off easy." And almost any parent can testify that boys are subject to a much earlier, more abrupt campaign to extinguish the compassion, empathy, and expression of feelings that young boys initially display as openly as girls. The list of derogatory words for boys who don't act masculine is miles longer than the list of disparaging words for girls who don't act feminine. Boys who don't get the message quickly enough are treated brutally. Those who do get the message find that the very success of their effort to "be a man" earns mistrust and fear as well as admiration. In an article that my male students invariably love, Eugene August points out that people always talk about "innocent women and children" in describing victims of war or terrorism. Is there no such thing as an innocent man?[18]

It's good to get past caricatures of female victims and male villains, but it is too simplistic to say that we just have to accept our differences. A man's fear of failure and discomfort with intimacy, for example, come from his socially structured need to constantly have others affirm his competence, self-reliance, or superiority. This is the downside of what he must do to exercise power and privilege. For women, lack of power often leads to fear of *success.* The downside of women's comfort with intimacy is discomfort with asserting authority.

As three researchers in the psychology of gender summarize the trade-offs, boys "get encouraged to be independent and powerful, possibly at the cost of distancing themselves from intimacy." The result is that boys "tend to be overrepresented in the psychopathologies involving aggression." Girls, by contrast, "get rewarded for being compliant and for establishing intimate relations, possibly at the cost of achieving autonomy and control over their choices." This may be why girls are "overrepresented in the psychopathologies involving depression."[19]

The solution suggested by historical and social analysis is not for men and women to feel each other's pain but to equalize their power and access to resources. That is the only way they can relate with fairness and integrity, so that unequal and therefore inherently dishonest relations do not deform their identities. Men must be willing to give up their advantages over women if they hope to build healthy relationships with either sex. Women must be willing to accept tough criticism and give up superficial "privileges" such as being able to cry their way out of a speeding ticket if they hope to develop the inner resources to be high achievers.

Getting Our Bearings on Family Issues

I have recounted my conversation about "situated social power" in many workshops and focus groups, and the feedback I've received has reassured me that historical and sociological approaches to these sorts of issues are helpful to many people. Three written responses I was handed after one talk were particularly meaningful for me. One was from a young couple who said they'd been trying very hard to develop a new and "liberated" relationship. I don't know which partner penned the words, but both signed the form, under the following comment: "Looking at history opened up new areas of communication and closed down unrealistic expectations of same. The discussion made me realize how conflicts with my partner are bigger than we can totally solve on our own, even with lots of talk. But it also let us see which of our expectations are historical baggage that maybe we could get rid of and lighten our load." Another person wrote: "It made me see there are reasons for what my parents did and why we fight. They grew up in a different world. What seems weird to me wasn't a whim but the rules they learned to play by." And still another individual, who I hope was the parent of the last one, wrote: "Now I can understand why my kids resent some of the things I say to them, and maybe they have some good reasons for living the way they do."

A historical and sociological perspective on the question of how families are changing in our society allows us to examine the forest we live in as well as the individual trees. It helps us distinguish issues specific to a particular family from those that are affecting homes all across the country. And in between the extremes of the entirely personal and the pervasively social, this approach helps us understand patterned differences among families that belong to different groups.

Trees that grow along the river lowlands of a forest, for example, encounter different parasites and develop different adaptations or resistance to disease than trees that grow on steep sunny slopes. The same thing holds true for families who live in different "social locations."[20] The issues facing impoverished black families are different from those facing poor whites: Low-income African Americans are much more likely than low-income whites to have an income only *half or less* of the poverty-level figure, and to be trapped in areas where at least 40 percent of the population is also poor.[21] Yet the concerns of these two groups overlap at more points than they do with affluent families who are more likely to worry about whether their kids have too many advantages too early.

More and more therapists are beginning to use such historical and structural analysis to help clients better understand their lives. They increasingly draw up not just a family genogram but a map of the family's social location, so they can identify the resources and danger points of the terrain on which their clients operate. Many therapists report that this approach helps them confront important problems that get pushed aside when the conversation focuses only on personal dynamics within the family. At the same time, it clarifies the immediate tasks that can be addressed, making constructive solutions possible.

For example, two cotherapists were recently working with a family where the father had been abruptly fired, along with hundreds of coworkers, without even a day's notice. The family talked openly about their anger at each other and their fears about the escalating hostility between father and son, but expressed no emotion about the firing. Only when the therapists confessed their own shock and outrage, not only about the father's own firing but about what was being done to the whole community, did family members finally allow themselves to see how much of their anger and fear was socially caused and how much of their resentment was justified.[22]

The therapists found that talking through these social issues made it possible to disentangle the unavoidable, even healthy, indignation family members felt about the firing from the preexisting patterns of hostility in the parent–child relations. Understanding that much of the tension they were experiencing came from social changes beyond their control did not solve everything for this family. But it led parents and children past personal blame and guilt, helping them more effectively address the personal problems that were making it harder to handle the challenges of their social situation.

Along similar lines, Marianne Walters, director of the Family Therapy Practice Center in Washington, D.C., describes how social analysis can help families sidestep mutual blame or guilt and reach constructive solutions to individual problems. For example, Walters recounts her work with a young African-American woman who initially saw herself as paralyzed by a fear of success rooted in her parents' failure to approve her accomplishments and foster her self-esteem.

"Using a wider lens," writes Walters, "my take was different. I saw a young woman caught between a rock and a hard place." As the first in the family to attend college, she has to justify her parents' hard work and sacrifice. But success will distance her from her parents and their community. Saving for college, then likely moving away to another town, will remove her from the networks of borrowing, lending, and exchanging services through which working-class and poor communities typically pool resources to survive. This recognition creates ambivalence on both sides. If her career takes off, it might also be hard to find an African-American man with equal earning power, or one who could accept that she earns more. All these dilemmas make her angry, "and her anger, however justifiable, sometimes interferes in relationships."[23]

Identifying the social origins of these tensions helped Walters determine the thrust of therapy: not to explore the pathologies of the client's "codependence" or assign mantras to build her self-esteem, or even to encourage her to confront her family for past failures, but to accept her ambivalence as valid. Therapist and client began to look for ways that this woman could become successful while staying connected to family and community—ways "to reduce the price she will have to pay for being young, black, beautiful . . . and smart."

Developing a historical and sociological perspective on such issues helps people get past painful family experiences and personal histories without either denying them or becoming trapped in a cycle of blame and victimhood. For example, psychologist John Snarey, comparing men who became effective fathers with those who did not, found that many men were able to overcome the legacy of very poor paternal role models and painful childhoods. What separated the men who were able to become effective child-rearing fathers from those who weren't is that the successful fathers "placed their own fathers' shortcomings in context and thus were able to take extenuating circumstances into account." By "transforming their anger with their own fathers into a sense of sadness for and understanding of the conditions under which their own fathers had functioned," these men were able to use the kind of parenting they *wished* they had had as a model for the parenting they offered their own children.[24] To understand all is *not* to forgive all, but it can prevent mistakes from being repeated over and over again.

In other words, historical and social analysis can help people achieve the wish of the old serenity prayer—that we may have the courage to change what can be changed, the patience to accept (or at least adjust to) what cannot, and the wisdom to know the difference. It's a way to boost what Daniel Goleman calls our emotional IQ. "Emotional intelligence," argues Goleman, in a book by that name, is possibly the most important component of both individual success and social cohesion. It helps us read correctly the inner feelings of others, rather than be taken in by passing moods or public postures, and enables us to handle relationships smoothly. It is what we use to fend off "emotional hijacking" by strong impulses that can snatch us away from a rational, constructive course. Emotional intelligence is the ability, as Aristotle put it, "to be angry with the right person, to the right degree, at the right time, for the right purpose, and in the right way." It is also the ability to be afraid of the right things, in the right degree, at the right time, or to be confident in the right people, for the right reason. Our society, says Goleman, underestimates the importance of emotional IQ and fails to encourage its development, even though it can clearly be enhanced.[25]

The same goes for social intelligence. Social intelligence allows us to be angry, afraid, or optimistic about the right trends and relevant social forces, to the right degree and for the right reason. It enables us to read social change correctly, so we are not misled by short-term fluctuations. It is also a powerful defense against ideological hijackers who try to use our fears, hopes, or impulses to divert us from rationally evaluating our options.

Boosting Our Social Intelligence: Putting Family and Personal Trends in Context

Understanding the history of families and the structural constraints under which they operate can prevent our emotional and social IQs from being stunted by what sometimes seems like a national campaign to "dumb us down." Politicians have become experts in squeezing the complexity out of issues to produce compressed, thirteen-second sound bites. Think-tank publicists bombard us with the out-of-context snippets of information sometimes called "factoids."

The word suggests little fragments of data, broken off from their original planetary moorings, zinging merrily through space and occasionally hurtling down into our atmosphere in a fleeting arc of light. And that's very much how the mass media deliver information. News outlets, every bit as much as advertising agencies, need to trumpet their wares as unprecedented or revolutionary. One way of giving the impression that every bit of news is "new" is by drawing comparisons from year to year, rather than over decades, so that temporary fluctuations can't be distinguished from long-range trends. "A Nation of Rolling Stones" is how a *New York Times* headline described America on December 12, 1994; "U.S. No Longer a Land Steeped in Wanderlust" declared the same paper nine months later. Had things really changed so drastically in nine months? No. Each article used different yardsticks to measure the same trends.[26]

Another source of confusion is failure to distinguish raw numbers from percentages. "Hello Ozzie and Harriet," "U.S. Family Stabilizing," "Traditional Families Making a Comeback," announced various news reports in March 1996. Less than a week later the message was: "Marriage an Eroding Institution." The first headlines were based on the fact that the absolute number of married couples with children had increased by 700,000 over the past five years. The second was based on the fact that the ratio of cohabitating couples to married couples rose sevenfold between 1970 and 1994. In the first news report, the use of absolute numbers instead of percentages left the impression that the relative decline in marriage had been reversed. In the second case, a dramatic percentage increase in cohabitation obscured the continuing importance of marriage: The sevenfold rise was from one cohabitating couple per 100 married ones in 1970 to 7 per 100 in 1994.[27]

A similar misconception was promulgated in a 1993 report that the percentage of "Murphy Brown" moms had tripled. Very impressive. But to put this dramatic finding in perspective, even after this rise only 8.3 percent of all women aged 18 to 44 who have children out of wedlock have managerial or professional jobs.[28]

Yet another method for repackaging long-term family trends as breathtaking new discoveries is to pick two extreme dates for comparison, while ignoring differences in the age structure of the population or other relevant facts that would put the differences in context. For example, a larger proportion of the marrying-age population is single today than in the 1950s, but in 1940 the proportion of the population that was single was 30 percent higher than in 1988. Today's fertility rates are much lower than in the 1950s, the high point of fertility in the twentieth century, but much higher than in the 1930s, the low point. While the number of children per family has fallen since the turn of the century, the percentage of women remaining childless is actually lower now than it was then.[29] So, taking your pick of comparisons, you can make totally opposite points about trends in U.S. birth rates.

Or consider the question of youthful violence. Teenage boys and young men are the group most likely to commit violent crime. But when the media report a rise in crime, they very seldom tell us whether this represents an increase in the proportion of young males in the population or a rise in the percentage of this group who commit crime. And when they can't find a percentage increase in *either* to report, they often throw raw numbers at us, since these are sure to rise as our population increases. During the 1980s, rates of crime reporting rose much faster than rates of crime.

What have the real trends been? There was an increase in murder rates among all age groups between 1965 and 1975. Some of this increase, says noted criminologist Alfred Blumstein, probably reflects a shift in recording methods, whereas another part was due to a surge in the most violent-prone sector of the population, as baby-boom boys entered adolescence. Murder rates leveled off, at a rather high plane, from 1970 to 1980. They actually fell from 1980 to 1985, though no one could have told this from most media reports. From 1985 to 1993, the murder rate stayed flat, and in some cases fell, for older individuals, but rose sharply for young teens.[30]

Shocking as this trend may be, we miss a lot of the real dilemmas facing youth if we blame it on a crisis in family relations or on some recent deterioration in morals. On balance, *most* teens today are no more violent than in the past. For one thing, much teen violence of earlier days went unreported because it was directed at what then were considered "legitimate targets," such as African Americans. Historians are only now uncovering the block-by-block guerilla war that greeted blacks who moved to northern cities seeking work after World War II.[31]

Oral histories I've taken over the past few years suggest that today's teenagers are *less* likely to get into fights than those of their grandparents' generation. Older men report almost daily fights behind the high school or the local movie theater. Their grandsons much less seldom report being drawn into such melees. Today's weaponry, however, means the fights that *do* occur are more likely to turn lethal. Thus the National Institute of Justice recently concluded that "virtually the entire increase" in gang-related homicides was caused by the increased use of high-calibre, automatic, and semiautomatic weapons.[32] The availability of such weapons sets into motion an escalating cycle of defensive arming, fear, and more arming. But this problem cannot be solved at the family level.

In addition, young people have now replaced elders as the sector of the population most likely to be poor. A higher proportion of children live in areas of concentrated poverty today than at any time since the Great Depression. The growth of such areas of condensed, undiluted poverty has paralleled the growth in youthful violence, which suggests that part of what we call the crisis of youth may in fact be a crisis of class.[33]

Similar care must be taken in interpreting headlines about the explosion of unwed motherhood. Unwed motherhood has increased dramatically since 1970, but it's easy to overstate *how* dramatically, because much illegitimacy was covered up in the past and reporting methods have recently become much more sophisticated. In the past, notes Sam Roberts, many unwed mothers would tell census workers that they were separated, "resulting in the anomaly of many more 'separated' women than men." At least 80 percent of the increase in unwed motherhood reported between 1981 and 1983, explains Steve Rawlings of the Census Bureau, came from "refinements in survey procedures that were introduced early in the 1980s. This represents 10 to 15 percent of the total increase between 1970 and 1993 (or 20 to 25 percent of the increase since 1980)." And though newspapers routinely use unwed motherhood and single parenthood interchangeably, many unwed mothers are part of cohabitating couples. Five states, including California, further distort the statistics by assuming a woman is unmarried if she has a different last name than the father listed on the birth certificate![34]

It's also important to distinguish between the ratio of unmarried to married births and the rate of births to unmarried women. Between 1960 and 1990, the nonmarital birth ratio increased by more than 500 percent, from 5.3 percent of all births to 28 percent. But birth rates to unmarried women only increased by a factor of 1.73, not quite twofold. What explains the larger figure is that births to unmarried women rose while births to married women fell, increasing the *relative* proportion of unmarried births much more than their *absolute* numbers. In some cases, a fall in marital fertility may be so large that unwed births become a larger proportion of all births even when rates of unwed childbearing are flat or falling. The probability that an unmarried African-American woman would have a child actually fell from 9.8 to 9.0 percent between 1960 and 1990, for example; but because married-couple childbearing decreased among African Americans even more sharply, the proportion of black children born to unwed mothers rose.[35]

I'm not saying that the media intend to mislead. But in many cases, lack of historical perspective makes intelligent, dedicated reporters vulnerable to manipulation by people who wish to magnify one particular set of the factoids that continuously streak across our information horizon. Too many media outlets dutifully report each factoid sighting to which their attention is directed. In consequence, passing blips on the historical radar screen are all too often mistaken for major vehicles of social change.[36]

Such blips generate waves of panic, followed by shouts of relief: "Marriage is about to crash!" "Oh, good, the rates are climbing again." "Working women are about to collide with their kids' needs." "No, look, here's a poll saying they want to spend more time at home." Meanwhile, the truly unprecedented changes in family life seem to be taking place too close to the ground for the radar watchers to notice. So while the smallest shift in yearly statistics or attitude polls gets blown up into a gigantic new trend or a stunning reversal, few commentators understand exactly how families, jobs, social and political institutions, and interpersonal relationships are being repositioned on the ground.

The result is that many pronouncements about the family, often by the same commentators, have a peculiarly manic-depressive quality. On the one hand, there are the doomsday predictions. New consensus spokesman David Popenoe warns that the decay of family life is "unique and unprecedented" and that the final collapse of "the last vestige of the traditional family unit" is imminent. "Marriage is dying," says Robert Rector of the Heritage Foundation; the next ten years will "decide whether or not marriage and family survive in this nation." Our failure to halt the decay of marriage, says the Council on Families in America, is "nothing less than an act of cultural suicide."[37]

On the other hand, these catastrophic assertions are periodically interspersed with cheerful assurances that things may be turning around. Popenoe sees hopeful signs of a "new familism" in "the nation as a whole." Charles Murray of the American Enterprise Institute thinks we may be moving toward "the restoration of a culture in which family, parenthood, . . . morality, and the virtues are all perceived and valued in ways that our grandparents would find familiar."[38]

Such wild fluctuations in assessments result from a lack of historical context. By contrast, once people understand the complicated *mix* of long-term changes in family trends, social institutions, and cultural mores, they are less likely to think that any one-size-fits-all quick fix can turn everything around, for better or for worse. They're more likely to be realistic about what can and can't be changed, what we need to adjust to and what we may be able to resist.

For example, take the question of whether marriage is a dying institution. In 1867 there were 9.6 marriages per 1,000 people. A hundred years later, in 1967, there were 9.7. The rate reached a low of 7.9 in 1932 and an all-time high of 16.4 in 1946, a peak quickly followed by a brief but huge surge in divorce. Marriage rates fell again from the early 1950s to 1958, rose slowly until the end of the 1960s, and then began to decline again. But the proportion of women who remain single all their lives is *lower* today than at the turn of the century, and fewer women now feel they have to forgo marriage entirely in order to do anything else in their lives. Periodic predictions to the contrary, it is unlikely that we will someday record the demise of the last married couple in America.[39]

Nevertheless, marriage is certainly a *transformed* institution, and it plays a smaller role than ever before in organizing social and personal life. One reason is that marriage comes much later, for most people, than in the past. Men's average age at first marriage today is not unprecedented, though it has now regained the previous record high of 1890. But the average age of marriage for contemporary women is two years higher than its historical peak in 1890 and almost four years higher than in the 1950s. This figure approaches the highest age ever recorded for Western Europe, a region where marriage has always taken place later than almost anywhere else in the world. And although fewer women stay single all their lives than in 1900, a higher proportion of women than ever before experience a period of independent living and employment before marriage. Women's expectations of both marriage and work are unlikely to ever be the same as in the past.[40]

The second reason for marriage's more limited role in people's lives is that it is no longer expected to last "until death do us part." Divorce rates in America rose steadily until World War II, fell briefly during the 1950s, and took off again during the late 1960s. The divorce rate crested near the end of the 1970s, leveled off in the 1980s, and very slightly receded from 1988 to 1993. This last trend was heralded by many commentators as a "real turnaround," a sign that Americans "are turning conservative, pro-family." But while demographers now say that only 40 percent, rather than 50 percent, of marriages will end in divorce, these remain among the highest divorce rates ever recorded. Furthermore, the cumulative effects of past divorces continue to mount. In 1960 there were 35 divorced men and women for every 1,000 married ones. By 1990 there were 140 divorced individuals for every 1,000 married ones.[41]

People often misunderstand what statisticians mean when they estimate that one in every two or three marriages will end in divorce. The calculations refer to the chances of a marriage ending in divorce within 40 years. While rising divorce rates have increased the number of marriages at risk for dissolution, the gradual extension of life spans ensures that a marriage today has the potential to last three times longer than one of 200 years ago. Thus while the number of people who divorce is certainly unprecedented, so is the number of couples who celebrate their fortieth wedding anniversaries. In fact, the chances of doing so have never been better.[42]

On the other hand, the average marriage that ends in divorce lasts only 6.3 years. We may be seeing more marriages that last longer and are more fulfilling than at any time in our history. But we are also seeing more marriages that are *less* committed and of shorter duration than in the past. Sociologist Valerie Oppenheimer suggests we are experiencing growing polarization between increasing numbers of very "high-quality," long-lasting marriages *and* increasing numbers of short-lived, medium- to "low-quality" ones where the partners are not committed enough to stay and work things through. Understanding this polarization helps explain some of the ambivalence Americans have about modern families. Very few people in a modern high-quality marriage would trade it for an older model where limited communication and a high degree of sexual dissatisfaction were taken for granted. And few adults in a very low-quality marriage, or their children, want to be trapped there for life. But the commitments and consequences of "medium-quality" marriages are more ambiguous, especially for kids, and this worries many Americans.[43]

Often their worry takes the form of a debate over whether we should return to the family forms and values of the 1950s. That decade is still close enough that many people derive their political position on the issue from personal experience. At forums I've conducted across the country, some people raised in 1950s families tell of tormented childhoods in alcoholic, abusive, or conflict-ridden families. They cannot understand, they say vehemently, why anyone would regret the passing of the 1950s for a single moment. My research validates their experience. These individuals were not alone.

But other people remember 1950s families that shielded them from adult problems and disputes. Many had unmistakably happy parents. Others had secure childhoods but learned later that one or both of their parents were miserable. Some of these individuals are now sorry that their parents stayed together, but many more say they are glad not to have known about their parents' problems and grateful for whatever kept their families together. They are also thankful that the media did not expose them to many adult realities that today's children see or read about every day. My research validates their experience too.

The only way to get past the polarized personal testimonies for and against 1950s families is to put their strengths and weaknesses into historical perspective. This permits a more balanced assessment of what we have gained and lost since then. It also helps us distinguish historical precedents we may be able to draw on from new issues requiring new responses.

2

What We Really Miss About the 1950s

In a 1996 poll by the Knight-Ridder news agency, more Americans chose the 1950s than any other single decade as the best time for children to grow up.[1] And despite the research I've done on the underside of 1950s families, I don't think it's crazy for people to feel nostalgic about the period. For one thing, it's easy to see why people might look back fondly to a decade when real wages grew more in any single year than in the entire ten years of the 1980s combined, a time when the average 30-year-old man could buy a median-priced home on only 15–18 percent of his salary.[2]

But it's more than just a financial issue. When I talk with modern parents, even ones who grew up in unhappy families, they associate the 1950s with a yearning they feel for a time when there were fewer complicated choices for kids or parents to grapple with, when there was more predictability in how people formed and maintained families, and when there was a coherent "moral order" in their community to serve as a reference point for family norms. Even people who found that moral order grossly unfair or repressive often say that its presence provided them with something concrete to push against.

I can sympathize entirely. One of my most empowering moments occurred the summer I turned 12, when my mother marched down to the library with me to confront a librarian who'd curtly refused to let me check out a book that was "not appropriate" for my age. "Don't you *ever* tell my daughter what she can and can't read," fumed my mom. "She's a mature young lady and she can make her own choices." In recent years I've often thought back to the gratitude I felt toward my mother for that act of trust in me. I wish I had some way of earning similar points from my own son. But much as I've always respected his values, I certainly wouldn't have walked into my local video store when he was 12 and demanded that he be allowed to check out absolutely anything he wanted!

Still, I have no illusions that I'd actually like to go back to the 1950s, and neither do most people who express such occasional nostalgia. For example, although the 1950s got more votes than any other decade in the Knight-Ridder poll, it did not win an outright majority: 38 percent of respondents picked the 1950s; 27 percent picked the 1960s or the 1970s. Voters between the ages of 50 and 64 were most likely to choose the 1950s, the decade in which they themselves came of age, as the best time for kids; voters under 30 were more likely to choose the 1970s. African Americans differed over whether the 1960s, 1970s, or 1980s were best, but all age groups of blacks agreed that later decades were definitely preferable to the 1950s.

Nostalgia for the 1950s is real and deserves to be taken seriously, but it usually shouldn't be taken literally. Even people who *do* pick the 1950s as the best decade generally end up saying, once they start discussing their feelings in depth, that it's not the family arrangements in and of themselves that they want to revive. They don't miss the way women used to be treated, they sure wouldn't want to live with most of the fathers they knew in their neighborhoods, and "come to think of it"—I don't know how many times I've recorded these exact words—"I communicate with my kids *much* better than my parents or grandparents did." When Judith Wallerstein recently interviewed 100 spouses in "happy" marriages, she found that only five "wanted a marriage like their parents'." The husbands "consciously rejected the role models provided by their fathers. The women said they could never be happy living as their mothers did."[3]

People today understandably feel that their lives are out of balance, but they yearn for something totally *new*—a more equal distribution of work, family, and community time for both men and women, children and adults. If the 1990s are lopsided in one direction, the 1950s were equally lopsided in the opposite direction.

What most people really feel nostalgic about has little to do with the internal structure of 1950s families. It is the belief that the 1950s provided a more family-friendly economic and social environment, an easier climate in which to keep kids on the straight and narrow, and above all, a greater feeling of hope for a family's long-term future, especially for its young. The contrast between the perceived hopefulness of the fifties and our own misgivings about the future is key to contemporary nostalgia for the period. Greater optimism *did* exist then, even among many individuals and groups who were in terrible circumstances. But if we are to take people's sense of loss seriously, rather than merely to capitalize on it for a hidden political agenda, we need to develop a historical perspective on where that hope came from.

Part of it came from families comparing their prospects in the 1950s to their unstable, often grindingly uncomfortable pasts, especially the two horrible decades just before. In the 1920s, after two centuries of child labor and income insecurity, and for the first time in American history, a bare majority of children had come to live in a family with a male breadwinner, a female homemaker, and a chance at a high school education. Yet no sooner did the ideals associated with such a family begin to blossom than they were buried by the stock market crash of 1929 and the Great Depression of the 1930s. During the 1930s domestic violence soared; divorce rates fell, but informal separations jumped; fertility plummeted. Murder rates were higher in 1933 than they were in the 1980s. Families were uprooted or torn apart. Thousands of young people left home to seek work, often riding the rails across the country.[4]

World War II brought the beginning of economic recovery, and people's renewed interest in forming families resulted in a marriage and childbearing boom, but stability was still beyond most people's grasp. Postwar communities were rocked by racial tensions, labor strife, and a right-wing backlash against the radical union movement of the 1930s. Many women resented being fired from wartime jobs they had grown to enjoy. Veterans often came home to find that they had to elbow their way back into their families, with wives and children resisting their attempts to reassert domestic authority. In one recent study of fathers who returned from the war, four times as many reported painful, even traumatic, reunions as remembered happy ones.[5]

By 1946 one in every three marriages was ending in divorce. Even couples who stayed together went through rough times, as an acute housing shortage forced families to double up with relatives or friends. Tempers frayed and generational relations grew strained. "No home is big enough to house two families, particularly two of different generations, with opposite theories on child training," warned a 1948 film on the problems of modern marriage.[6]

So after the widespread domestic strife, family disruptions, and violence of the 1930s and the instability of the World War II period, people were ready to try something new. The postwar economic boom gave them the chance. The 1950s was the first time that a majority of Americans could even *dream* of creating a secure oasis in their immediate nuclear families.

There they could focus their emotional and financial investments, reduce obligations to others that might keep them from seizing their own chance at a new start, and escape the interference of an older generation of neighbors or relatives who tried to tell them how to run their lives and raise their kids. Oral histories of the postwar period resound with the theme of escaping from in-laws, maiden aunts, older parents, even needy siblings.

The private family also provided a refuge from the anxieties of the new nuclear age and the cold war, as well as a place to get away from the political witch-hunts led by Senator Joe McCarthy and his allies. When having the wrong friends at the wrong time or belonging to any "suspicious" organization could ruin your career and reputation, it was safer to pull out of groups you might have joined earlier and to focus on your family. On a more positive note, the nuclear family was where people could try to satisfy their long-pent-up desires for a more stable marriage, a decent home, and the chance to really enjoy their children.

The 1950s Family Experiment

The key to understanding the successes, failures, and comparatively short life of 1950s family forms and values is to understand the period as one of *experimentation* with the possibilities of a new kind of family, not as the expression of some longstanding tradition. At the end of the 1940s, the divorce rate, which had been rising steadily since the 1890s, dropped sharply; the age of marriage fell to a 100-year low; and the birth rate soared. Women who had worked during the depression or World War II quit their jobs as soon as they became pregnant, which meant quite a few women were specializing in child raising; fewer women remained childless during the 1950s than in any decade since the late nineteenth century. The timing and spacing of childbearing became far more compressed, so that young mothers were likely to have two or more children in diapers at once, with no older sibling to help in their care. At the same time, again for the first time in 100 years, the educational gap between young middle-class women and men increased, while job segregation for working men and women seems to have peaked. These demographic changes increased the dependence of women on marriage, in contrast to gradual trends in the opposite direction since the early twentieth century.[7]

The result was that family life and gender roles became much more predictable, orderly, and settled in the 1950s than they were either twenty years earlier or would be twenty years later. Only slightly more than one in four marriages ended in divorce during the 1950s. Very few young people spent any extended period of time in a nonfamily setting: They moved from their parents' family into their own family, after just a brief experience with independent living, and they started having children soon after marriage. Whereas two-thirds of women aged 20 to 24 were not yet married in 1990, only 28 percent of women this age were still single in 1960.[8]

Ninety percent of all the households in the country were families in the 1950s, in comparison with only 71 percent by 1990. Eighty-six percent of all children lived in two-parent homes in 1950, as opposed to just 72 percent in 1990. And the percentage living with both biological parents—rather than, say, a parent and stepparent—was dramatically higher than it had been at the turn of the century or is today: seventy percent in 1950, compared with only 50 percent in 1990. Nearly 60 percent of kids—an all-time high—were born into male breadwinner–female homemaker families; only a minority of the rest had mothers who worked in the paid labor force.[9]

If the organization and uniformity of family life in the 1950s were new, so were the values, especially the emphasis on putting all one's emotional and financial eggs in the small basket of the immediate nuclear family. Right up through the 1940s, ties of work, friendship, neighborhood, ethnicity, extended kin, and voluntary organizations were as important a source of identity for most Americans, and sometimes a *more* important source of obligation, than marriage and the nuclear family. All this changed in the postwar era. The spread of suburbs and automobiles, combined with the destruction of older ethnic neighborhoods in many cities, led to the decline of the neighborhood social club. Young couples moved away from parents and kin, cutting ties with traditional extrafamilial networks that might compete for their attention. A critical factor in this trend was the emergence of a group of family sociologists and marriage counselors who followed Talcott Parsons in claiming that the nuclear family, built on a sharp division of labor between husband and wife, was the cornerstone of modern society.

The new family experts tended to advocate views such as those first raised in a 1946 book, *Their Mothers' Sons,* by psychiatrist Edward Strecker. Strecker and his followers argued that American boys were infantalized and emasculated by women who were old-fashioned "moms" instead of modern "mothers." One sign that you might be that dreaded "mom," Strecker warned women, was if you felt you should take your aging parents into your own home, rather than putting them in "a good institution . . . where they will receive adequate care and comfort." Modern "mothers" placed their parents in nursing homes and poured all their energies into their nuclear family. They were discouraged from diluting their wifely and maternal commitments by maintaining "competing" interests in friends, jobs, or extended family networks, yet they were also supposed to cheerfully grant early independence to their (male) children—an emotional double bind that may explain why so many women who took this advice to heart ended up abusing alcohol or tranquilizers over the course of the decade.[10]

The call for young couples to break from their parents and youthful friends was a consistent theme in 1950s popular culture. In *Marty,* one of the most highly praised TV plays and movies of the 1950s, the hero almost loses his chance at love by listening to the carping of his mother and aunt and letting himself be influenced by old friends who resent the time he spends with his new girlfriend. In the end, he turns his back on mother, aunt, and friends to get his new marriage and a little business of his own off to a good start. Other movies, novels, and popular psychology tracts portrayed the dreadful things that happened when women became more interested in careers than marriage or men resisted domestic conformity.

Yet many people felt guilty about moving away from older parents and relatives; "modern mothers" worried that fostering independence in their kids could lead to defiance or even juvenile delinquency (the recurring nightmare of the age); there was considerable confusion about how men and women could maintain clear breadwinner–homemaker distinctions in a period of expanding education, job openings, and consumer aspirations. People clamored for advice. They got it from the new family education specialists and marriage counselors, from columns in women's magazines, from government pamphlets, and above all from television. While 1950s TV melodramas warned against letting anything dilute the commitment to getting married and having kids, the new family sitcoms gave people nightly lessons on how to make their marriage or rapidly expanding family work—or, in the case of *I Love Lucy,* probably the most popular show of the era, how *not* to make their marriage and family work. Lucy and Ricky gave weekly comic reminders of how much trouble a woman could get into by wanting a career or hatching some hare-brained scheme behind her husband's back.

At the time, everyone knew that shows such as *Donna Reed, Ozzie and Harriet, Leave It to Beaver,* and *Father Knows Best* were not the way families really were. People didn't watch those shows to see their own lives reflected back at them. They watched them to see how families were *supposed* to live—and also to get a little reassurance that they were headed in the right direction. The sitcoms were simultaneously advertisements, etiquette manuals, and how-to lessons for a new way of organizing marriage and child raising. I have studied the scripts of these shows for years, since I often use them in my classes on family history, but it wasn't until I became a parent that I felt their extraordinary pull. The secret of their appeal, I suddenly realized, was that they offered 1950s viewers, wracked with the same feelings of parental inadequacy as was I, the promise that there were easy answers and surefire techniques for raising kids.

Ever since, I have found it useful to think of the sitcoms as the 1950s equivalent of today's beer ads. As most people know, beer ads are consciously aimed at men who *aren't* as strong and sexy as the models in the commercials, guys who are uneasily aware of the gap between the ideal masculine pursuits and their own achievements. The promise is that if the viewers on the couch will just drink brand X, they too will be able to run 10 miles without gasping for breath. Their bodies will firm up, their complexions will clear up, and maybe the Swedish bikini team will come over and hang out at their place.

Similarly, the 1950s sitcoms were aimed at young couples who had married in haste, women who had tasted new freedoms during World War II and given up their jobs with regret, veterans whose children resented their attempts to reassert paternal authority, and individuals disturbed by the changing racial and ethnic mix of postwar America. The message was clear: Buy these ranch houses, Hotpoint appliances, and child-raising ideals; relate to your spouse like this; get a new car to wash with your kids on Sunday afternoons; organize your dinners like that—and you too can escape from the conflicts of race, class, and political witch-hunts into harmonious families where father knows best, mothers are never bored or irritated, and teenagers rush to the dinner table each night, eager to get their latest dose of parental wisdom.

Many families found it possible to put together a good imitation of this way of living during the 1950s and 1960s. Couples were often able to construct marriages that were much more harmonious than those in which they had grown up, and to devote far more time to their children. Even when marriages were deeply unhappy, as many were, the new stability, economic security, and educational advantages parents were able to offer their kids counted for a lot in people's assessment of their life satisfaction. And in some matters, ignorance could be bliss: The lack of media coverage of problems such as abuse or incest was terribly hard on the casualties, but it protected more fortunate families from knowledge and fear of many social ills."

There was tremendous hostility to people who could be defined as "others": Jews, African Americans, Puerto Ricans, the poor, gays or lesbians, and "the red menace." Yet on a day-to-day basis, the civility that prevailed in homogeneous neighborhoods allowed people to ignore larger patterns of racial and political repression. Racial clashes were ever-present in the 1950s, sometimes escalating into full-scale antiblack riots, but individual homicide rates fell to almost half the levels of the 1930s. As nuclear families moved into the suburbs, they retreated from social activism but entered voluntary relationships with people who had children the same age; they became involved in PTAs together, joined bridge clubs, went bowling.

There does seem to have been a stronger sense of neighborly common-alities than many of us feel today. Even though this local community was often the product of exclusion or repression, it sometimes looks attractive to modern Americans whose commutes are getting longer and whose family or work patterns give them little in common with their neighbors.[12]

The optimism that allowed many families to rise above their internal difficulties and to put limits on their individualistic values during the 1950s came from the sense that America was on a dramatically different trajectory than it had been in the past, an upward and expansionary path that had already taken people to better places than they had ever seen before and would certainly take their children even further. This confidence that almost everyone could look forward to a better future stands in sharp contrast to how most contemporary Americans feel, and it explains why a period in which many people were much worse off than today sometimes still looks like a better period for families than our own.

Throughout the 1950s, poverty was higher than it is today, but it was less concentrated in pockets of blight existing side-by-side with extremes of wealth, and, unlike today, it was falling rather than rising. At the end of the 1930s, almost two-thirds of the population had incomes below the poverty standards of the day, while only one in eight had a middle-class income (defined as two to five times the poverty line). By 1960, a majority of the population had climbed into the middle-income range.[13]

Unmarried people were hardly sexually abstinent in the 1950s, but the age of first intercourse was somewhat higher than it is now, and despite a tripling of nonmarital birth rates between 1940 and 1958, more then 70 percent of nonmarital pregnancies led to weddings before the child was born. Teenage birth rates were almost twice as high in 1957 as in the 1990s, but most teen births were to married couples, and the effect of teen pregnancy in reducing further schooling for young people did not hurt their life prospects the way it does today. High school graduation rates were lower in the 1950s than they are today, and minority students had far worse test scores, but there were jobs for people who dropped out of high school or graduated without good reading skills—jobs that actually had a future. People entering the job market in the 1950s had no way of knowing that they would be the last generation to have a good shot at reaching middle-class status without the benefit of postsecondary schooling.

Millions of men from impoverished, rural, unemployed, or poorly educated family backgrounds found steady jobs in the steel, auto, appliance, construction, and shipping industries. Lower middle-class men went further on in college during the 1950s than they would have been able to expect in earlier decades, enabling them to make the transition to secure white-collar work. The experience of shared sacrifices in the depression and war, reinforced by a New Deal–inspired belief in the ability of government to make life better, gave people a sense of hope for the future. Confidence in government, business, education, and other institutions was on the rise. This general optimism affected people's experience and assessment of family life. It is no wonder modern Americans yearn for a similar sense of hope.

But before we sign on to any attempts to turn the family clock back to the 1950s we should note that the family successes and community solidarities of the 1950s rested on a totally different set of political and economic conditions than we have today. Contrary to widespread belief, the 1950s was not an age of laissez-faire government and free market competition. A major cause of the social mobility of young families in the 1950s was that federal assistance programs were much more generous and widespread than they are today.

In the most ambitious and successful affirmative action program ever adopted in America, 40 percent of young men were eligible for veterans' benefits, and these benefits were far more extensive than those available to Vietnam-era vets. Financed in part by a federal income tax on the rich that went up to 87 percent and a corporate tax rate of 52 percent, such benefits provided quite a jump start for a generation of young families. The GI bill paid most tuition costs for vets who attended college, doubling the percentage of college students from prewar levels. At the other end of the life span, Social Security began to build up a significant safety net for the elderly, formerly the poorest segment of the population. Starting in 1950, the federal government regularly mandated raises in the minimum wage to keep pace with inflation. The minimum wage may have been only $1.40 as late as 1968, but a person who worked for that amount full-time, year-round, earned 118 percent of the poverty figure for a family of three. By 1995, a full-time minimum-wage worker could earn only 72 percent of the poverty level.[14]

An important source of the economic expansion of the 1950s was that public works spending at all levels of government comprised nearly 20 percent of total expenditures in 1950, as compared to less than 7 percent in 1984. Between 1950 and 1960, nonmilitary, nonresidential public construction rose by 58 percent. Construction expenditures for new schools (in dollar amounts adjusted for inflation) rose by 72 percent; funding on sewers and waterworks rose by 46 percent. Government paid 90 percent of the costs of building the new Interstate Highway System. These programs opened up suburbia to growing numbers of middle-class Americans and created secure, well-paying jobs for blue-collar workers.[15]

Government also reorganized home financing, underwriting low down payments and long-term mortgages that had been rejected as bad business by private industry. To do this, government put public assets behind hous-

ing lending programs, created two new national financial institutions to facilitate home loans, allowed veterans to put down payments as low as a dollar on a house, and offered tax breaks to people who bought homes. The
National Education Defense Act funded the socioeconomic mobility of
thousands of young men who trained themselves for well-paying jobs in
such fields as engineering.[16]

Unlike contemporary welfare programs, government investment in
1950s families was not just for immediate subsistence but encouraged long-
term asset development, rewarding people for increasing their investment
in homes and education. Thus it was far less likely that such families or individuals would ever fall back to where they started, even after a string of
bad luck. Subsidies for higher education were greater the longer people
stayed in school and the more expensive the school they selected. Mortgage
deductions got bigger as people traded up to better houses.[17]

These social and political support systems magnified the impact of the
postwar economic boom. "In the years between 1947 and 1973," reports
economist Robert Kuttner, "the median paycheck more than doubled, and
the bottom 20 percent enjoyed the greatest gains." High rates of unioniza-
tion meant that blue-collar workers were making much more financial
progress than most of their counterparts today. In 1952, when eager home
buyers flocked to the opening of Levittown, Pennsylvania, the largest
planned community yet constructed, "it took a factory worker one day to
earn enough money to pay the closing costs on a new Levittown house,
then selling for $10,000." By 1991, such a home was selling for $100,000 or
more, and it took a factory worker *eighteen weeks* to earn enough money for
just the closing costs.[18]

The legacy of the union struggle of the 1930s and 1940s, combined
with government support for raising people's living standards, set limits
on corporations that have disappeared in recent decades. Corporations
paid 23 percent of federal income taxes in the 1950s, as compared to just
9.2 percent in 1991. Big companies earned higher profit margins than
smaller firms, partly due to their dominance of the market, partly to
America's postwar economic advantage. They chose (or were forced) to
share these extra earnings, which economists call "rents," with employees. Economists at the Brookings Institution and Harvard University estimate that 70 percent of such corporate rents were passed on to workers at
all levels of the firm, benefiting secretaries and janitors as well as CEOs.
Corporations routinely retained workers even in slack periods, as a way
of ensuring workplace stability. Although they often received more generous tax breaks from communities than they gave back in investment, at
least they kept their plants and employment offices in the same place.
AT&T, for example, received much of the technology it used to finance

its postwar expansion from publicly funded communications research conducted as part of the war effort, and, as current AT&T Chairman Robert Allen puts it, there "used to be a lifelong commitment on the employee's part and on our part." Today, however, he admits, "the contract doesn't exist anymore."[19]

Television trivia experts still argue over exactly what the fathers in many 1950s sitcoms did for a living. Whatever it was, though, they obviously didn't have to worry about downsizing. If most married people stayed in long-term relationships during the 1950s, so did most corporations, sticking with the communities they grew up in and the employees they originally hired. Corporations were not constantly relocating in search of cheap labor during the 1950s; unlike today, increases in worker productivity usually led to increases in wages. The number of workers covered by corporate pension plans and health benefits increased steadily. So did limits on the work week. There is good reason that people look back to the 1950s as a less hurried age: The average American was working a shorter workday in the 1950s than his or her counterpart today, when a quarter of the workforce puts in 49 or more hours a week.[20]

So politicians are practicing quite a double standard when they tell us to return to the family forms of the 1950s while they do nothing to restore the job programs and family subsidies of that era, the limits on corporate relocation and financial wheeling-dealing, the much higher share of taxes paid by corporations then, the availability of union jobs for noncollege youth, and the subsidies for higher education such as the National Defense Education Act loans. Furthermore, they're not telling the whole story when they claim that the 1950s was the most prosperous time for families and the most secure decade for children. Instead, playing to our understandable nostalgia for a time when things seemed to be getting better, not worse, they engage in a tricky chronological shell game with their figures, diverting our attention from two important points. First, many individuals, families, and groups were excluded from the economic prosperity, family optimism, and social civility of the 1950s. Second, the all-time high point of child well-being and family economic security came not during the 1950s but *at the end of the 1960s.*

We now know that 1950s family culture was not only nontraditional; it was also not idyllic. In important ways, the stability of family and community life during the 1950s rested on pervasive discrimination against women, gays, political dissidents, non-Christians, and racial or ethnic minorities, as well as on a systematic cover-up of the underside of many families. Families that were harmonious and fair of their own free will may have been able to function more easily in the fifties, but few alternatives existed for members of discordant or oppressive families. Victims of child abuse, incest, alcoholism, spousal rape, and wife battering had no recourse, no place to go, until well into the 1960s.[21]

At the end of the 1950s, despite ten years of economic growth, 27.3 percent of the nation's children were poor, including those in white "underclass" communities such as Appalachia. Almost 50 percent of married-couple African-American families were impoverished—a figure far higher than today. It's no wonder African Americans are not likely to pick the 1950s as a golden age, even in comparison with the setbacks they experienced in the 1980s. When blacks moved north to find jobs in the postwar urban manufacturing boom they met vicious harassment and violence, first to prevent them from moving out of the central cities, then to exclude them from public space such as parks or beaches.

In Philadelphia, for example, the City of Brotherly Love, there were more than 200 racial incidents over housing in the first six months of 1955 alone. The Federal Housing Authority, such a boon to white working-class families, refused to insure homes in all-black or in racially mixed neighborhoods. Two-thirds of the city dwellers evicted by the urban renewal projects of the decade were African Americans and Latinos; government did almost nothing to help such displaced families find substitute housing.[22]

Women were unable to take out loans or even credit cards in their own names. They were excluded from juries in many states. A lack of options outside marriage led some women to remain in desperately unhappy unions that were often not in the best interests of their children or themselves. Even women in happy marriages often felt humiliated by the constant messages they received that their whole lives had to revolve around a man. "You are not ready when he calls—miss one turn," was a rule in the Barbie game marketed to 1950s girls; "he criticizes your hairdo—go to the beauty shop." Episodes of *Father Knows Best* advised young women: "The worst thing you can do is to try to beat a man at his own game. You just beat the women at theirs." One character on the show told women to always ask themselves, "Are you after a job or a man? You can't have both."[23]

The Fifties Experiment Comes to an End

The social stability of the 1950s, then, was a response to the stick of racism, sexism, and repression as well as to the carrot of economic opportunity and government aid. Because social protest mounted in the 1960s and unsettling challenges were posed to the gender roles and sexual mores of the previous decade, many people forget that families continued to make gains throughout the 1960s and into the first few years of the 1970s. By 1969, child poverty was down to 14 percent, its lowest level ever; it hovered just above that marker until 1975, when it began its steady climb up to contemporary figures (22 percent in 1993; 21.2 percent in 1994). The high point of health and nutrition for poor children was reached in the early 1970s.[24]

So commentators are being misleading when they claim that the 1950s was the golden age of American families. They are disregarding the number of people who were excluded during that decade and ignoring the socio-economic gains that continued to be made through the 1960s. But they are quite right to note that the improvements of the 1950s and 1960s came to an end at some point in the 1970s (though not for the elderly, who continued to make progress).

Ironically, it was the children of those stable, enduring, supposedly idyllic 1950s families, the recipients of so much maternal time and attention, that pioneered the sharp break with their parents' family forms and gender roles in the 1970s. This was not because they were led astray by some youthful Murphy Brown in her student rebel days or inadvertently spoiled by parents who read too many of Dr. Spock's child-raising manuals.

Partly, the departure from 1950s family arrangements was a logical extension of trends and beliefs pioneered in the 1950s, or of inherent contradictions in those patterns. For example, early and close-spaced childbearing freed more wives up to join the labor force, and married women began to flock to work. By 1960, more than 40 percent of women over the age of 16 held a job, and working mothers were the fastest growing component of the labor force. The educational aspirations and opportunities that opened up for kids of the baby boom could not be confined to males, and many tight-knit, male-breadwinner, nuclear families in the 1950s instilled in their daughters the ambition to be something other than a homemaker.[25]

Another part of the transformation was a shift in values. Most people would probably agree that some changes in values were urgently needed: the extension of civil rights to racial minorities and to women; a rejection of property rights in children by parents and in women by husbands; a reaction against the political intolerance and the wasteful materialism of 1950s culture. Other changes in values remain more controversial: opposition to American intervention abroad; repudiation of the traditional sexual double standard; rebellion against what many young people saw as the hypocrisy of parents who preached sexual morality but ignored social immorality such as racism and militarism.

Still other developments, such as the growth of me-first individualism, are widely regarded as problematic by people on all points along the political spectrum. It's worth noting, though, that the origins of antisocial individualism and self-indulgent consumerism lay at least as much in the family values of the 1950s as in the youth rebellion of the 1960s. The marketing experts who never allowed the kids in *Ozzie and Harriet* sitcoms to be shown drinking milk, for fear of offending soft-drink companies that might sponsor the show in syndication, were ultimately the same people who slightly later invested billions of dollars to channel sexual rebelliousness and a depoliticized individualism into mainstream culture.

There were big cultural changes brewing by the beginning of the 1970s, and tremendous upheavals in social, sexual, and family values. And yes, there were sometimes reckless or simply laughable excesses in some of the early experiments with new gender roles, family forms, and personal expression. But the excesses of 1950s gender roles and family forms were every bit as repellent and stupid as the excesses of the sixties: Just watch a dating etiquette film of the time period, or recall that therapists of the day often told victims of incest that they were merely having unconscious oedipal fantasies.

Ultimately, though, changes in values were not what brought the 1950s family experiment to an end. The postwar family compacts between husbands and wives, parents and children, young and old, were based on the postwar social compact between government, corporations, and workers. While there was some discontent with those family bargains among women and youth, the old relations did not really start to unravel until people began to face the erosion of the corporate wage bargain and government broke its tacit societal bargain that it would continue to invest in jobs and education for the younger generation.

In the 1970s, new economic trends began to clash with all the social expectations that 1950s families had instilled in their children. That clash, not the willful abandonment of responsibility and commitment, has been the primary cause of both family rearrangements and the growing social problems that are usually attributed to such family changes, but in fact have *separate* origins.

The reversal of the wage and family bargain of the 1950s began in the late 1960s, with a gradual rise in inequality among young male workers. As inflation picked up toward the end of the Vietnam War, young male breadwinner families started losing ground in real wages. In the cities, the labor supply grew faster than the manufacturing jobs that African Americans and Latinos had moved there to find. Then in the early 1970s, the biggest generation in history hit the housing market, setting off a bidding war for single-family homes. While overall price increases averaged 170 percent between 1972 and 1987, the average price of a new home rose by 294 percent. People who had bought homes before the rise saw their personal worth climb dramatically, especially since the cost of maintaining a home actually fell. But other people were saddled with crushing mortgages. Meanwhile, as Europe and Japan recovered from the devastation of World War II, America's competitive international position began to weaken. Sharp increases in oil prices in 1973 helped kick off a series of three recessions. Average weekly earnings of U.S. workers, on the rise since 1950, peaked in 1972 and 1973, then started a steady decline that has yet to be checked.[26]

How did families handle these pressures? As economists Gordon Berlin and Andrew Sum explain, most families "kept their standard of living up even while individual real wages were falling by doing the following four things: they postponed marriage, both spouses entered the labor market, they had fewer children, and they went into debt."[27]

Often, these behaviors led to changed family values, but they hardly represented a conscious rebellion against the past. Instead, American families were facing a *conflict* between two values they had dutifully absorbed in the 1950s. On the one hand, experts had told them that the best way to have a happy family was to have the husband work and the wife stay home. On the other hand, the media's descriptions of happiness had revolved around mother using the latest cooking and cleaning appliances, dad washing the car with the kids, and the kids hanging out in the comforts and spaciousness of an up-to-date home. By the mid-1970s, maintaining the prescribed family *lifestyle* meant for many couples giving up the prescribed family *form*. They married later, postponed children, and curbed their fertility; the wives went out to work. Such changes in family forms and values in the early 1970s were just as widespread among people who *accepted* the 1950s family dream as among those who rebelled against it.

Because more people went to work in the 1970s, or worked longer hours, per capita income continued to increase even while real wages fell. But this created other problems. Disruptions of the old pathways from school to marriage to childbearing became more common. Marital conflict and breakup increased. For two-parent families, rising household income, soaring housing values, and growing payroll and excise taxes left them paying more in taxes without seeing any payoffs in government investments that increased their personal security, their leisure, or their access to social capital. Back in the late 1940s, points out political analyst Kevin Phillips, the tax rate gap between a median-income family and a rich family "was enormous." By the 1970s, moderate- and middle-income taxpayers were paying almost as much as the rich. As rich families and corporations paid a smaller share of the tax burden, and middle-income families watched a larger proportion of their stagnant incomes go to taxes, antigovernment and antispending sentiment grew. By 1974–1975, bankers and bondholders in New York City began demanding layoffs of city workers and cutbacks of social services as a condition for lending the money that had historically financed urban growth.[28]

Unfortunately, the tax revolts of the 1970s were a good example of what happens when people seek legitimate goals with no historical or sociological perspective on the means they employ. Traditional antitax sentiment in America stemmed from egalitarian and antiwar sentiments. During the revolutionary period, Americans were horrified by the taxation system of Europe, in which the aristocracy taxed working people to finance the upper class, and by British attempts to pass the costs of their imperial wars on to the colonists. Standing this revolutionary antitax tradition on its head, the tax cuts of the 1970s and 1980s disproportionately benefited the wealthy, while cutbacks in investment and services curtailed the creation of jobs and social capital that moderate-income families needed most. Lower-income families had been losing ground since the early 1970s; in the 1980s the rich began to *gain* ground, at the expense of both the poor and the middle class. At the same time, government funding for parks and forest protection, highway building, urban investment, and school construction was steadily reduced, making people ever more dependent on private investments in schools, home security, and recreation to maintain the quality of their lives.[29]

From 1965 to 1969, net investment in public works by federal, state, and local governments averaged 2.3 percent of the gross national product. From 1975 to 1979 it averaged only 0.7 percent; between 1980 and 1984 it was 0.4 percent. Cutbacks in unemployment insurance programs caused the proportion of unemployed workers receiving unemployment compensation "to drop to record lows in seven of the ten years from 1980 to 1990." Welfare ceased to provide anything remotely resembling a viable fallback for families in economic distress. Cash benefits in the typical state lost more than half their purchasing power between 1970 and 1996. Meanwhile real wages continued to slide, resulting in a dramatic rollback of the gains made from 1947 to 1973. In each year from 1991 to 1994, average real wages were lower than they had been at any time between 1963 and 1990![30]

Of course, there were other important factors working to change family life in the 1960s and 1970s, such as the civil rights movement, the sexual revolution, government military spending, the controversy over the war in Vietnam, the women's movement, and the acceleration of individualism. The impact of these is a subject of much controversy. But it is vital to remember the economic backdrop against which the reconfiguration of family life and gender roles proceeded in the 1970s and 1980s.

Under the pressures of these economic conditions, many good innovations in family life were distorted, while some already problematic changes were made worse. Liberating and positive changes in gender roles and family relations continued to occur, but people often had to pay a higher price for their gains than they might otherwise have expected. Behaviors that would have been purely emancipating options in the earlier economic climate sometimes became grinding necessities, as when women who had fought for the choice to work suddenly found that they couldn't choose not to. The resultant strains, turmoil, and confusion about the future drastically affected people's family options and attitudes. But these value changes cannot be understood apart from the economic pressures that families and individuals increasingly faced.

Initially, many economists thought that the economic reverses of the 1970s were an ironic but temporary consequence of 1950s family patterns. Richard Easterlin has argued that young men entering the job market in the 1950s were in an especially fortunate position because the low fertility of their parents' generation put them in a seller's market as the postwar economy expanded its demand for labor. Companies seeking to increase production were competing for workers and therefore had to raise wages.[31]

But the workers hired in the 1950s gave birth to the baby-boom generation. Between 1950 and 1970, the school-age population more than doubled. In the postwar economic and political climate, this population boom fueled prosperity, stimulating the construction of roads, schools, homes, sewer systems, and factories to churn out family consumer goods.[32] Baby-boom children benefited from this economic expansion, and in the process developed high expectations about their own standard of living. When these youngsters became the next generation of workers, however, they faced a very different situation than their parents. With many more young men in competition for good jobs and resources, says Easterlin, the job and housing markets were far less favorable to young men starting families than they had been in the 1950s and 1960s. In consequence, the real wages of baby-boom workers began to fall, and their chances of experiencing poverty began to rise.

There are two interesting implications to this argument. The first supports the view that many changes in family forms and gender roles during the 1970s were an outgrowth of 1950s family values, though Easterlin makes the birth rate a stronger causal factor than I suggested earlier. Thus for Easterlin, the rise of dual-earner families and divorce during the 1970s was the direct result of an oversupply of workers produced by the family-oriented fifties. Because their parents had raised them with high expectations about home ownership and material goods, even relative deprivation was enough to dramatically change these young adults' family behavior. Many couples postponed having children, while more and more wives went to work. Conflicts over work, in turn, produced marital discord, thus leading to a rise in the divorce rate.

I think this is a relatively accurate *description* of what happened during the 1970s. But if an oversupply of baby-boom workers was the primary *cause* of falling real wages and unemployment, the second implication of Easterlin's argument is that these trends should have been reversed in the post–baby-boom generation, at least for male workers. As the next, smaller, generation of male workers entered the labor market, wages should have risen again, even if the female-headed families formed as a result of divorce or blocked marriage opportunities remained poor. But this prediction about male wages has not come true, suggesting that something bigger and more long term than a temporary oversupply of labor is behind the economic setbacks since the early 1970s. Sociologist Irene Browne reports that the chance of poverty has increased for each group of workers born *after* the baby boom.[33]

Some people might say that incomes would have risen and poverty fallen for the post–baby-boom generation if the averages hadn't been held down by the growth of African-American and single-parent families, both of which are more likely to be poor than white families or two-parent families. But Browne controlled for this in her calculations. While it is true that rising percentages of African-American families and single-mother families (in all racial or ethnic groups) have contributed to the overall growth of poverty, there is an *independent trend toward increasing poverty even among white, male-headed households*—the group that should have bounced back since the 1970s if the reversal of 1950s economic prosperity was just a temporary adjustment to an oversupply of labor. Browne finds that the odds of being poor for whites are more than five times higher for workers who entered the labor market *after* the baby boom "than for household heads born at the peak of the baby boom"—even after eliminating single-parent families from the calculations.

These trends in the wages of male household heads suggest that even if it were possible to revive 1950s family forms in the social context of the 1990s, this would not solve the problems of falling real wages and declining job security that so many Americans face today. Nevertheless, many people believe that we could at least alleviate the stress associated with our changing economy if we could restore marriage to a more central place in society and re-create the interdependence between men and women that seemingly made child rearing easier in the 1950s. So the question is, Which aspects of 1950s family life and parenting behaviors could or should be reinstated? Unfortunately, most of the answers currently being proposed lack a historical perspective. The result is that they often create more problems for families than they solve.

3

Why Working Mothers
Are Here to Stay

The 1950s was clearly out of balance in one direction, with almost half the adult population restricted in their access to economic and political roles beyond the family. But the last few decades have been out of balance in the opposite direction. Many of us now feel that our expanding roles beyond the family have restricted our access to family life.

At first glance, it appears that the new imbalance results from women, especially mothers, entering the workforce. Certainly, that trend has produced a dramatic change in relation to the decade that most people use as their measure of "traditional" family life. In 1950, only a quarter of all wives were in the paid labor force, and just 16 percent of all children had mothers who worked outside the home. By 1991, more than 58 percent of all married women, and nearly two-thirds of all married women with children, were in the labor force. Of the total number of children in the country, 59 percent, including a majority of preschoolers, had mothers who worked outside the home.[1]

But to analyze today's family imbalance as a conflict between work and mothering is to misread family history and to misdirect future family policy. Historically, productive work by mothers as well as fathers (and by young people) has not only been compatible with family life but has also strengthened family relationships. What's really out of balance is the relationship between market activities and nonmarket ones (including community as well as family ties). Our jobs don't make room for family obligations. The purchase of goods and services often substitutes for family or neighborhood activities. Phone calls, beepers, faxes, and e-mail constantly intrude into family time. To correct this imbalance, we need to reorganize work to make it more compatible with family life. We need to reorganize family life to make sure that all members share in the work needed to sustain it. We need to redirect technology so that it serves rather than dominates our social and interpersonal relationships.

Instead, however, the family consensus brokers encourage us to cobble together personal marital arrangements that combine what they consider to be the best family features from both the 1950s and the 1990s. They reason that if we could convince women to take time off from work while their children are young, bolster male wages enough that more families could afford to make this choice, increase the incentives for marriage, and combat the excesses of individualism that lead to divorce or unwed motherhood, then surely we could solve the conflicts that parents now experience in balancing work and family. While recommending that men should help out more at home and expressing abstract support for equal pay and promotion opportunities for women on the job, the family values think tanks nevertheless propose that parents revive "relatively traditional marital gender roles" for the period "when children are young," cutting back on mothers' paid work.[2]

In the absence of wider social change in work policies and family support systems, this is the individual solution that many men and women try to work out. And it may be a reasonable stopgap measure for parents who can afford it. But when such personal accommodations are put forward as an overarching political program for family life, they cease to sound quite so reasonable.

Although the family values instruction manual for how you should organize your marital and parenting roles claims to be a common-sense route to the balance most Americans are looking for, its actual prescriptions may surprise you. When leaders of the National Fatherhood Initiative announce that "fatherlessness" is "*the* crisis of our age," for instance, their definitions of a "fatherless" family are extraordinarily broad, and their directions for "recovering fatherhood" are extraordinarily narrow.[3]

"Every child deserves a father," write the authors of "Marriage in America," a report put together by the entire range of the family consensus spokespeople quoted here. But *real* fathers, by their definition, are found only in "intact" families—and only certain *kinds* of intact families at that. Stepfamilies "are inherently fraught with bad outcomes for children." Even some married fathers living at home with their own kids don't count as *real* fathers, because they allow "role convergence" to occur with their wives. When a father tries to act too much like a mother, giving up his distinctive breadwinning role, claims David Blankenhorn of the Institute for American Values, he "becomes no father."[4]

I'd be the first to agree that children need support and involvement from fathers and that children who do not receive it face a significant disadvantage. But the family values crusaders are asserting something far more controversial. They argue that most men cannot be good fathers, or even good citizens, if they are not married and living in the same household with the mother of their children. And they think men are unlikely to commit to marriage unless a woman validates the man's identity as primary family breadwinner. Their view of masculine nature is, ironically, far more cynical than that of any radical feminist you're likely to meet.

"Every society must be wary of the unattached male," writes David Popenoe of the Council on Families in America, "for he is universally the cause of numerous social ills." Only marriage and fatherhood, says Blankenhorn, channel men's natural tendencies toward violence and promiscuity into "pro-social" activities. When a magazine editor asked him if there were any other ways men could overcome their antisocial nature, Blankenhorn replied that they might "become a priest or a military officer. But mostly it's the fatherhood role."[5]

Women, the argument goes, are happy to care for children, but men's biological drives point them in a different direction. Men have to be coaxed and guided into responsible fatherhood, and societies have historically achieved this by granting husbands special status as moral educators, family authority figures, and breadwinners. When society stops viewing breadwinning "as a father's special task," we lose our most powerful way "to motivate fathers to provide for their children."[6]

The family values crusaders believe that all men and women, at least during their parenting years, should organize their families with the man as primary provider and protector and the wife as primary nurturer. Before and after child rearing, a woman is welcome to work; but unless she has no other option, she should engage in "sequencing"—alternating work and child raising rather than trying to combine them. Popenoe proposes the wife take "at least a year" off work, then work part-time until her children are in their early to mid-teens. Even when both husband and wife are employed, the woman should remain primarily responsible for nurturing, with the man as "junior partner" at home. Husbands should help out more than in the past, but anything that smacks of "androgyny" is to be avoided like the plague. Society, he argues, must "disavow the popular notion of radical feminists that 'daddies can make good mommies.'"[7]

Hostility to women's economic independence is a consistent subtext in "new consensus" writing. "Policies that encourage mothers to work instead of marry" are a large part of America's social problem, says Wade Horn of the National Fatherhood Initiative. Without providing any evidence, Dan Quayle claims studies show "that children whose parents work are *less likely* to have Mommy's undivided attention than children whose mothers stay home." Isn't it odd how quickly a discussion of working *parents* becomes an indictment of *Mommy*? According to this agenda, a male breadwinner–female homemaker division of labor is not an individual family choice but the correct model for every family. Women are told that there are compensations for giving up their aspirations to economic equality: "Even though the man is the head of the family, the woman is the neck, and she turns the head any way she wants." But if women are not willing to "give back" family leadership, groups such as the Promise Keepers advise men to "take it back. . . . Be sensitive. Treat the lady gently and lovingly. But lead!"[8]

While we can debate the *merits* of these proposals for America's families, I am more interested in examining their *practicality*. How likely is it that a majority of mothers will once more withdraw from paid employment during the early years of child rearing? What can historical and sociological analysis teach us about how realistic it is to propose that we revive the breadwinner identity as the basis for men's commitment to marriage and child raising?

The Late Birth and Short Life of the Male Breadwinner Family

One of the most common misconceptions about modern marriage is the notion that coprovider families are a new invention in human history. In fact, today's dual-earner family represents a return to older norms, after a very short interlude that people mistakenly identify as "traditional."

Throughout most of humanity's history women as well as men were family breadwinners. Contrary to cartoons of cavemen dragging home food to a wife waiting at the campfire, in the distant past of early gathering and hunting societies women contributed as much or more to family subsistence as men. Mothers left the hearth to forage for food, hunt small animals, trade with other groups, or tend crops.[9]

On this continent, neither Native American, African-American, nor white women were originally seen as economic dependents. Among European colonists, men dominated women, but their authority was based on legal, political, and religious coercion, not on men's greater economic importance. The most common words for wives in seventeenth- and eighteenth-century colonial America were "yoke-mates" or "meet-helps," labels that indicated women's economic partnership with men. Until the early nineteenth century, men and women worked together on farms or in small household businesses, alongside other family members. Responsibility for family life and responsibility for breadwinning were not two different, specialized jobs.[10]

But in the early 1800s, as capitalist production for the market replaced home-based production for local exchange and a wage-labor system supplanted widespread self-employment and farming, more and more work was conducted in centralized workplaces removed from the farm or home. A new division of labor then grew up within many families. Men (and older children) began to specialize in work outside the home, withdrawing from their traditional child-raising responsibilities. Household work and child care were delegated to wives, who gave up their older roles in production and barter. While slaves and free blacks continued to have high labor force participation by women, wives in most other ethnic and racial groups were increasingly likely to quit paid work outside the home after marriage.[11]

But it's important to remember that this new division of work between husbands and wives came out of a *temporary* stage in the history of wage labor and industrialization. It corresponded to a transitional period when households could no longer get by primarily on things they made, grew, or bartered, but could not yet rely on purchased consumer goods. For example, families no longer produced their own homespun cotton, but ready-made clothing was not yet available at prices most families could afford. Women still had to sew clothes from cloth that men purchased with their pay. Most families still had to grow part of their food and bake their own bread. Food preparation and laundering required hours of work each day. Water often had to be hauled and heated.

Somebody had to go out to earn money in order to buy the things the family needed; but somebody else had to stay home and turn the things they bought into things they could actually use. Given the preexisting legal, political, and religious tradition of patriarchal dominance, husbands (and youths of both sexes) were assigned to work outside the home. Wives assumed exclusive responsibility for domestic matters that they had formerly shared with husbands or delegated to older children and apprentices. Many women supplemented their household labor with income-generating work that could be done at or around home—taking in boarders, doing extra sewing or laundering, keeping a few animals, or selling garden products. But this often arduous work was increasingly seen as secondary to wives' primary role of keeping house, raising the children, and getting dinner on the table.

The resulting identification of masculinity with economic activities and femininity with nurturing care, now often seen as the "natural" way of organizing the nuclear family, was in fact a historical product of this nine-teenth-century transition from an agricultural household economy to an industrial wage economy. So even as an ideal, the male breadwinner family was a comparatively late arrival onto the historical scene. As a reality—a family form in which most people actually lived—it came about even later.

Throughout the nineteenth century, most families still depended on child labor or the work of wives on farms and in family businesses. It was not until the 1920s that a bare majority of American children lived in a home where the children did not have to work and where they had both a father who was the sole wage earner and a mother who was a full-time homemaker. Yet no sooner was the male breadwinner family established as a norm for children than it began to erode as a norm for wives.

The Revival of Women's Role as Family Coprovider

During the 1920s, an expansion of office jobs in the new urban economy drew thousands of women into the workforce. In the unstable economic and political climate of the 1930s and 1940s, married women found them-selves pulled into work for economic or political emergencies and shoved out when pressures to reemploy men mounted. The result was that more and more women gained work experience, and wives, even with young children, were increasingly seen as a legitimate reserve labor pool, available for use in a pinch. In World War II, women were exhorted to join the workforce. When the war ended, they were bumped to make room for re-turning veterans. Some women responded to being yanked around this way by resolving to quit their jobs and start a family as soon as they were finan-cially able; others felt regretful about the postwar pressure to make way for the male provider.[12]

Either way, though, it was during the 1950s, the height of the Ozzie and Harriet family ideal, that wives began their most rapid movement into the labor force. Mothers of young children still tended to withdraw from the labor force until their children were well established in school. But the need of both families and businesses for female labor soon outstripped the sup-ply of childless married women. After 1970, mothers—especially mothers of young children—became the fastest-growing group of female workers.[13]

For approximately 50 years, from the 1920s through the 1960s, the growth in married women's work outside the home was smaller than the decline in child labor, so that the male breadwinner family became increas-ingly dominant. But even at its high point in the 1950s, less than 60 percent of American children spent their youth in an Ozzie and Harriet–type family where dad went to work and mom stayed home. And by the 1970s the fifty-year reign of this family form was definitely over.[14]

Economists and sociologists cite many reasons for the sharp rise in the employment of mothers. Some mothers were coaxed out of the home by increases in the availability and pay of service work. Others took jobs to put their husbands through school or save for their children's education. Still others found that modern housework was just not a full-time occupation, and they wanted more to do. It's also possible that a critical mass had been reached in the seventy-year-long rise of paid work for married women: As more women believed they would have to work through much of their married lives, many felt they could not afford to postpone that work until they had gotten their children off to school.[15]

After 1973, real wages for young men began falling, creating a larger proportion of families where the mother worked just to keep the family afloat. Housing inflation meant that families with young children were especially likely to need the wife to work, in order to afford the new home that their growing family motivated them to buy. By 1989, almost 80 percent of all home buyers came from two-income households. Another incentive was the rising cost of higher education, which increased nearly three times faster than household income between 1980 and 1994.[16]

Today most families can no longer think of the earnings that wives and mothers bring home as a bonus that can be put aside when family needs call. Nor, increasingly, do the jobs women hold allow them the luxury of choosing to cut back or quit when family priorities change, any more than their husbands' jobs would. By 1993, married women working full-time contributed 41 percent of their families' incomes. Indeed, in 23 percent of two-earner couples, the wives earned *more* than their husbands.[17]

The sequencing of mothering and paid employment that characterized many women's activities over the past 100 years is becoming a thing of the past. Through most of this century, even though labor participation rates for women rose steadily, they dropped significantly when women were in their twenties and thirties. By 1990, however, labor-force participation rates no longer dipped for women in their child-raising years. Today, fewer and fewer women leave their jobs while their children are very young.[18]

Proponents of the modified male breadwinner family believe that if we could drastically reduce the number of single-mother households, raise wages for men, and convince families to get by on a little less, we might be able to get wives to quit work during their child-raising years. Polls consistently show that many women would like to cut back on work hours, though not quit entirely (and it's interesting that an almost equal number of men would also like to cut back their hours).[19] But a return to the norm of male breadwinner families is simply not feasible for most Americans.

Why Wives and Mothers Will Continue to Work Outside the Home

It's not just a dollars-and-cents issue. Most women would not give up the satisfactions of their jobs even if they could afford to quit. They consistently tell interviewers they like the social respect, self-esteem, and friendship networks they gain from the job, despite the stress they may face finding acceptable child care and negotiating household chores with their husbands. In a 1995 survey by Louis Harris & Associates, for example, less than a third of working women said they would prefer to stay home even if money were no object.[20]

Another reason women do not want to quit work is that they are not willing to surrender the increased leverage it gives them in the family. The simple truth is that women who do not earn income have much less decision-making power in marital relations than women who do. And no amount of goodwill on the part of husbands seems to lessen this imbalance. In one in-depth study of American families, researchers found that the primary determinant of power in all couples was who brings in the money. The only exception was among lesbians. Lesbian couples might be persuaded to have one partner stay home with the kids and the other earn the money, but I doubt that the Institute for American Values would consider this a positive step in the direction of "marital role complementarity."[21]

Aside from women's own motivations to remain at work, the issue of whether a family can afford to have the wife stay home is quite debatable. One of the most longstanding American traditions, much older than the ideal of the male breadwinner, is the search for socioeconomic mobility. That's why many families came to America in the first place. It's what people were seeking when they crossed the plains in covered wagons, why farmers switched from diversified family crops to specialized market production, what parents have expected education to provide for their children.

From the mid-nineteenth to the mid-twentieth century, there were three main routes to family economic advancement. One was child labor, allowing parents to accumulate enough to buy a house and possibly send a later generation to school. Another was the move from farm to city, to take advantage of higher wage rates in urban areas. The third was investment in increased training and education for male members of the family.

But child labor was abolished in the early twentieth century, and even before 1950 most men had already obtained nonfarm jobs. By the mid-1960s there were diminishing returns to the gains families could expect from further education or training for men. As these older strategies ceased to guarantee continued mobility, women's employment became so central to family economic advancement that it could less and less often be postponed or interrupted for full-time child raising.[22]

In other words, even for families where the uninterrupted work of wives isn't essential for minimum family subsistence, it is now the main route to even a modest amount of upward mobility. Those who tell women who "don't need to work" that they should go back to full-time child rearing are contradicting many of the other ideals most Americans hold dear. We're talking about abandoning the American dream here. The only way to get a significant number of families to make this choice would be to foster a thoroughly untraditional—some might even say un-American—acceptance of a stationary standard of living, a no-growth family economy. Some families may harbor such subversive ideals; yet the chances are slim that this will become a mass movement any time soon.

But can't women make up for their lost wages by saving on child care and transportation costs, combined with making meals from scratch and sewing their kids' clothes? Economist Joan Smith points to yet another reason that working wives and mothers are here to stay. Back when wives first started working outside the home, it was much easier to withdraw from wage work when they desired, substituting homemade goods or services for those purchased from wages. Many families still could grow much of their food or keep animals. People didn't need a car to do their shopping. A woman could sew clothes for her kids that weren't immediately distinguishable from those she might otherwise have bought with her paycheck.

The postwar economic boom fundamentally changed the internal economy of the household, making it less possible for families to move back and forth between women's waged and unwaged labor. Even in the least developed, most rural areas of the world, families are finding that women's household work can no longer substitute for wages. Modernization, for example, means children need more advanced schooling, which are not goods or services most mothers can produce at home. As one international development expert points out, "they can farm for food, [but] they can't farm for school fees."[23]

There are even greater obstacles facing American families wishing to substitute household production for waged labor. One of the driving forces behind rising family living standards since World War II has been the expansion of credit. In the 1950s and 1960s, credit cards, installment plans, and consumer loans democratized the enjoyment of such items as automobiles, lawn mowers, washing machines, and freezers. But once these items were no longer restricted to the rich, the mass market for *alternatives* to such items disappeared, ironically making such alternatives prohibitively expensive.

Prior to the 1950s, door-to-door peddlers, fruit and vegetable carts, knife grinders, ice and milk deliveries, and corner stores meant people did-n't need big refrigerators, cars, or a lot of privately owned tools to provide for their families and keep up their homes. Public transportation was once so widely used that construction decisions were made with that in mind. But with widespread access to the automobile, alternatives to car travel de-clined; jobs, homes, and shops are increasingly located without regard to the availability of public transportation. This makes it hard for families to pull back from waged labor and do without the cars, freezers, and washing machines that were once supposed to be extra conveniences. Yet the depen-dence of households on these commodities often locks them into a finan-cial treadmill that reinforces their need for more than one household earner.[24]

"Just jump off the treadmill," advise pundits and politicians who haven't had to compare food, furniture, or medical insurance costs since sixth-grade math class. During the 1996 presidential primaries, for exam-ple, one family values candidate was heard telling an aide: "I need to know the price of a gallon of milk and a dozen eggs. I need to know right now."[25]

Of course it's possible to cut back in some areas. Many families tell me they have gotten rid of their dishwasher so they can share the task of wash-ing and drying dishes with their children. Others mention the rewards of learning to do without conveniences they once thought indispensable. Families with young children often buy a VCR but disconnect the cable or television antenna, so their kids can't watch advertisements, cartoons, or daytime talk shows but can see videos the parents consider educational and age appropriate. And many parents of teenagers will testify that an old-fashioned deck of cards is a far better family togetherness investment than a fancy toy or expensive outing.

But there are limits to how fully most of us can opt out of the great American marketplace. Pro-child goals such as saving for a college educa-tion generally require two incomes. Even one-earner families often need two cars so they can take advantage of the wife's availability to run errands and chauffeur children. And very few families buy cars with cash. So de-pendence on purchased goods and credit is here to stay, and with this, the need for wives and mothers to work. As for "sequencing," sociologist Phyl-lis Moen notes, the "child-nurturing years are also the career-nurturing years."[26] Women who quit work to raise children very seldom catch up later—in today's economy, they may not get their jobs back at all.

Making the New Coprovider Family Work: What Can We Learn from the Past?

The massive entry of mothers into the paid workforce may be in some respects a return to an earlier family model, but that earlier model can't teach us much about raising children or maintaining stable marriages today. First, the requirements for child care are quite different now than in the earlier coprovider family, where much of the work that men and women did took place at the same location, often at home. Neither fathers nor mothers in such families spent the bulk of their time on child care, but either could more easily keep an eye on a child while working, and many children were gradually initiated into adult roles by participating in some of the work their parents did. There was also what you might call on-the-job child care, provided by older siblings or servants in the household. Alternatively, many families sent their kids away from home at a relatively early age to live or work in another household. Either way, supervision and socialization of children were less of a problem for working parents in the earlier coprovider family.

Today's coproducer family does not offer the same opportunity for combining productive and reproductive tasks. Men and women both work outside the home, at different locations. Rarely is on-the-job child care available, as it was in colonial days, for either parent. The apprenticeship and child-exchange customs that used to provide adult mentoring and supervision for children no longer exist. Prolongation of schooling has partly substituted for these traditional nonfamilial sources of care and education, but schools cannot cope with ill children, and school schedules do not match parents' work schedules, leaving gaps during critical hours of the day. Youths are far more likely to get into trouble between 3 and 6 P.M., for example, than after midnight.[27] There are no precedents from the earlier coprovider family that we can use to solve these problems.

The way that early coprovider families ensured marital stability would be unacceptable to most contemporary Americans. Although colonial women were no more dependent on men for subsistence than men were on women, wives could not translate their economic parity into personal or social equality. Law, religion, and politics enforced wives' subordination to husbands through everything from seating plans at church to domestic rituals at home. Husbands had the legal right to physically "chastise" their wives and government could not interfere unless "permanent injury or excessive violence" was used.[28]

For these reasons, women's coprovider roles did not increase wives' leverage in the household as they do today. Husbands had outside support for refusing to renegotiate the marriage relationship with an unhappy wife, and women had few possibilities for leaving a brutish husband. There is little we would want to learn from the earlier coprovider family about how to organize stable, harmonious marriages, despite attempts by groups such as the Promise Keepers to reestablish male leadership and female deference within the family.

But the earlier coprovider model bequeaths us two useful precedents that contradict the alarmist predictions of those who cannot accept modern family realities. The first is the knowledge that women in the past successfully combined child rearing with uninterrupted, lifelong participation in the wider economy. Conflict between work and motherhood was a consequence of the nineteenth-century reorganization of work, gender roles, and cultural values; it is not a natural fact of life. Historically, in most cultures, it has been extremely exceptional for women to withdraw from subsistence work after childbirth in order to take exclusive responsibility for child rearing. In the past, mothers engaged in production and exchange of goods throughout their lives, sharing child care with both kin and nonkin, without producing generations of dysfunctional kids. Even though we must coordinate work, parenting, and child care differently today, history shows that it can be done successfully.[29]

History also demonstrates that men do *not* need their wives to teach them how to relate to their children. Men have both the ability and the motivation to care for children at their own initiative. English and American fathers in the seventeenth and eighteenth centuries, historian John Gillis reports, were active in all aspects of domestic life, from monitoring their wives' pregnancies to taking responsibility for the daily socialization of children. In many contemporary families, the wife keeps track of all significant occasions, even reminding her husband of his parents' birthdays. But prior to the nineteenth century, fathers, not mothers, "carried on the bulk of family correspondence and were the masters of ceremonies for baptisms, weddings, and funerals." The idea that fathers are "junior partners" in domestic matters and that women have unique, irreplaceable roles in nurturing infants has "no precedent in earlier notions of parenthood."[30]

The memoirs of Cotton Mather, the most famous Puritan clergyman in colonial America, reveal that when he or his siblings got sick during the night, they went to their father, not their mother, for comfort and relief. "Thomas Jefferson's earliest recollections," history professor Mary Frances Berry reports, "included being physically cared for by slaves and nurtured by his father." Many children raised in the eighteenth and early nineteenth centuries recalled that their fathers were their primary nurturers, even when their mothers were around. And the stepfather relationship did not preclude such paternal involvement. When James Madison married the widow Dolly Payne Todd, he took personal responsibility for tutoring her son by her first marriage until they sent the youngster away to school at age 11.[31]

In England, it was not until the "bastardy" law of 1834 that fatherhood was made subsidiary to husbandhood. From that time on, a man's claim to paternity depended on his legal relationship to the mother. This was the judicial counterpart of an emotional reorganization of family life that made mothers the primary experts in child rearing. In the United States as well, courts, legislatures, and opinion makers gradually increased the domestic sway of women during the 1800s, fostering a new prejudice that men could not nurture children effectively and could only relate to them as adjuncts of their wives.[32]

The nineteenth-century male breadwinner family limited men's coercive power over wives and children, but highlighted their economic power. Family rituals and fables stopped stressing the subservience of women and children to the father's will and focused instead on their gratitude for his support. Among working-class families, some fathers formally turned their pay packets over to the wife, reserving an amount for personal use; others doled out allowances to women and children (even when the allowances came out of the children's wages). Either way, the weekly ceremony of redistribution emphasized the family's economic dependence on the man. In the middle class, children's birthdays, which had not previously been occasions for celebration, became an institution that underscored the father's role in passing out gifts. "Look what daddy gave us. Aren't we lucky to have such a good provider?"

But the bribe that so many family values crusaders want to offer modern men—reviving their prestige as providers in return for commitment to marriage—costs more, historically speaking, than most people realize. In the nineteenth century, fathers were displaced from the center of the family circle, their parenting skills were disparaged, and they lost the direct emotional access to their children that colonial fathers had possessed. The nurturing of husbands and fathers only came to be recognized when expressed in a paycheck. At the same time, the labor of wives and mothers came not to be recognized at all. It was relabeled as love, even though women continued to work very hard at home and to contribute substantially to family subsistence. According to the new male breadwinner ideology, mothers didn't *give to* their families; they *did for* their loved ones.

This polarized view of marital roles has caused us, for at least 100 years, to consistently underestimate the importance of work to women and of nurturing to men. But the historical evidence from earlier coprovider families demonstrates that fathers can take a much larger share of child rearing and mothers a much larger share of economic support without needing to feel inadequate or guilty.

The Good News: Benefits of Coprovider Families

These historical precedents are not merely of antiquarian interest. It turns out that women's yearning to engage in productive work and men's desire to participate in child rearing were not extinguished during the sway of the male breadwinner model, and they are now emerging with renewed vigor. We've already seen how committed working mothers are to their jobs today, even when they experience guilt, time stress, and marital conflict in juggling work and family life. And despite strong institutional and emotional pressures on men to place work above family, there is evidence that men want to reclaim the active parenting role that history tells us they are perfectly capable of playing.

Research shows that men as well as women increasingly find their "primary emotional, personal and spiritual gratification in the family setting" rather than on the job. A recent study of dual-earner couples conducted by the National Institute of Mental Health showed that a close relationship with children was just as important to a man's mental and physical health as to a woman's. Growing numbers of men are willing to make sacrifices at work to enhance such relationships. For example, a 1991 survey by the Families and Work Institute found that one-third of men under age 40—twice the number from just five years earlier—said they would consider giving up raises and promotions for more time at home. A study of Du Pont company employees, released in 1995, found that 47 percent of the women employed at the management or professional level, and 41 percent of the men, had told their supervisors they would not be available for relocation, while 45 percent of the women and 39 percent of the men in manufacturing jobs had refused to work overtime. "We've asked those questions in about 40 surveys of larger companies, and what we're seeing over time is that more men are making these trade-offs," said the president of the firm that conducted the survey. "Du Pont is not out of line. There is increasing convergence between men's answers and women's."[33]

Although men have been reluctant to assume their fair share of household chores, they are generally enthusiastic about doing more child rearing. Two federal agencies in Washington, D.C., found that half the fathers they employed changed their work hours in order to spend more time with wives and children when management introduced flextime. There are still many obstacles to men's full involvement in domestic life, but both historical and contemporary research support the belief that, as a majority of men told Gallup pollsters in 1991, "fathers . . . are just as capable as women of being good parents."[34]

Current investigation also reaffirms the historical lesson that women can work and share child care with others without harming their children.

Given America's undeveloped state of family-friendly work policies and our pitifully inadequate investment in quality child care, it is all the more impressive that contemporary research finds no negative effects of maternal employment or use of day care on children's economic, educational, or emotional life. Good parenting and effective child rearing, as one researcher sums up the evidence, "can be accomplished in a variety of work and family contexts. . . . There are few signs of difference in family processes as a function of maternal employment status per se."[35]

One of the most important benefits that working women bring to families with children is monetary. Not only do working women increase the total family resources available to children but families with a working woman may devote a higher proportion of their resources to children than families with a male breadwinner. International surveys have found that "women consistently contribute a higher percentage of their income to household maintenance than do men." Among low-income populations, children's nutritional status is often more closely connected to the *percent* of family income earned by the mother than to the absolute income of the family. And at higher economic levels, a wife's employment frequently makes a critical difference in children's educational options.[36]

The economic benefits of maternal employment may be important for families who need extra income, people often say, but in families that don't need the money, aren't there big psychological and social costs for both working mothers and their children? For women, there are certainly stresses involved in juggling work and family, especially when there are problems organizing child care. But in many instances, balancing work and motherhood can be more rewarding for women than specializing in one or the other. One prominent researcher found that there is a group of parents who might be termed "the blessedly stressed." The more roles they had, the happier and healthier they reported themselves to be and the less anxiety or depression they exhibited. Women who work, including mothers, are consistently found to be healthier, less depressed, and less frustrated than women who do not.[37]

Nor is it true that working women are selfishly choosing their own fulfillment over their children's needs. In fact, a certain amount of "selfishness" seems to be good for kids as well as moms. A woman's satisfaction with her role as worker, homemaker, or spouse, *whatever* that role may be, is one of the best predictors both of a good relationship with her child and of the child's own well-being.[38]

The benefits of working mothers for children are especially striking when the parents' income or educational background is lower than average. Initially, some researchers reported that children from the most economically and educationally advantaged families, with high levels of mental stimulation in the home, were by contrast somewhat disadvantaged by early maternal employment. More recent studies, however, have been unable to replicate this finding. The general consensus among researchers today is that no children are set back by maternal employment, in and of itself, and that some children are actively helped by it.[39]

There is no historical or contemporary evidence to suggest that mothers should choose to work *or* choose to stay home "for the sake of the kids." Mothering, contrary to the beliefs of family values crusaders, is not a zero-sum game. The more choice and autonomy women have, assuming a basic commitment to their children, the *better* their children do.

A large body of research finds that children whose mothers are employed do better in school, on average, than children with at-home mothers. Of course, a woman who stays home and devotes herself to enrichment programs may improve her child's academic skills, but women who are unhappy away from work or simply lack the temperament to handle all-day, one-on-one interactions with a child may find that their kids suffer from *too much* maternal attention. There is evidence that children of employed mothers show more responsibility and independence than children whose mothers stay home. However, a few women have told me that they felt so guilty about working that they produced *more* dependence in their children, doing too much for the kids in an attempt to make up for going off to work. These variations just go to show that today's diverse families are not helped by prefabricated proclamations about what's best for the kids.[40]

Working mothers often beat up on themselves for not spending more time with their children, but they may be romanticizing how they would use their day if they were not at work. The time loss experienced by children whose mothers work has been greatly exaggerated. In the first place, fathers often make up for mothers' reduced time at home, and this has extremely positive effects on children. Second, the difference in the amount of time spent on child care by working mothers and at-home mothers is surprisingly small. One large study in the 1980s found that the average full-time mother spent less than ten minutes a day playing with or reading to her child; the rest was spent on chores or television watching. Working women spent as much direct, one-on-one time with their children as nonemployed women, though they shared less time and space over the course of a weekday and loaded in more time on weekends. Furthermore, working women generally take special care to set aside periods of special, uninterrupted time for their children, sacrificing housework, leisure, or sleep rather than interactions with children when something has to give.[41]

One recent investigation found that mothers who spent more time working outside the home did spend "significantly less time doing what is traditionally defined as child care," but they spent more time in "nontraditional" parent–child interactions, such as sharing housework and leisure time with their children. When mothers work, the researchers concluded, "it is the *mix* of parent–child time that changes, rather than the overall amount of shared time."[42]

Tremendous anxiety was raised in 1986 when psychologist Jay Belsky suggested that infants under a year old who spent more than twenty hours a week in day care formed weaker attachments to their mothers than babies whose mothers stayed home. Belsky noted that his findings were probably a result not of day care per se but of the uneven quality of American day care. In Sweden, he pointed out, where child care centers are better funded and more closely controlled for quality, there was no evidence of negative effects on children when mothers returned to work full-time before their child's first birthday. Belsky expressed concern, though, about early return to work by mothers in the United States, where families have less desirable child care options.[43]

Ten years of research since Belsky's study should have allayed much of this anxiety. In April 1996 the National Institutes of Health released the most comprehensive study so far of families and day care. Conducted by 25 researchers who began their work with sharp disagreements about child care, the study has followed more than 1,300 families since 1991. The results show that children's attachment to their mothers is not affected by whether or not they are in day care, what age they enter, or how many hours they spend there. Researchers will continue to follow these children to see whether any differences in intellectual, emotional, and social developments appear at later ages. In the meantime, though, the study suggests that there is no reason for most parents to worry about the effects of day care on their children, so long as the parents are responsive and sensitive to their children's needs while they are at home.[44]

As with maternal employment, sometimes day care is actively beneficial to the children involved. Researcher Alison Clarke-Stewart has found that the social and intellectual development of children in day care is six to nine months ahead of children who remain at home. Impoverished children seem to get substantial long-term advantages from early childhood programs. In two long-term studies of low-income urban children, those enrolled in preschool were much more likely than their counterparts to avoid teenage pregnancy, to stay in school, and to find jobs in future years, and they were far less likely to be arrested. And at all income levels, child care may be especially helpful to small families, where children who stay home are not exposed to many ongoing interactions with other kids.[45]

The Bad News: Problems Facing
Coprovider Families Today

Contemporary studies reinforce the historical evidence that it is possible to construct healthy families that don't follow the male breadwinner–female caretaker model. But there are still tremendous strains associated with the emergence of the new coprovider family. Two parents have to hold down three essentially full-time jobs (or a single parent has to hold down two), all of which take place in different locations, require different skills, and involve people in different social networks. The result, as any parent can testify, is stress, both as a parent and a partner.

Finding affordable, quality child care, for example, is one of the biggest problems. In 1993, nearly 10 million children under age 5 needed day care while their mothers were at work. Thirty percent of these were enrolled in organized day care centers or preschools, 22 percent were cared for by nonrelated caregivers, and 48 percent were kept by relatives while their mothers were on the job—down from 53 percent with relatives in 1991. In many families, parents work opposing shifts so that one parent is home while the other is at work.[46]

None of these solutions is ideal. Tag-team care by parents can undermine the adults' relationship and well-being. Center care is extremely uneven, and low-income families, who spend almost a quarter of their total family income on child care costs, often cannot afford decent facilities. Preschools are frequently unavailable in rural areas and economically distressed neighborhoods. Many home care arrangements escape regulation by their states' licensing system, resulting in higher ratios of children to adults than researchers say is best. Some relatives do day care to earn extra money or to help out the mother, rather than because they enjoy working with children or have any skills at doing so. In consequence, children are no more likely to be securely attached to child care providers who are kin than to those who are nonkin. All these arrangements can be difficult for children where providers change frequently or the care is of low quality.[47]

In addition to the 9.9 million children under age 5 who need day care, another 22.3 million children aged 5 to 14 with working mothers need supplemental after-school care. Some researchers note that fears about "latch-key" kids have been exaggerated, and many youngsters do very well in some form of "self-care." Yet the fact remains that children of this age do need monitoring, and a lot of them are not getting it. Research on young and mid-adolescent children indicates that "the type of after-school supervision a child experiences is more critical than whether or not the mother is employed." Even many families where the mother does not work would benefit from quality after-school programs.[48]

But after-school programs have recently been labeled "pork" by cost-cutting politicians, and many have been severely cut back. Parents with long commutes, evening shifts, or irregular hours face special problems finding consistent child care; they often patch together a "crazy quilt" of multiple care combinations that cause stress for both parents and children. When inadequate after-school care interacts with poverty or with deprived neighborhoods, the results can be high levels of family distress and added risks to children.[49]

Even affluent families face child care problems. Some rely on low-paid nannies or maids who have few options other than to be almost continuously available to their employers, and this exploitative work situation is often harmful to children. It certainly damages the caregivers' *own* family lives. It can also produce resentments by the caregivers, sabotaging the care received by the more privileged children as well.[50]

Even for families with access to high-quality child care, another source of stress comes in the form of long work hours and commutes, combined with an unequal division of labor at home. Three out of every ten men and four out of every ten women "often" or "very often" feel "used up" at the end of the workday. Working mothers are especially likely to report feeling overwhelmed; they are more likely to get sick than their husbands. While men have increased their child care activities significantly, especially when their wives work a different shift than they do, child care is still far from evenly shared, and housework remains even more imbalanced.[51]

Arlie Hochschild calls it "the stalled revolution." Women's family roles have changed far more than men's, so many women who now work equal hours with their husbands still come home to a domestic second shift at night and on weekends. Women have cut back their housework from an average of thirty hours a week just two decades ago to about twenty hours a week today. But married fathers have failed to make up the difference, increasing their household work from five to about ten hours a week. Men's failure to change their domestic roles as much as women have changed their work ones is a major source of discord between men and women.[52]

Men whose wives work outside the home perform more housework than men whose wives do not, and on average, the higher the wife's contribution to household income, the more equally shared is the housework. Rarely, though, is the work equally divided. The greater the man's income, the less likely he is to do chores. At the other end of the continuum are husbands whose wives contribute the bulk of the family's economic support: Many find this so threatening to their definition of masculinity that they attempt to reassert their "manhood" by refusing to do "women's work" around the house.[53]

Even with good intentions, men face pressures against taking equal parenting responsibilities with their wives. In a study by the National Institute of Mental Health about why so few fathers took parental leaves when their babies were born, 63 percent of the men reported that their supervisors would not like it, and 43 percent said they feared negative repercussions from coworkers. The fact that most leaves in the United States are unpaid, unlike in Europe, is also a major difficulty for families. When dads do take time off, they generally have to use accumulated paid vacation time or personal days rather than unpaid parental leave—a fact that some politicians and businesses then cite to show that fathers are uninterested in parental leave.[54]

It's not just employers and coworkers who sabotage men who desire to play a stronger parenting role. In a sample of families studied a few years ago, the more fathers attempted to take active roles in caring for their own children, "the more mixed or negative feedback" they received from the grandparents. Two other research projects on married parents in the United States found that the majority of women resisted their husbands' efforts to get more involved in child care, even when the fathers *wanted* to do so.[55]

Whether the resistance comes from women or men, or from some interaction between them, the main barriers to fathers' fuller involvement in child care and housework are the values held over from the male breadwinner–female caretaker family model. This legacy increases the stress on working mothers and denies children the benefit of fully involved fathers. Until the imbalance between women's expanded work roles and men's lagging domestic roles is corrected, neither pocket dictionaries for interpreting male–female language differences nor pep talks about the sanctity of marriage will significantly reduce the incidence of divorce and separation.

But instead of confronting this imbalance, the "new consensus" crusaders want working mothers to back off from their demands on men. The linchpin of the family values campaign in the 1990s has been the argument that though the expansion of male–female equality over the past four decades has generally been good, the early years of child rearing trigger a "parental emergency" that requires a temporary return to so-called traditional gender roles. It's okay for wives to work before the children come, the crusaders concede. And "role convergence" may be healthy in mid-life or old age when "each sex can 'reclaim' exactly those aspects of human potentiality that, during the parental emergency, were ceded to the other sex in the interest of the child." But in between, the best way to reduce marital stress and meet children's needs is for father and mother to specialize in what they naturally do best. Men should take on most of the breadwinning during the child-rearing years; women should devote their primary attention to nurturing the children and orchestrating the husband's relationship with them.[56]

The Parental Emergency: Why a Traditional Response to Child Rearing Makes Things Worse for Modern Families

Two-earner couples *do* experience strain, and the arrival of a child intensi-fies the pressures. Ironically, though, couples who attempt to solve the new problems of coprovider families by returning to old patterns often end up worse off in the long run.

Consider what happens to women who try to go back to the sequenc-ing of child rearing and work that has characterized women's lives for the past 100 years. By taking traditionally "feminine," low-paid, dead-end work that can be easily interrupted "for the sake of the kids," women find them-selves in jobs that are *less* likely than nontraditional occupations to offer the flexibility and autonomy that working mothers need.[57]

Many studies suggest that part-time jobs have a negative impact on women's mental health, possibly because they encourage families to oper-ate under the fiction that the wife can "do it all," rather than pressing the husband to pitch in or forcing both parents to recognize that they may need outside help. The risk of behavior problems for children of working mothers is greater for women who work a smaller number of hours rather than a larger number. The best outcomes for children occur when mothers and fathers have good jobs, especially jobs that improve over time. Work-ing mothers and their children do best when the women are skilled, long-term employees, valued enough by their employers to be able to command good vacation benefits and time off to attend to family needs. Unfortu-nately, these are not the kind of jobs that women get by working part-time, curtailing their investment in education and work, or quitting work for a year or two at a stretch.[58]

It may *feel* logical to the family values crusaders that the best way for couples to respond to the parental emergency is to fall back on familiar gender roles for a while, but at this point in the historical transformation of family life, retreating from shared marital responsibilities is exactly the wrong thing to do. Philip and Carolyn Cowan have devoted many years of research to discovering what happens to marital partners as they become parents, and they have experimented with different ways of reducing the stress of the transition. Their studies show that parenthood frequently trig-gers a decline in marital satisfaction precisely *because* couples tend to revert to a male breadwinner–female nurturer mode after the birth of a child. Women resent the backsliding in equality, while men are either stressed by their heightened breadwinning responsibilities or confused by their wives' lack of appreciation for their resumption of the main provider role. The more different men and women become in their experiences and attitudes after childbirth, the Cowans found, the more dissatisfied they are likely to be in their marital relationship and the more conflict they are likely to report. Conversely, when couples work to *decrease* the divergence between husband and wife, the partners are less likely to experience conflict and disenchantment with the marriage.[59]

Family values spokesman David Blankenhorn worries that attempts to involve men equally in fathering will just lead to fathers experiencing the same conflicts between work and parenthood that women do. He thinks we can contain such conflicts by confining them to women. We should not, he argues, undermine one of the great advantages men bring to family life— that they *don't* feel torn between work and family but instead see work as the main way they serve their family.[60]

But it's too late to protect men from this stress. Role strain is currently a fact of life for fathers as well as mothers. One survey of a public utility in the Northeast found that almost the same proportion of fathers as mothers (36 percent as compared to 37 percent) reported "a lot of stress" in balancing work and parenting. Another study of 1,200 employees found that 72 percent of the men said they were having trouble juggling child care and career issues.[61]

We need to reduce role strain for *both* men and women. This can only be done by addressing the need of many women for more help from their husbands, the need of many fathers for more recognition of their family responsibilities, and the need of all working parents for flexible work policies and accessible, quality child care.

What Today's Coprovider Families Really Need

The answer to the role strain and marital conflicts that occur in modern families is not to refurbish old gender relationships, however comforting they seem on the surface. Rather, we must reorganize both marriage and work to accommodate the needs of working parents and their children. Changes in cultural and personal values about marriage are essential if we are to move past the "stalled revolution" in male–female relations that leads to so much stress. As therapist Betty Carter has commented, if any other institution in this country was failing half the people who entered it, we'd demand that the institution change to fit people's new needs, not the other way around.

But changes in the personal relations of marriage require adjustments in institutional support systems so men can act on their emerging parenting values and women can let go of their increasingly embattled sense that they are completely responsible for managing child care. Both men and women need and want to work; neither sex can or will agree to withdraw from work. Therefore employers have to stop assuming they can hire a full-time homemaker along with a full-time wage worker for the price of one employee. They must organize their work policies on the assumption that *all* their workers have caretaking responsibilities. The best comment I've heard on this issue was raised in a TV show where I debated a business executive who claimed this adjustment would be prohibitively expensive. A female audience member in her sixties stood up and told him: "Look at it this way. You had women's free labor for years to let you pay our husbands less than it really costs to raise a family. Count yourself lucky we traditional housewives aren't suing for back pay."

Some companies object that reorganizing their work policies to meet family needs will put them at a disadvantage in our competitive economy. But government can create a level playing field by requiring all companies to adopt such policies as a condition of receiving the legal rights and tax privileges of conducting a business. Workers need paid parental leaves and time-off days to care for sick children (or parents). These should be considered part of the normal costs of doing business.

Alternative work schedules, such as flextime, are also essential. Many parents tell me that, given the problems of after-school supervision even for older children, they would take advantage of policies such as Sweden's law granting parents the option to work three-fourths time, for less pay but without losing benefits or seniority. On-site child care should be routinely provided by employers, perhaps encouraged by tax incentives or outright subsidies such as are routinely given for shipbuilding, oil exploration, and the like. Government agencies need to make sure that accessible, regulated, and well-staffed child care centers or home care arrangements are available in all communities.

Such mandated family benefits are a fact of life in every European country today. Every Western European nation provides *paid* maternity leaves; most have legislated paid sick leaves for parents who need to stay home with ill children. The United States shares with South Africa the distinction of being the only two developed economies without a national insurance program for families.[62]

There is no historical reason to think that the construction of family-friendly policies and regulations can be entrusted solely to private companies. As with airplane safety and meat preparation, the regulation of child care centers and the provision of family benefits cannot be left to people whose profits depend on cutting costs.

In some cases, farsighted companies have demonstrated that they can provide high-quality child care (and sometimes elder care as well) for their employees, along with flextime, reduced hours, and other family-friendly options, while actually increasing worker productivity and morale. But the parents most likely to be stressed by low-paid employment and inflexible work hours are also least likely to have the leverage to get such services from their employers. For these reasons, some federal subsidy will undoubtedly be required.[63]

Many people oppose government funding for matters such as child care. But history amply demonstrates the necessity of public investment in social health and well-being. Even Adam Smith, the father of the free market, insisted that government must build and maintain education systems and other "advantageous" public works whose expenses are too high to yield a profit to private individuals or companies.[64]

During the transition to the male breadwinner family during the early nineteenth century, government funded the transportation systems that were essential for the development of a national market. In today's transition to a coprovider family system, child care, paid parental leaves, and family-friendly work policies are equally vital social and economic investments as were canals and railroads then. We don't ask individual families and businesses to pay *per use* for roads, fire protection, disease control, or meat inspection. Instead, we consider such investment a form of social capital. What social capital could be more essential to society than the care and education of our children?

Many European countries have already answered this question by developing comprehensive family support systems, combining high-quality child care with generous family leave and assistance programs. We can build on their experiences to meet the needs of American families. One very practical incentive to do so is the fact that availability of child care is often the critical factor in moving families off welfare and out of poverty.[65]

Picking Our Family-Friendly Priorities

Despite overwhelming public support for such family-friendly reforms, none of the so-called family values organizations will lead a crusade to implement these policies. Some oppose them outright. "Providing child care is a distraction from our main goal of helping married women stay home to raise their kids," a member of the misnamed Family Research Council told me at a forum in Washington, D.C. "If you make it easier for mothers to have careers, you also reward divorce and illegitimacy."

The Family Research Council and several individuals affiliated with the Council on Families in America oppose mandated parental leaves on the grounds that these "inhibit the flexibility" of employers. People's birth control, abortion, and divorce options cannot be left to personal choice, they believe, but employers' work and family leave policies cannot be regulated.

More moderate family values leaders express support for workplace reforms in the abstract, but they are reluctant to actively press for policies that might place single-parent or cohabiting families on the same footing as married-couple ones, even when such measures would also make it easier for married women to combine work and motherhood. They fear such measures will contribute to the undermining of the married, coresidential nuclear family as the exclusive place for rearing children. Therefore their first priority is not to win concrete reforms for working parents but to roll back divorce and unwed motherhood. Before we start requiring employers and government to adopt policies favoring working parents, they argue, we must first "rewrite the cultural script" of American life to favor lifetime marriage.

Browsing on the computer at my library recently, I found 11 books, 209 articles, and hundreds of interviews put out by the new consensus crowd between 1994 and early 1996, all of which insisted that the most important task for the 1990s was to convince people that divorce and unwed motherhood are wrong or even shameful. As Don Eberly of the National Fatherhood Initiative put it: "Whatever else the debate is about, it must be primarily and predominantly about shoring up and rebuilding the intact two-parent family. Everything else is secondary."[66]

The campaign to rekindle disapproval of divorce has had considerable success in influencing attitudes, if not behavior. Polls show a growing concern about "too much" and "too easy" divorce. Several states have introduced legislation to repeal no-fault divorce or slow down the divorce process for couples with children. These trends fill the family values crowd with optimism. Young people "are yearning for restabilization," William Galston, Clinton's former domestic policy advisor, told an interviewer in 1996. "Sociologists think this might be the Great Awakening."[67]

But getting people to worry about the effects of divorce is not the same as ending divorce, and it does nothing for children in families that are already divorced. After all, "rebuilding the intact two-parent family" is a contradiction in terms. It is also no more realistic a solution to America's family dilemmas than the proposal to revive the male breadwinner family. Just as working mothers are here to stay, diversity in family forms and marriage arrangements is also going to remain a fact of life. Ignoring the historical and sociological trends that produce such diversity in favor of a cheerleading campaign to promote enduring marriage is no service to *any* type of family.

4

The Future of Marriage

M ost Americans support the emergence of alternative ways of organizing parenthood and marriage. They don't want to reestablish the supremacy of the male breadwinner model or to define masculine
and feminine roles in any monolithic way. Many people worry, however,
about the growth of alternatives to marriage itself. They fear that in some of
today's new families parents may not be devoting enough time and resources to their children. The rise of divorce and unwed motherhood is
particularly worrisome, because people correctly recognize that children
need more than one adult involved in their lives.

As a result, many people who object to the "modified male breadwinner" program of the "new consensus" crusaders are still willing to sign on
to the other general goals of that movement: "to increase the proportion of
children who grow up with two married parents," to "reclaim the ideal of
marital permanence," to keep men "involved in family life," and to establish the principle "that every child deserves a father."[1]

Who could disagree? When we appear on panels together, leaders of
"traditional values" groups often ask me if I accept the notion that, on the
whole, two parents are better than one. If they would add an adjective such
as two *good* parents, or even two *adequate* ones, I'd certainly agree. And of
course it's better to try to make a marriage work than to walk away at the
first sign of trouble.

As a historian, however, I've learned that when truisms are touted as stunning new research, when aphorisms everyone agrees with are presented as a courageous political program, and when exceptions or complications are ignored for the sake of establishing the basic principles, it's worth taking a close look for a hidden agenda behind the cliches. And, in fact, the new consensus crowd's program for supporting the two-parent family turns out to be far more radical than the feel-good slogans might lead you to believe.

Members of groups such as the Council on Families in America claim they are simply expressing a new consensus when they talk about "reinstitutionalizing enduring marriage," but in the very next breath they declare that it "is time to raise the stakes." They want nothing less than to make lifelong marriage the "primary institutional expression of commitment and obligation to others," the main mechanism for regulating sexuality, male–female relations, economic redistribution, and child rearing. Charles Murray says that the goal is "restoration of marriage as an utterly distinct, legal relationship." Since marriage must be "privileged," other family forms or child-rearing arrangements should not receive tax breaks, insurance benefits, or access to public housing and federal programs. Any reform that would make it easier for divorced parents, singles, unmarried partners, or stepfamilies to function is suspect because it removes "incentives" for people to get and stay married. Thus, these groups argue, adoption and foster care policies should "reinforce marriage as the child-rearing norm." Married couples, and only married couples, should be given special tax relief to raise their children. Some leaders of the Institute for American Values propose that we encourage both private parties and government bodies "to distinguish between married and unmarried *couples* in housing, credit, zoning, and other areas." Divorce and illegitimacy should be stigmatized.[2]

We've come quite a way from the original innocuous statements about the value of two-parent families and the importance of fathers to children. Now we find out that we must make marriage the only socially sanctioned method for organizing male–female roles and fulfilling adult obligations to the young. "There is no realistic alternative to the one we propose," claims the Council on Families in America. To assess this claim, we need to take a close look at what the consensus crusaders mean when they talk about the need to reverse the "deinstitutionalizing" of marriage.[3]

Normally, social scientists have something very specific in mind when they say that a custom or behavior is "institutionalized." They mean it comes "with a well-understood set of obligations and rights," all of which are backed up by law, customs, rituals, and social expectations. In this sense, marriage is still one of America's most important and valued institutions.[4]

But it is true that marriage has lost its former monopoly over the organization of people's major life transitions. Alongside a continuing commitment to marriage, other arrangements for regulating sexual behavior, channeling relations between men and women, and raising children now exist. Marriage was once the primary way of organizing work along lines of age and sex. It determined the roles that men and women played at home and in public. It was the main vehicle for redistributing resources to old and young, and it served as the most important marker of adulthood and respectable status.

All this is no longer the case. Marriage has become an option rather than a necessity for men and women, even during the child-raising years. Today only half of American children live in nuclear families with both biological parents present. One child in five lives in a stepfamily and one in four lives in a "single-parent" home. The number of single parents increased from 3.8 million in 1970 to 6.9 million in 1980, a rate that averages out to a truly unprecedented 6 percent increase each year. In the 1980s, the rate of increase slowed and from 1990 to 1995 it leveled off, but the total numbers have continued to mount, reaching 12.2 million by 1996.[5]

These figures understate how many children actually have two parents in the home, because they confuse marital status with living arrangements. Approximately a quarter of all births to unmarried mothers occur in households where the father is present, so those children have two parents at home in fact if not in law. Focusing solely on the marriage license distorts our understanding of trends in children's living arrangements. For example, the rise in cohabitation between 1970 and 1984 led to more children being classified as living in single-parent families. But when researchers counted unmarried couples living together as two-parent families, they found that children were spending *more* time, not less, with both parents in 1984 than in 1970. Still, this simply confirms the fact that formal marriage no longer organizes as many life decisions and transitions as it did in the past.[6]

Divorce, cohabitation, remarriage, and single motherhood are not the only factors responsible for the eclipse of marriage as the primary institution for organizing sex roles and interpersonal obligations in America today. More people are living on their own before marriage, so that more young adults live outside a family environment than in earlier times. And the dramatic extension of life spans means that more people live alone after the death of a spouse.[7]

The growing number of people living on their own ensures that there are proportionately fewer families of *any* kind than there used to be. The Census Bureau defines families as residences with more than one householder related by blood, marriage, or adoption. In 1940, under this definition, families accounted for 90 percent of all households in the country. By

1970, they represented just 81 percent of all households, and by 1990 they represented 71 percent. The relative weight of marriage in society has decreased. Social institutions and values have adapted to the needs, buying decisions, and lifestyle choices of singles. Arrangements other than nuclear family transactions have developed to meet people's economic and interpersonal needs. Elders, for example, increasingly depend on Social Security and private pension plans, rather than the family, for their care.[8]

Part of the deinstitutionalization of marriage, then, comes from factors that few people would want to change even if they could. Who wants to shorten the life spans of the elderly, even though that means many more people are living outside the institution of marriage than formerly? Should we lower the age of marriage, even though marrying young makes people more likely to divorce?[9] Or should young people be forced to live at home until they do marry? Do we really want to try to make marriage, once again, the only path for living a productive and fulfilling adult life?

Working Women, Singlehood, and Divorce

If the family values crusaders believe they are the only people interested in preserving marriages, especially where children's well-being is involved, self-righteousness has blinded them to reality. I've watched people of every political persuasion struggle to keep their families together, and I've met very few divorced parents who hadn't tried to make their marriages work. Even the most ardent proponents of reinstitutionalizing marriage recognize that they cannot and should not force everyone to get and stay married. They do not propose outlawing divorce, and they take pains to say that single parents who were not at fault should not be blamed. Yet they still claim that moral exhortations to take marriage more seriously will reduce divorce enough to "revive a culture of enduring marriage."

This is where the radical right wing of the family values movement is far more realistic than most moderates: So long as women continue to make long-term commitments to the workforce, marriage is unlikely to again become the lifelong norm for the vast majority of individuals unless draconian measures are adopted to make people get and stay married. Paid work gives women the option to leave an unsatisfactory marriage. In certain instances, much as liberals may hate to admit it, wives' employment increases dissatisfaction with marriage, sometimes on the part of women, sometimes on the part of their husbands. When a wife spends long hours at work or holds a nontraditional job, the chance of divorce increases.[10]

I'm not saying we can't slow down the divorce rate, lessen emotional and economic disincentives for marriage, and foster longer-lasting commitments. But there is clearly a limit to how many people can be convinced to marry and how many marriages can be made to last when women have the option to be economically self-supporting. In this sense, the right-wing suspicion that women's work destabilizes marriage has a certain logic.

There is, however, a big problem with the conclusion that the radical right draws from this observation. To say that women's employment has *allowed* divorce and singlehood to rise in society as a whole does not mean that women's work *causes* divorce and singlehood at the level of the individual family, or that convincing women to reduce their work hours and career aspirations would reestablish more stable marriages.[11]

Trying to reverse a historical trend by asking individuals to make personal decisions opposing that trend is usually futile. When individuals try to conduct their personal lives as if broader social forces were not in play, they often end up worse off than if they adapted to the changing times. What traditional values spokesman in his right mind would counsel his own daughter not to prepare herself for higher-paid, nontraditional jobs because these might lead to marital instability down the road?

After all, even if a woman *prefers* to have a male breadwinner provide for her, the fact that people can now readily buy substitutes for what used to require a housewife's labor changes marriage dynamics in decisive ways. Most individuals and families can now survive quite easily without a full-time domestic worker. If this frees women to work outside the home, it also frees men from the necessity of supporting a full-time homemaker.

Before the advent of washing machines, frozen foods, wrinkle-resistant fabrics, and 24-hour one-stop shopping, Barbara Ehrenreich has remarked, "the single life was far too strenuous for the average male." Today, though, a man does not really need a woman to take care of cooking, cleaning, decorating, and making life comfortable. Many men still choose marriage for love and companionship. But as Ehrenreich notes, short of outlawing TV dinners and drip-dry shirts, it's hard to see how we can make marriage as indispensable for men as it used to be. And short of reversing laws against job discrimination, there's no way we can force women into more dependence on marriage. Neither men nor women need marriage as much as they used to. Asking people to behave as if they do just sets them up for trouble.[12]

Wives who don't work outside the home, for instance, are at much higher economic and emotional risk if they *do* get deserted or divorced than women who have maintained jobs. They are far more likely to be impoverished by divorce, even if they are awarded child support, and they eventually recover a far lower proportion of the family income that they had during marriage than women who had been working prior to the divorce.[13]

Women who refrain from working during marriage, quit work to raise their children, or keep their career aspirations low to demonstrate that "family comes first" are taking a big gamble, because there are many factors other than female independence that produce divorce. Some of them are associated with women's decisions or expectations *not* to work or *not* to aspire to higher education. For example, couples who marry in their teens are twice as likely to divorce as those who marry in their twenties. Women who marry for the first time at age 30 or more have exceptionally low divorce rates, despite their higher likelihood of commitment to paid work. Women who don't complete high school have higher divorce rates than women who do, and high school graduates have higher divorce rates than women who go on to college. With further higher education, divorce rates go up again, but should we advise a woman to abandon any aspirations she may have developed in college because her statistical chance of staying married will rise if she quits her education now? Besides, the statistics may confuse the impact of higher education with what is called the "glick effect"—people who have started toward *but failed to complete* a particular degree or diploma, whatever its level, are more likely to divorce than those who secure a precise diploma or degree. A more useful piece of advice might be that if you *are* going to do graduate work, hang in there until you've finished.[14]

Highly educated and high-paid women may have a greater chance of divorcing, but women with low earnings and education have lower prospects of getting married in the first place. Men increasingly choose to marry women who have good jobs and strong educational backgrounds. In the 1980s, reversing the pattern of the 1920s, "women with the most economic resources were the most likely to marry." But of course these are also the women most able to leave a bad marriage.[15]

The Issue of No-Fault Divorce

Some people believe we could stabilize families, and protect homemakers who sacrifice economic independence, by making divorce harder to get, especially in families with children. This sounds reasonable at first hearing. Divorce tends to disadvantage women economically, and to set children back in several ways. It is hardest of all on women who committed themselves and their children to the bargain implied by the 1950s marriage ideal—forgoing personal economic and educational advancement in order to raise a family, and expecting lifetime financial support from a husband in return. A 47-year-old divorced mother describes what happened to her: "Instead of starting a career for myself, I helped my husband get his business started. I had four children. I made the beds. I cooked the meals. I cleaned the house. I kept my marriage vows. Now I find myself divorced in midlife with no career. My husband makes $100,000 a year, and we're struggling to get by on a quarter of that."[16]

We could avoid such inequities, say the family values crusaders, if today's marriage contract was not "considerably less binding than, for example, a contract to sell a car or a cow." "The first step is to end unilateral divorce," says Maggie Gallagher of the Institute for American Values. She advocates imposing a five- to seven-year waiting period for contested divorces.[17]

The argument that "we ought to enforce marriage just like any other contract" sounds reasonable until you take a historical and sociological perspective on the evolution of divorce law. Then a number of problems become clear. First, requiring people to stay together has nothing to do with enforcing contract law. When someone breaks a contract, the courts don't normally force the violator to go back and provide the services; they merely assign payment of money damages. If an entertainer refuses to perform a concert, for example, no matter how irresponsibly, the pro-moter cannot call the police to haul the performer into the theater and stand over him while he sings, or even impose a cooling-off period so he can rethink whether he wants to honor the contract. Instead, the pro-moter is awarded damages. The contract analogy may make a case for seeking damages, but it has no relevance to the issue of making divorce harder to get.

A woman who has sacrificed economic opportunities to do the bulk of child raising ought to get compensation for that when a marriage breaks up, no matter whose "fault" the failure is. Even full-time working wives of-ten give up higher-paying jobs or education in order to take the lion's share of responsibility for family life. The tendency of many courts during the 1970s to reduce alimony and maintenance allowances for wives was based on the mistaken assumption that because more women were working, male–female equality had already been achieved. Maintenance awards need to be rethought, as well as separated from child support payments, a process now occurring in many states. But improving maintenance provi-sions for the spouse who did family caregiving is a separate question from forcing someone to remain in a marriage against his or her will—or to do *without* support for a protracted period of time while the courts sort through who was "at fault."[18]

Second, making divorces harder to get would often exacerbate the bit-terness and conflict that are associated with the *worst* outcomes of divorce for kids. One of the hot new concepts of the consensus school is that we need to preserve the good-enough marriage—where there is not abuse or neglect but merely an "acceptable" amount of adult unhappiness or dis-content in comparison to the benefits for children in keeping the family together. But what government agency or private morals committee will decide if a marriage is "good enough"?

One author suggests we might require parents with children under 18 to "demonstrate that the *family* was better off broken than intact. Unhappiness with one's spouse would not then be a compelling argument for divorce. Domestic violence would be." Yet what would prevent the person who wanted out of the marriage from upping the ante—for example, from threatening domestic violence to get his or her way?[19]

Furthermore, it is *women* more than men who have historically needed the protection of divorce. And yes, I mean protection. Because of men's greater economic and personal power, one divorce historian points out, husbands traditionally handled marital dissatisfaction by intimidating or coercing their wives into doing what the men wanted, such as accepting an extramarital affair or living with abuse. Alternatively, the man simply walked away, taking no legal action. Women, with less social and domestic power, "turned to an external agency, the law, for assistance." Women were the majority of petitioners for divorce and legal separation in English and American history long before the emergence of a feminist movement. Access to divorce remains a critical option for women.[20]

Finally, sociological research finds little evidence that no-fault laws have been the main cause of rising divorce rates, or that, on average, women do worse with no-fault than they did in the days when spouses had to hire detectives or perjurers to prove fault. While more than half the states enacted some form of no-fault divorce legislation in the 1970s, the rates of marital dissolution in most of these states were no higher in the 1970s than would be expected from trends in states that did *not* change their laws. Researcher Larry Bumpass suggests that, in some instances, no-fault has speeded up "cases that were already coming down the pipeline," but the rise in divorce seems to be independent of any particular legal or social policy. And, of course, making divorce harder to get does nothing to prevent separation or desertion.[21]

Work on preventing unnecessary divorces, separations, and desertions needs to happen *before* a marriage gets to the point of rupture. We can experiment with numerous ways to do that, from marriage education to moral persuasion to parenting classes to counseling. We can educate young people about the dangers of our society's throwaway mentality, pointing out that it creates emotional as well as material waste. We should certainly warn people that divorce is never easy for the partners or for their children. Still, history suggests that no amount of classes, counseling, or crusades will reinstitutionalize marriage in the sense that the family values crusaders desire.

Divorce rates are the product of long-term social and economic changes, not of a breakdown in values. Individual belief systems are a comparatively minor factor in predicting divorce. Despite the Catholic Church's strong opposition to divorce, for example, practicing Catholics are as likely to divorce as non-Catholics. Studies have shown that prior disapproval of divorce has little bearing on a person's later chance of divorce, although people who do divorce are likely to modify their previous disapproval. Once again, we have a situation where many intricately related factors are involved. Neither legal compulsions nor moral exhortations are likely to wipe out historical transformations that have been building for so long.[22]

Unwed Motherhood

Many people I talk with think the place we should draw the line on family diversity is at the question of unwed motherhood. If we could just take care of this problem, they say, society could survive even a fairly large number of divorces.

The growth of unwed motherhood is an even more complicated story than that of divorce, because some of it stems from expanding options for women and some from worsening constraints, especially for low-income or poorly educated women. Often, it's a messy mix, with increased sexual freedom interacting in explosive ways with decreased economic opportunities for both sexes and continuing inequities between men and women.

For example, many people consider the rise in pregnancy among very young teens a symptom of what's wrong with today's "liberated" sexuality. But men over age 20 father five times more births among junior high school girls, and two and a half times more births among senior high school girls, than do the girls' male peers. When the mother is 12 years old or younger, the father's average age is 22. These girls may be responding to new sexual options, but they are doing so within a very old pattern of unequal, exploitative power relations. Three-fourths of girls who have sex before age 14 say they were coerced, and research suggests that a majority of teens who give birth have been physically or sexually abused at some point in their past.[23]

Contrary to what you might guess, the most rapid increase in the rate of nonmarital childbearing occurred between 1940 and 1958, when the rate *tripled* from 7.1 births per 1,000 unmarried women to 21.2. The rate of unwed childbearing rose very slowly from 1958 to 1971, then declined until 1976. Then it rose steadily again until 1992, not quite doubling to reach 45.2 unwed births per 1,000 unmarried women in 1992.[24]

This timing obviously calls into question the popular perception that

1960s permissiveness started the rise in unwed childbearing. Indeed, the increase in unwed motherhood between 1960 and 1975 was *not* due to a significant increase in birth rates among unmarried women but to a combination of two other factors. One was the fact that married women's fertility fell by more than 40 percent during the period, which increased the proportion of unwed births among the total number of births. The second was that the absolute number of single women was rising, putting more women "at risk" for an out-of-wedlock birth. Only after 1975 did the *proportion* of unmarried women who gave birth begin to rise—not just their absolute numbers or their contribution to total births in comparison to married women.[25]

So it's wrong to blame the rise of unwed births on the sexual revolution of the 1960s and 1970s. While it's true that the decision to raise a child born out of wedlock is related to changing cultural values, it appears that changing economic relations between men and women are more important than is usually realized. The renewed increase in rates of unmarried childbearing after 1975 *followed* the fall in real wages for young men that began in 1973. Men with low or irregular wages are far less likely to marry a woman they impregnate than men who have a steady job and earn a family wage. Women are less likely to see such men as desirable marriage partners.

The interactions between economic, social, and cultural factors are too complicated to support any single generalization about *the* cause of unwed motherhood. In a small though highly publicized number of cases, women's new economic independence has allowed them to choose to bear children out of wedlock. Contrary to conventional wisdom, this choice is more common for women in their twenties and thirties than for teens, and the proportion of such cases remains small. Unwed motherhood is seldom actively pursued by women. National statistics reveal that more than 80 percent of pregnancies among unmarried women are unplanned.

Although the consensus crowd may call for a campaign of stigmatization to prevent women from keeping an unplanned child, it is unlikely that women "of independent means" will give up their hard-earned freedom of choice. And stigmatization would not necessarily prevent unwed motherhood among impoverished women. Historically, out-of-wedlock births have often soared during times of economic stress, and the main result of stigmatization or punitive social policy has been child abandonment or even murder.[26]

Economic stress remains a critical factor in many out-of-wedlock births. The overwhelming majority of single mothers have only a high school education or less. Only one in seven unmarried mothers has a family income above $25,000 the year her child is born; 40 percent have incomes of less than $10,000.[27]

I understand why people worry about women who seem not to plan their childbearing wisely. But I also know, both from sociological research and from participating in parenting workshops across the country, that there are hundreds of paths to becoming a single mother. Some of the tales I hear would seem irresponsible to even the most ardent proponent of women's right to choose; others stem from complicated accidents or miscalculations that even the most radical right winger would probably forgive; still others flow from carefully thought-out choices. But I fail to see how we can draw a hard and fast line between the decisions of unmarried and married women. As one unwed mother said to me, "I made some stupid choices to get where I am. But my reasons for having a kid were no worse than my sister's, who had a baby she didn't want in order to save her marriage. Why should I be the one they stand up and preach against on TV?"

Take the three never-married mothers I met at a workshop in Georgia. One was a young girl who had gotten pregnant "by accident/on purpose" in hopes that her unfaithful boyfriend would marry her. It hadn't worked, and in the ensuing year she sometimes left her baby unattended while she went out on new dates. Shocked into self-examination by being reported for neglect, she concluded that going back to school and developing some job skills might be more help in escaping her own neglectful parents than chasing after a new boyfriend. Another, 25 years old at the time we met, had been 15 when she got pregnant. She considered abortion, but she would have had to drive 300 miles, by herself, to the nearest provider, and she didn't even have money for a hotel room.

Both these young mothers had gone onto welfare. The first had gotten off in three years, and never expected to need it again. The second had stayed on for only a year the first time, then married and found her first job. Shortly afterward, though, her husband left her and she went back on welfare because her work didn't cover child care or medical benefits. Within a year she had found another job and left welfare again. But the company relocated. Twice more she had cycled on and off Aid to Families with Dependent Children because of layoffs or ill health.

At one low point in her welfare days, she told me, she tried prostitution, planning to accumulate some cash she could hide from the welfare agency so she'd have a small financial cushion once she landed a new job. Unfortunately, she said wryly, she hadn't anticipated the job-related expenses in that occupation. For a while she spent a lot of her extra earnings on drugs and alcohol, "to get the dirty taste out of my mouth." She was straight and sober now, and she had a job, but she wasn't willing to stand up and make any testimonials, as her minister had urged her to do during the workshop at which we met. "It's going to be one day at a time for a long time."

These two stories are quite typical. Three-fourths of welfare recipients leave welfare within two years (half get out within a year), but the scarcity and instability of the jobs they find often drive them back to welfare in a few years. Even if they keep their jobs, they seldom earn enough to rise above the poverty line. In light of the hardships facing poor and near-poor mothers, including lack of jobs, child care, and work training, the fact that such a tiny proportion of women stay on welfare continuously for five years (about 15 percent) is testimony to a work ethic and determination that many of us, more fortunately placed, have never tested so severely.[28]

The third woman, by contrast, was an older, well-paid professional who superficially fit the stereotype of the selfish, liberated woman "mocking the importance of fatherhood" by choosing to have a child on her own. But this woman had had three wedding plans fall through before she decided to go ahead on her own. She attributed her failures with men to having been caught between two value systems. Old-fashioned enough in her romantic fantasies to be attracted only to powerful, take-charge men, she was modern enough in her accomplishments that such men generally found her threatening once the early excitement of a relationship died down. At age 35, her last fiancé had walked away, leaving her pregnant. With her biological clock ticking "now or never" in her ear, she decided to have the child.

I have also met men who tell angry stories about having been tricked by a woman into thinking it was "safe" to have sex. "Why should I have to pay child support?" demanded one. "Doesn't that just encourage women to have babies outside of marriage?" It is, of course, totally unethical for a woman to assure a man that sex is "safe" when it isn't. But what is the alternative? If a man could get off the hook by claiming "she told me it was safe," no unmarried father would pay child support.

Charles Murray of the American Enterprise Institute thinks that would be just fine. He advocates denying child support to any woman who bears a baby out of wedlock: Girls, he declares, need to grow up knowing that if they want any legal claims whatsoever on the father of their child, "they must marry." Answering objections that this gives men free reign to engage in irresponsible sex, Murray offers a response straight out of a Dickens novel. A man who gets a woman pregnant, he observes, "has approximately the same causal responsibility" for her condition "as a slice of chocolate cake has in determining whether a woman gains weight." It is *her* responsibility, not the cake's, to resist temptation.[29]

The analogy works nicely if you think of sexual behavior in terms of greedy women cruising an erotic dessert buffet, trying to decide which sperm-filled slice of temptation to sample. But it misses something important about the dynamics of courting. For centuries, parents have had to teach their daughters that it was ultimately their responsibility to avoid pregnancy, whatever promises a boy might make. Now we will have to teach our sons the same thing, and strict child support just might drive the lesson home.

Meanwhile, though, unwed motherhood, like divorce, is rising around the world. In places as diverse as Southern Africa and Northern Europe, more than 20 percent of all births are to unwed mothers. Part of the reason is the rise in women's economic independence. Part is the decline in society's coercive controls over personal life. And part is simply that with falling marital fertility, even comparatively low rates of unmarried childbearing create higher proportions of children born to unwed mothers.

Unwed motherhood creates tremendous hardships in some situations, while it is far less damaging in societies that pay women decent wages and make a commitment to providing parental leave and quality child care. Half of all births in Sweden and a quarter of all births in France are to unmarried women, for example, but the children do not face the same poverty and limited life options as their counterparts in the United States. We will not abolish unwed motherhood; but we can affect its outcome.[30]

Unwed Motherhood and the New Welfare Experiment

It may also be possible to reduce unmarried, or at least unpartnered, childbearing through educational campaigns, stiffened child support, and restructured relations between men and women. We have particular reason to think we can reduce unwed births among teenagers, by teaching young people of both sexes to take more personal responsibility for sexual behavior, making birth control available, and improving education or job opportunities in poverty-stricken areas.[31]

In order to accomplish this end, though, we need to reject the incredibly widespread double-barreled myth that unwed motherhood has been both cause and effect of out-of-control welfare spending. In 1996 a new welfare bill passed Congress, largely because of this myth. There was good reason to dislike the way that the welfare system had developed over the past few decades, but it is quite astonishing that the politicians who decided to "end welfare as we know it" knew so little about what they voted to end.

When many people think of unwed motherhood among impoverished women, the image that springs to mind is of a black teenager popping out babies to get the average $65 a month hike this entitles her to in states that have not frozen benefits. But the idea that welfare benefits cause unwed motherhood, *especially* among African Americans, is one of the most ill-founded notions in contemporary political discourse. Recently a group of seventy-six leading researchers on welfare and out-of-wedlock childbearing felt compelled to issue a public statement correcting the assumptions that both Democratic and Republican politicians bring to this question. They pointed out that few studies have found any correlation at all between welfare and unwed motherhood, and those few have found at most only a small link. Interestingly, when such a link has been discerned, it has been found only for *whites,* not for African Americans.[32]

In the absence of factual correlations between welfare and unwed motherhood, politicians and pundits have relied on a few personal anecdotes and some "common sense." Conservative columnist George Will says there's "surely" a relationship between welfare and unwed motherhood, and reporters can always find some youngster ignorant and deprived enough to think welfare gives her the option to have a baby without working. Yet researchers who have studied the issue estimate that at most the welfare system might have been responsible for 15 percent of the increase in unwed motherhood. Sociologist Mark Rank reports that the typical woman on welfare has 1.9 children, fewer than her counterpart who is not on welfare, and the longer she stays on welfare the *less* likely she is to have more children.[33]

Out-of-wedlock birth rates were stationary or falling from 1960 to the early 1970s, the period when welfare benefits were rising. Increases in rates of unmarried motherhood occurred in the late 1970s and the 1980s, a period when welfare benefits were dropping sharply. In fact, illegitimacy rates in America historically have been lowest in the states with the *highest* welfare benefits, and mothers living in states with higher AFDC payments have returned to work *more* quickly than those in states with less generous payments.[34]

A recent study of New York City, challenging both barrels of the myth at once, found that only one in four poor households in the city is headed by a single parent today, and that welfare spending in the city, adjusted for inflation, had declined by 30 percent between 1970 and 1992. Most poverty spending in the city went to pay Medicaid bills for the elderly and disabled. Medical costs of welfare have indeed been rising around the country. Yet while such increases may benefit hospitals and clinics, patient care remains the same or even deteriorates when the price tag goes up.[35]

This is not an issue of "a welfare culture" based on "rampant immorality." International comparisons show that Americans are more likely to be religious, to disapprove of premarital sex, and to limit welfare benefits than people in any of the European nations or Canada. Yet our rates of unwed teen parenthood are *far* higher than theirs. The two factors most likely to produce high percentages of unwed teenage births in a country are high absolute rates of poverty and a big gap between rich and poor. America has become a leader of the industrial world in both.[36]

The new welfare bill is unlikely to improve our dismal record, despite some improvements in child support collection. It cuts approximately $55 billion, spread over the next six years, from programs serving low-income Americans. The largest "savings" are achieved by reducing spending for food stamps and assistance to disabled and elderly poor people, as well as declaring individuals who legally immigrated to America ineligible for Medicaid, food stamps, and other aid programs.[37]

AFDC has been replaced with a program called Temporary Assistance for Needy Families. This program ends the commitment the federal government made during the Great Depression to respond when poverty and economic hardship rise. States will receive a fixed grant for income support and work programs, based on what they spent in 1994. If unemployment continues to fall, this may seem like an improvement, but there are no provisions for an increase if economic conditions deteriorate further. And the money involved is already inadequate. Arkansas will have less than $12 per week per child for cash support, parental work training, and child care. The wealthiest states will have over three times as much—but that still works out to just $40 per week for each poor child.

No family who receives any service or cash assistance for a period that adds up to a total of five years will be eligible for any further aid, ever—even if the assistance was spread over many years of intermittent layoffs and illnesses and even if members work for years before being laid off again. States are also allowed to make the time limit shorter than five years.

Proponents hail the bill as a victory for the work ethic. No one, they say proudly, will be "entitled" to public funds. Since the biggest entitlement programs, from Social Security to mortgage deductions, have not been touched, what they really mean is that everyone in the United States is guaranteed government assistance except the people who need help the most. And these people have no right to assistance even if they have made every effort to find work or if their jobs do not pay enough to keep them out of poverty. More than 93 percent of the budget reductions in entitlements come from programs for low-income Americans.

Ironically, most of the children likely to fall into poverty due to these cutbacks live in families with a working parent. Children with unemployed parents are typically already poor, even with welfare. The theory is that the cutbacks will not push them even deeper into poverty but will force their parents to get a job. However, no state or federal agency is required to help create jobs.

The new program does provide states with more funding for child care than the Congressional Budget Office estimates they would have received under previous child care programs. Unfortunately, the increase in funding does not meet the increase in the need for child care resulting from the bill's more stringent work requirements for parents of young children. The bill also repeals an older provision that gave child care assistance to families during their first year after leaving AFDC. In an effort to provide the subsidized child care slots needed by former AFDC mothers, several states are reducing subsidies to poor families who are already working.[38]

Proponents herald the "flexibility" that will result from states being able to set their own grants and work requirements. In some cases this may well lead to innovative programs. But the new flexibility includes the right of states to deny aid to any category of poor families. It also allows states to divert funds to uses other than income or work support without facing penalties or cutbacks in federal matching funds. History offers no reassurance that most states will withstand the temptation to cut back. Those that are inclined to maintain services or benefits may hesitate for fear that needy people from more miserly states may move in.

Regardless of what states may desire, the bill also cuts $28 billion from the food stamp program. Only 2 percent of these savings come from provisions to diminish administrative costs or fraud. When fully complete, the cuts will reduce food stamp benefits by nearly 20 percent, from the current average level of 80 cents per meal per person to 66 cents. About two-thirds of the benefit reductions will be borne by families with children. Laid-off adults who don't have children will be limited to only three months of food stamp assistance in any three-year period.

Whatever one's views on the new welfare rules, the idea that such changes will help restore a culture of "enduring marriage," far less a culture that cares about children, is absurd. The historic increase in divorce and unwed motherhood has developed independently of the welfare system. It will not disappear no matter how punitive we get with the poor.

The Reproductive Revolution

The final obstacle to reinstitutionalizing traditional marriage is the recent revolution in reproductive techniques. The main beneficiaries of this revolution have been heterosexual married couples with infertility problems. But the methods developed to aid such couples in conceiving have shattered what we might quite literally call older "preconceptions" about the links between marriage, childbirth, and child raising. Reproduction has been separated not just from marriage but from gender, age, and even sex itself.

Consider the possibilities of in vitro fertilization, which involves fertilizing a woman's eggs in a Petri dish and then transferring them to the woman's womb. The eggs may come from the woman herself or from a female donor; the sperm can come from the woman's partner or another male donor. An ovum transfer involves moving a five-day-old embryo from one female to another, who then carries the embryo to term. When these are combined, it means that a "child can have at least five parents," not counting any later changes with remarriage: a donor mother, a birth mother, a social mother (the one who raises the child), a donor father, and a social father.[39]

Traditional definitions of marriage and parental rights will not resolve the issues raised by such medical and technological change. Surrogate custody disputes have pitted the claims of biological mothers against biological fathers. In one court case a woman who went through pregnancy and birth with someone else's egg was termed a "prenatal foster mother." A man who participated with his wife in freezing embryos for in vitro fertilization sued (unsuccessfully) after the divorce to prevent her from implanting them, charging that he was being forced to become a father against his will.[40]

Ethicists debate whether it is fair for older mothers and fathers to take advantage of the new technology, given that they may die before their child even reaches adolescence. Issues of privacy and obligation arise for the biological parents of embryo transplants. Social parents move into uncharted territory in explaining "the facts of life" to their children. Payments for egg donors complicate the question of what is a free and informed choice. Yet many donors speak of the joy of helping another woman have a child; and the parents of children conceived by unconventional fertilization methods are as loving and caring as those who conceive by "natural" means. Obviously, our definitions of parental rights and responsibilities must change to encompass these new possibilities and danger spots.[41]

Reality Bites

It makes little sense to whip up hysteria about an issue if you don't have any concrete solutions. Yet for people who believe we're on the verge of "cultural suicide," the measures proposed by the family values crusaders are curiously halfhearted. Amitai Etzioni urges individuals to make "supervows," voluntary premarriage contracts indicating "that they take their marriage more seriously than the law requires." One of the few concrete reforms David Blankenhorn proposes to ensure "a father for every child" is that we forbid unmarried women access to sperm banks and artificial insemination. In addition, he asks men to take pledges that "marriage is the pathway to effective fatherhood," wants the president to issue an annual report on the "state of fatherhood," and thinks Congress should designate "Safe Zones" for male responsibility. Can anyone who looks at the historical trends in divorce, unwed motherhood, and reproductive technology seriously think such measures will bring back the married-couple–biological-parent monopoly over child rearing?[42]

Barbara Dafoe Whitehead of the Institute for American Values advocates "restigmatization" of divorce and unwed motherhood; "stigmatization," she argues, "is a powerful means of regulating behavior, as any smoker or overeater will testify." But while overeaters may now feel "a stronger sense of shame than in the past," this has hardly wiped out the problem of obesity. Indeed, the proportion of overweight Americans has increased steadily since the 1950s. As for curbing smoking, the progress here has come from stringent public regulations against smoking, combined with intensive (and expensive) interventions to help people quit. The pretended "consensus" of the new family values crusaders would quickly evaporate if they attempted to institute an equally severe campaign against single parents. After all, 90 percent of the people in a 1995 Harris poll believe society "should value all types of families."[43]

Besides, stigmatization is a blunt instrument that does not distinguish between the innocent and the guilty any better than no-fault divorce. Dan Quayle's latest book, for example, includes a divorced family among five examples he gives of the "strong" families that still exist in America. He puts a divorced single mother into a book intended to prove that "intact" families are ideal because, "Though Kathy experienced divorce, she did not foresee or want it." It was not this woman's intent, Quayle explains, to pursue "a fast-track career." She "expected to play the traditional role, to raise her children and create a home for a husband of whom she was proud." Such distinctions put the consensus brokers in the tricky business of examining people's motives to decide which divorced or single parents had good intentions and therefore should be exempt from stigmatization.[44]

It would be easy to dismiss the flimsy reforms proposed by the "new consensus" proponents as fuzzy-headed wishful thinking were it not for the fact that their approach opens such a dangerous gap between practice and theory. At best, affirming lifelong marriage as a principle while issuing exceptions for people whose *intentions* were good encourages a hypocrisy that is already far too common in today's political and cultural debates. Consider Congressman Newt Gingrich, who was born into a single-parent family, made his ex-wife a single mom by divorcing her, and has a half-sister who is gay. "I'm not sitting here as someone who is unfamiliar with the late twentieth century," he has said. "I know life can be complicated." Yet that didn't stop him from blaming Susan Smith's murder of her two children in

1994 on lack of family values—though he considered it irrelevant that the stepfather who abused her was a member of the Christian Coalition.[45]

At worst, this approach offers right-wing extremists moderate-sounding cover for attempts to penalize or coerce families and individuals that such groups find offensive. Insisting that everyone give lip service to lifelong marriage as an ideal while recognizing in practice that life is complicated is like having a law on the books that *everyone* breaks at one time or another. Authorities can use it selectively to discipline the poor, the powerless, or the unpopular, while letting everyone else off the hook.

The family values crusade may sound appealing in the abstract. But it offers families no constructive way to resolve the new dilemmas of family life. Forbidding unmarried women access to sperm banks, for instance, is hardly going to put the package of child rearing and marriage back together. It would take a lot more repression than that to reinstitutionalize lifelong marriage in today's society.

As Katha Pollitt argues, "we'd have to bring back the whole nineteenth century: Restore the cult of virginity and the double standard, ban birth control, restrict divorce, kick women out of decent jobs, force unwed pregnant women to put their babies up for adoption on pain of social death, make out-of-wedlock children legal nonpersons. That's not going to happen."[46] If it did happen, American families would be worse off, not better, than they are right now.

5

Putting Divorce in Perspective

We have already accepted the fact that aging Americans are increasingly unlikely to live out their lives in "traditional" nuclear families, where they can be supported and cared for entirely by a spouse or a child. We can no longer assume that a high enough proportion of kids grow up with both biological parents that society can continue to ignore the "exceptions" that were there all along. Nor can our school schedules, work policies, and even emotional expectations of family life continue to presume that every household has a husband to earn the income and a wife to take care of family needs.

The social and personal readjustments required by these changes can seem awfully daunting. Here's what a spokesman for the Institute for American Values told me during a tape-recorded debate over whether it was possible to revive male breadwinning and restore permanent marriage to its former monopoly over personal life: "The strongest point in your argument is that the toothpaste is out of the tube. There's no longer the subordinate status of women to the extent there was in earlier eras—there is simply too much freedom and money sloshing around. We may be heading into what some sociologists call a 'postmarriage society,' where women will raise the children and men will not be there in any stable, institutional way. If so, we'd better build more prisons, even faster than we're building 'em now."[1]

I don't think the consequences of facing reality are quite so bleak. As my grandmother used to say, sometimes problems are opportunities in work clothes. Changes in gender roles, for example, may be hard to adjust to, yet they hold out the possibility of constructing far more honest and satisfying relationships between men and women, parents and children, than in the past. But this doesn't mean that every change is for the better, or that we don't pay a price for some of the new freedoms that have opened up. Divorce is a case in point. While divorce has rescued some adults and children from destructive marriages, it has thrown others into economic and psychological turmoil.

For the family values crusaders, this is where the discussion of how to help families begins and ends. "Let's face it," one "new consensus" proponent told me privately, "the interests of adults and children are often different, and there are too many options today for parents to pursue personal fulfillment at the expense of their children's needs. Sure there are other issues. But unless we keep the heat on about the dangers of divorce, parents will be tempted to put their own selfish concerns above the needs of their children." Fighting the "divorce culture" has to be the top priority, he argued, because "it's the one thing we can affect" by making parents realize what disastrous consequences divorce has for the future of their kids.

I have met only a tiny handful of divorced parents who didn't worry long and hard about the effects of divorce on their children (almost a third of divorced women, for example, attempted a reconciliation between the time of initial separation and the final divorce, according to data from 1987–1988).[2] And while it's true that a few pop psychologists have made irresponsible claims that divorce is just a "growth experience," I don't believe we are really a culture that "celebrates" divorce, even if well-meaning people sometimes issue overly rosy reassurances to those who have undergone this trauma.

But for the record, let me be clear. Ending a marriage is an agonizing process that can seriously wound everyone involved, especially the children. Divorce can interfere with effective parenting and deprive children of parental resources. Remarriage solves some of the economic problems associated with divorce but introduces a new set of tensions that sometimes, at least temporarily, make things even more difficult.

Surely, however, it's permissible to put the risks in perspective without being accused of glorifying single parenthood or attempting, in Barbara Dafoe Whitehead's words, "to discredit the two-parent family." And the truth is that there has been a lot of irresponsible doom-saying about "disrupted" families. In a widely distributed article in the *Atlantic Monthly*, for example, Whitehead spends eight pages explaining why kids from divorced families face almost insurmountable deficits. Then, when she's convinced the average single mom to run out immediately to find a father for her child, she lowers the boom: Children in stepfamilies turn out even worse.[3]

While it is true that children in divorced and remarried families are more likely to drop out of school, exhibit emotional distress, get in trouble with the law, and abuse drugs or alcohol than children who grow up with both biological parents, most kids, from *every* kind of family, avoid these perils. And to understand what the increased risk entails for individual families, we need to be clear about what sociologists mean when they talk about such children having more behavior problems or lower academic achievement. What they really mean to say is *not* that children in divorced families have more problems but that *more* children of divorced parents have problems.

It's an important distinction, especially if you are a divorced or divorcing parent. It doesn't mean that all kids from divorced families will have more problems. There will be outstanding kids and kids with severe problems in both groups, but there will be a slightly higher proportion of kids from never-disrupted families in the outstanding group and a slightly lower proportion of them in the group with severe problems.

As family researcher Paul Amato notes, in measures of both achievement and adjustment, "a large proportion of children in the divorced group score *higher* than the average score of children in the nondivorced group. Similarly, a large proportion of children in the nondivorced group score *lower* than the average score of children in the divorced group." Comparing the average outcomes of children in various types of families obscures the fact that there is "more variability in the adjustment of children in divorced and remarried families than in nondivorced families." So knowing there are more divorced kids who do poorly is not really helpful. The question is how many more children from divorced and never-married parents are doing poorly, and what accounts for this, since some divorced children do exceptionally well and most are within normal range.[4]

Researchers who use clinical samples, drawn from people already in therapy because their problems are severe enough that they have sought outside help, tend to come up with the highest estimates of how many children are damaged by divorce. In 1989, for example, Judith Wallerstein published a long-term study of middle-class children from divorced families, arguing that almost half experienced long-term pain, worry, and insecurity that adversely affected their love and work relationships. Her work was the basis for Whitehead's claim in the *Atlantic Monthly* that "the evidence is in: Dan Quayle was right." But this supposedly definitive study, based on a self-selected sample of only sixty couples, did not compare the children of divorced couples with those of nondivorced ones to determine whether some of their problems might have stemmed from other factors, such as work pressures, general social insecurities, or community fragmentation. Moreover, the sample was drawn from families already experiencing difficulty and referred to the clinic for therapy. Only a third of the families were judged to be functioning adequately *prior* to the divorce.[5]

Research based on more representative samples yields much lower estimates of the risks. Paul Amato and Bruce Keith recently reviewed nearly every single quantitative study that has been done on divorce. Although they found clear associations with lower levels of child well-being, these were, on average, "not large." And the more carefully controlled the studies were, the smaller were the differences reported. The "large majority" of children of divorce, wrote eleven family researchers in response to Whitehead's misuse of their data, do not experience severe or long-term problems: *Most* do not drop out of school, get arrested, abuse drugs, or suffer long-term emotional distress. "Examining a nationally representative sample of children and adolescents living in four diverse family structures," write researchers Alan Acock and David Demo, "we find few statistically significant differences across family types on measures of socioemotional adjustment and well-being."[6]

Sara McLanahan, often cited by family values crusaders for her research on the risks of divorce, points out that divorce does not account for the majority of such social problems as high school dropout rates and unwed teen motherhood. "Outlawing divorce would raise the national high school graduation rate from about 86 percent to 88 percent. . . . It would reduce the risk of a premarital birth among young black women from about 45 percent to 39 percent."[7]

To be sure I'm not minimizing the risks, let's take a comparatively high estimate of divorce-related problems, based on the research of Mavis Hetherington, one of the most respected authorities in the field. She argues that "20 to 25 percent of kids from divorced families have behavior problems—about twice as many as the 10 percent from nondivorced families. You can say, 'Wow, that's terrible,'" she remarks, "but it means that 75 to 80 percent of kids from divorced families *aren't* having problems, that the vast majority are doing perfectly well."[8]

The fact that twice as many children of divorce have problems as children in continuously married families should certainly be of concern to parents. But it's important to remember that the doubling of risk is not evenly distributed among all families who divorce. Some of the families who contribute to these averages have had several divorces and remarriages. A study of boys who had been involved in divorce and remarriage found that those who had experienced many transitions, such as two or more divorces and remarriages, "showed the poorest adjustment." But even here the causal relationship involved more than divorce alone. It was "antisocial mothers" who were most likely *both* to experience many marital transitions and to engage in unskilled parenting practices that in turn placed their sons at risk for maladjustment.[9]

Many of the problems seen in children of divorced parents are caused not by divorce alone but by other frequently coexisting yet analytically separate factors such as poverty, financial loss, school relocation, or a prior history of severe marital conflict. When Rand Institute researchers investigated the relation between children's test scores and residence in a female-headed family, for example, the gross scores they obtained showed a significant deficit, but the disadvantage of children in mother-headed families was reduced to "essentially zero" when they controlled for other factors. "Apparently," they concluded, "a lot of the gross difference is . . . due to income, low maternal education, and other factors that frequently characterize single-parent families, rather than family structure itself."[10]

Income differences account for almost 50 percent of the disadvantage faced by children in single-parent homes. The tendency of less-educated women to have higher rates of divorce and unwed motherhood also skews the statistics. In fact, a mother's educational background has more impact on her child's welfare than her marital status. Other research suggests that the amount of television kids watch affects aggressive behavior whether or not their parents are divorced; one survey found that eating meals together was associated with a bigger advantage in school performance than was having two parents.[11]

Researchers who managed to disentangle the effects of divorce itself from the effects of a change in residence found that relocation and loss of peer support were more likely to interfere with school completion than parental separation. McLanahan's research with Gary Sandefur suggests that up to 40 percent of the increased risk of dropping out of school for children in single-parent families is attributable to moving after the divorce. A 1996 study found that the impact of family structure on schooling is "reduced substantially" when the number of school changes is controlled.[12]

Obviously, divorce often triggers financial loss, withdrawal of parental attention, and change of residence or schools. In this sense it is fair to say that divorce causes many childhood problems by creating these other conditions. But it makes more sense to adopt policies to minimize income loss or school and residence changes than to prohibit divorce across the board, for there are no hard and fast links between family structure, parental behaviors, and children's outcomes. One pair of leading researchers in the field conclude that there is "*no* clear, consistent, or convincing evidence that alterations in family structure per se are detrimental to children's development."[13]

The worst problems for children stem from parental conflict, before, during, and after divorce—*or within marriage*. In fact, children in "intact" families that are marked by high levels of conflict tend to do worse than children in divorced and never-married families. Two researchers who compared family types and child outcomes over a period of five years found that children who remained in highly conflicted marriages had more severe behavior problems than children in any other kind of family. They "were more depressed, impulsive, and hyperactive" than children from either low-conflict marriages or divorced families.[14]

In the first two years after a divorce, says Hetherington, children of divorce "look worse off than kids from intact families, even bad intact families." But after two or three years, "the kids who lived in one-parent households, with a competent mother, were doing better—with half as many behavioral problems—than the kids in the conflict-ridden homes."[15]

Furthermore, the problems found in children of divorced parents were often there months, or even years, *prior* to the parental separation. Eight to twelve years before a family breakup, researchers have found, parents who would eventually divorce were already reporting significantly more problems with their children than parents who ended up staying together. This finding suggests that "the association between divorce and poor parent–child relationships may be spurious; the low quality of the parents' marriage may be a cause of both." Alternatively, severely troubled children may help to precipitate a divorce, further distorting the averages.[16]

Some behaviors that make kids look worse off in the first few years after divorce may actually be the first steps toward recovery from damaging family patterns. For example, psychologist Richard Weissbourd cites the case of Ann, a 10-year-old girl who had become the family caretaker to cope with her father's alcoholism and her mother's long work hours. This role gave her many satisfactions and a strong sense of importance within the family, but it cut her off from friends and schoolmates. After the divorce, Ann's mother recovered from her own stress, spent more time at home, and resumed her parental role. Ann resented her "demotion" in the family and began to throw temper tantrums that landed her in a therapist's office. Yet her turmoil, far from being evidence of the destructive effects of divorce, was probably a necessary stage in the move to healthier relations with both parents and peers.[17]

One long-term study found that divorce produced extremes of *either* negative or positive behavior in children. At one end of the spectrum were children who were aggressive and insecure. These children were likely to have been exposed to a disengaged or inconsistently harsh parenting style.

A significant number of these children were boys who had been temperamentally difficult early in life and whose behavior problems were made worse by family conflict or divorce.

At the other extreme were caring, competent children who were exceptionally popular, self-confident, well behaved, and academically adept. These children had the most stable peer friendships and solid relations with adults. And a high proportion—more than half—of the girls in this group came from divorced, female-headed families. Their mothers were typically warm, but not always available, and most of these girls had had to assume some caretaking responsibility for siblings, grandparents, or even their mothers at a young age. "Experiences in a one-parent, mother-headed family seemed to have a positive effect for these girls."[18]

As Mavis Hetherington sums up the research, most family members go through a period of difficulty after a divorce but recover within two to three years. Some exhibit immediate and long-term problems, while others adapt well in the early stages but have problems that emerge later. "Finally, a substantial minority of adults and children . . . emerge as psychologically enhanced and exceptionally competent and fulfilled individuals."[19] It should be reassuring for divorced parents to realize that such enhancement is possible, and that we also know a lot about how to avoid the *worst* outcomes for children.

When Divorce Has Long-Term Effects, and How to Minimize Them

I don't want to trivialize the consequences of divorce. Transitions of any kind are stressful for kids, mostly because they are stressful for parents and therefore disrupt parental functioning. But it is important to point out the variability in the outcomes of divorce. Divorce is only one part of a much larger group of factors affecting parental functioning and child well-being. In many cases, the conditions imperiling children existed in the family prior to the divorce and would not be solved by convincing the parents to get back together. In other cases, divorce does create new problems but parents can minimize the disruptions if they set their minds to it. For these reasons, researchers have begun to emphasize that divorce is an ongoing process beginning long before physical separation and continuing long after the divorce is finalized. It is the *process*, not the divorce itself, that "is most significant in shaping subsequent family dynamics and individual adjustment."[20]

A critical factor in children's adjustment to divorce is how effectively the custodial parent functions. Usually this means the mother. The main problem for children of divorce is when depression, anger, or economic pressures distract their mothers' attention. A recent study of 200 single-parent families in Iowa found that somewhere between 20 and 25 percent of mothers became preoccupied in the aftermath of divorce, paying less attention to what their children were doing or focusing too much on negative behavior and responding to it harshly. A large part of their reactions stemmed from economic stress. But many of these distracted mothers had always been more self-centered, impatient, disorganized, and insensitive than the other mothers, traits that may have triggered their divorces in the first place. Only a small amount of dysfunctional parenting seemed to be associated with family structure alone, yet there were enough incidences for researchers to conclude that divorce does make it harder for many mothers to parent well, even when they are stable individuals who are not overwhelmed by economic stress.[21]

The main danger for children is conflict between parents during and after divorce. Few marriages disintegrate overnight; the last few months or years are often marked by severe strife. More than half of divorced couples in one national survey reported frequent fighting prior to separation. More than a third of those who fought said that the fights sometimes became physical. And children were often present during these incidents.[22]

Divorce may allow parents to back off, but sometimes it produces continuing or even escalating conflict over finances and custody. And post-divorce marital conflict, especially around issues connected with the children, is the largest single factor associated with poor adjustment in youngsters whose parents have divorced. A study of more than 1,000 divorcing families in California found that children in disputed custody cases (about 10 percent of the sample) seemed the most disturbed. They were two to four times more likely than the national average to develop emotional and behavioral problems, with boys generally displaying more symptoms than girls.[23]

Parents certainly should be educated about the potential problems associated with divorce and with raising children alone. But outlawing divorce or making it harder to get would not prevent parents from fighting or separating, and could easily prolong the kinds of conflict and disrupted parenting that raise the risks for children. While people who are simply discontented or bored with their relationship should be encouraged to try and work things out, campaigns to scare parents into staying married for the sake of the kids are simply out of touch with the real complexities and variability in people's lives. As psychologist Weissbourd writes, "divorce typically has complex costs and benefits" for children. They may be more vulnerable in some ways after the divorce and more protected in other ways.[24]

Studies show that fathers in unhappy marriages tend to treat their daughters negatively, especially when the daughters are young. These girls may benefit by getting away from this negative spillover, even if their brothers go through a hard period. Women who are dissatisfied with their marriage are at high risk of developing a drinking problem. Divorce or separation lowers such women's stress and tends to reduce their alcohol dependence. Getting sober may improve their parenting enough to counteract the negative effects of divorce on their children.[25]

As such examples reveal, open conflict is not the only process that harms children in a bad marriage. One recent study of adolescent self-image found the *lowest* self-esteem in teens of two-parent families where fathers showed little interest in their children. Such youngsters, lacking even the excuse of the father's absence to explain his lack of interest, were more likely than kids in divorced families to internalize the problem in self-blame.[26]

Given these kinds of trade-offs, it is not enough to just reiterate the risks of divorce. We also need to tell people what they can do to minimize these risks. The most important thing is to contain conflict with the former spouse and to refrain from "bad mouthing" the other parent to the children. Divorcing parents must not involve their children in the hostilities between them or demand that the child choose sides. They should not ask children to report on the other's activities, or to keep secrets about what's going on in one household.[27]

Leaders of the "new consensus" crusade are fond of saying that trying to teach people how to divorce with less trauma is like offering low-tar cigarettes to people instead of helping them quit smoking. But this is a sound bite, not a sound argument. Yes, there are clearly people who could save their marriages, or at least postpone their divorces, and should be encouraged to do so by friends, colleagues, or professionals who know their situation. But there are others whose marriages are in the long run more damaging to themselves and their children than any problems associated with divorce. In between there are many more people for whom it's a close call. Yet since "most divorced mothers are as effective as their married counterparts once the parenting boundaries are renegotiated," and since most families recover from divorce within a few years, it is neither accurate nor helpful to compare divorce to a carcinogenic substance.[28]

Is it possible for divorced parents to behave civilly? A national sample of parents who divorced in 1978 and were interviewed one, three, and five years later found that half of the couples were able to coparent effectively. The other half, unfortunately, were unable "to confine their anger to their marital differences; it infused all the relationships in the family" and made cooperative or even civil coparenting extremely rare. A more recent

California study found that three to four years after separation, only a quarter of divorced parents were engaged in such "conflicted coparenting," marked by high discord and low communication. Twenty-nine percent were engaging in cooperative coparenting, characterized by high communication and low dissension, while 41 percent were engaging in a kind of parallel parenting, where there was low communication between parents but also low conflict.[29]

Time helps. In one study of couples splitting up, "strong negative feelings among women dropped from 43 to 19 percent in the two years following separation, while for men they declined from 22 to 10 percent." There are encouraging signs that more immediate results can be obtained when parents are shown how their behavior affects their children. A recent study found that simply having children fill out a questionnaire and then sending that information to their divorced parents was enough to effect "significant change in the behavior of the parents." Specialists in divorce research recommend early intervention strategies to encourage parents to think of themselves as a "binuclear" family and separate their ongoing parenting commitments from any leftover marital disagreements.[30]

We know that people can learn to manage anger, and this seems to be the key to successful coparenting. It is not necessary for parents to like each other or even to "make up." The difference between divorced parents who were and were not able to coparent effectively, writes researcher Constance Ahrons, "was that the more cooperative group *managed* their anger better. They accepted it and diverted it, and it diminished over time." Establishing boundaries between the parents' relationship with each other and their relationships with their children is critical. For instance, it helps if parents have a friend to whom they can vent about all the crazy or terrible things they think their former partner has done. This is not something that should be discussed with the children. Most parents know this in the abstract, but they often need a friend, colleague, or professional to help them prevent their feelings about the partner from spilling over into interactions with their children.[31]

What about the problem of father absence? Surveys at the beginning of the 1980s found that more than 50 percent of children living with divorced mothers had not seen their fathers within the preceding year, while only 17 percent reported visiting their fathers weekly. But more recent studies show higher levels of paternal contact. A 1988 sample found that 25 percent of previously married fathers saw their children at least once a week, and only 18 percent had not visited their children during the past year. This may mean that as divorce has become more common, fathers have begun to realize that they must work out better ways of remaining in touch with their children, while mothers may be more willing to encourage such involvement.[32]

One of the puzzling findings of much divorce research is how little impact frequent visitation with fathers has on children's adjustment after divorce. But one recent study found evidence that while divorce weakened the significance of fathers for children's overall psychological well-being, a close relationship to a father, even when contact was minimal, seemed to have a strong association with a child's happiness. Other research shows that nonresidential fathers help their children best when they continue to behave as parents, "monitoring academic progress, emphasizing moral principles, discussing problems, providing advice, and supporting the parenting decisions of the custodial mother," rather than behaving as a friendly uncle who shows up to have fun with the children for a day.[33]

People need to know this kind of information, and a truly pro-family social movement would spend much more time publicizing such findings than making sweeping pronouncements about what's good and bad for children in the abstract. Again, it's a matter of coming to terms with reality. Historically speaking, the rise of alternatives to marriage is a done deal. Right here, right now, 50 percent of children are growing up in a home with someone other than two married, biological parents. It is not a pro-child act to deny divorced parents the information they need to help them function better or to try so hard to prevent divorce that we suppress research allowing parents to weigh their options, both pro and con.

Of course we should help parents stay together where possible, but the evidence suggests that we will save more marriages by developing new family values and support systems than by exhorting people to revive traditional commitments. And the fact remains that we will never again live in a world where people are compelled to stay married "until death do us part." Some couples will not be willing to go through the hard work of renegotiating traditional gender roles and expectations. Some individuals will choose personal autonomy over family commitments. Some marriages will fail for other reasons, such as abuse, personal betrayals, or chronic conflict—and often it is in no one's interest that such marriages be saved.

That is why, shocking though it may sound to the family values think tanks, we need, as researcher William Goode suggests, to "institutionalize" divorce in the same way that marriage remains institutionalized—to surround it with clear obligations and rights, supported by law, customs, and social expectations. To institutionalize divorce is not the same as advocating it. It simply means society recognizes that divorce will continue to occur, whether we like it or not. Reducing the ambiguity, closing the loopholes, and getting rid of the idea that every divorce case is a new contest in which there are no accepted ground rules will *minimize* the temptation for individuals to use divorce to escape obligations to children. Setting up clear expectations about what is civilized behavior will cut back on the adversarial battles that bankrupt adults and escalate the bitterness to which children are exposed.[34]

As one divorce lawyer writes, "I see couples every day who never lay a hand on one another but are experts in using children as instruments of psychological torture." Such children are not served well, she argues, by a high-minded refusal to sanction divorce or a rear-guard battle to slow it down. As the president of the Family and Divorce Mediation Council of Greater New York puts it: "Blaming children's problems on a megalith called 'Divorce' is a bit like stating that cancer is caused by chemotherapy. Neither divorce nor chemotherapy is a step people hope to have to take in their lives, but each may be the healthiest option in a given situation." He suggests that mediation "can restore parents' and children's sense of well-being" better than attempts to keep people locked in unhappy marriages where pent-up frustrations eventually make postdivorce cooperation even harder to obtain.[35]

Similarly, we need to institutionalize remarriage. Experts on stepfamilies argue that clearer norms and expectations for stepparents would facilitate easier adjustments and more enduring relationships. At the legal level, we must recognize and support the commitments that stepparents make, rather than excluding them from rights and obligations to their stepchildren. In one court case, for example, a boy named Danny was raised by his stepfather from the age of one, after his mother died. The biological father did not ask for custody until Danny was seven. Although a lower court ruled that Danny should be allowed to stay with his stepparent, who had been the primary parent for six of Danny's seven years, a higher court overruled this decision, calling the stepfather "a third party" whose claims should not be allowed to interfere with the rights of the biological parent.[36]

While we must adjust our laws to validate ties between stepparents and stepchildren, we also need to develop flexible models of various ways to achieve a "good" relationship. The worst problems facing stepfamilies, experts on remarriage now believe, are produced by unrealistic fantasies about re-creating an exclusive nuclear family unit in a situation where this is impossible because the child has at least one parent who lives outside the home. The best way to succeed, researchers in the field agree, is to reject the nuclear family model and to develop a new set of expectations and behaviors.[37]

What it all comes down to is this. Today's diversity in family forms, parenting arrangements, and sex roles constitutes a tremendous sea change in family relations. We will not reverse the tide by planting our chair in the sand like King Canute and crying, "Go back! Go back!" There are things we can do to prevent the global tide of changing work situations and gender roles from eroding as many marriages as it presently does, but our primary task is to find new and firmer ground on which to relocate family life.

6

How Holding on to Tradition Sets Families Back

M any of the problems commonly blamed on breakdown of the traditional family exist not because we've changed too much but because we haven't changed enough. As Betty Carter argues, pronouncements about the "revolution" in traditional marriage often work to *hold back* needed change in marriages. Because couples believe that their stresses come from how much gender roles have already changed, they don't realize how much more they still need to change.[1]

The failure of men to share housework and child care with their partners, for example, is a primary source of overload for working mothers and a major cause of marital conflict. Yet one recent study comparing the housework done by men and women in six different living situations found that married men did less housework than men in any other living arrangement, including cohabitation. Meanwhile, outdated expectations about marriage continue to be perpetuated among young men. In 1994, a national survey reported that 86 percent of 13- to 17-year-old girls expected to work after marriage, but only 58 percent of boys the same age expected to have an employed wife.[2]

Over and over, we find that it is the *lag* in adjusting values, behaviors, and institutions to new realities that creates problems in contemporary families. Marital dissatisfaction and divorce frequently originate when modern parents backslide into traditional roles after the birth of a child. And men who accept the Victorian notion that their wives are their main link to their children are the ones most likely to abandon those children after divorce or remarriage. Similarly, many incest and battering incidents seem to be triggered when traditional masculine notions of entitlement are resisted by wives or children. But the solution is hardly for wives to submit. A recent nationwide study of assaults against wives and cohabiting partners found that the greater the social, economic, and educational status of women in any state, the less likely that state was to have a high rate of wife assault.[3]

Moving Forward Instead of Back

Family sociologist Arlene Skolnick suggests that social and cultural transformations typically go through a series of stages. The first is a period of "individual and family stress" that occurs because old "understandings and practices are disrupted long before new ones have taken shape." In this stage, most people do not recognize that they are facing irreversible social changes or new structural dilemmas that may be forcing them or others to behave in new ways. If we just tried harder, people think, we could get back to the way things used to be. They search their hearts, make new resolutions, and berate themselves for failing to keep them. Growing numbers of individuals "show signs of psychological stress—personality disturbance, drinking and drug problems." People experiment with ways of coping that may appear irrational or self-destructive, but in fact reflect the harsh reality that there is as yet simply *no right way* to behave.[4]

The second stage of transformation, Skolnick suggests, is one of public debate and cultural struggle, as competing definitions of the problem are raised by different groups. Political and social movements arise, attempting to hold back the changes, push them in new directions, or shift their costs to someone else. This is often, I would add, a period when the previous denial of new realities turns into a search for scapegoats. Having redoubled their efforts to preserve the old ways without much success, people get tired of feeling guilty or inadequate. The next step is to conclude that most of us *have* been doing the right thing all along, but that someone else has been undermining our efforts. If we could just bring those individuals or groups under control, the old patterns would fall back in place. There are always demagogues waiting in the wings to encourage this blaming impulse, and they often manage to whip it into a frenzy.

Only after the two stages of personal distress and social conflict have been worked through, Skolnick argues, does society reach a period of

restabilization. When people gain an understanding of why change is occurring and what parts of it cannot be reversed, they begin to adapt their
institutions, values, and cultural norms to the new realities. Most of the
turmoil associated with the transitional period recedes. It's not that the
new equilibrium is conflict-free, or that it represents everyone's interests
equally. But acceptance that the transformation is here to stay establishes a
new baseline from which further change, modification, and adjustments
can occur.

It is practically a historical truism that the longer the denial and
scapegoating go on, the more the casualties of social transformation
mount. A historical and sociological perspective can be of tremendous
help to both individuals and society as a whole in getting us past the destructive stages more quickly, so we can move on to the period of reconstruction and restabilization.

A good example of these stages can be found in the early nineteenth
century, when Americans made the transition from the old coprovider
family to the new breadwinner family. This passage *into* the male breadwinner family system kicked off the same syndrome of distress, denial, and
scapegoating that we have seen in our current move *away* from that family
system.

The breakdown of the old coprovider family disrupted domestic
arrangements between men and women. It was also part of a larger socioeconomic transformation that changed the way people conducted work
and family life. In the earlier pattern of agricultural and household production, much exchange took place "in kind." With goods and services traded
directly, people had less need for cash. Farm families worked at a pace determined by the weather, the season, and their own needs, taking paid employment when necessary to supplement their production, but not bound
to full-time, year-round wage work for others. They also did not specialize
in a single crop for the market, so although they depended on trade, they
were not left without means of subsistence if one crop failed or the market
broke down. Even workers whose primary occupation was making manu-
factured goods (the word originally meant hand produced, not factory produced) expected eventually to work for themselves as master craftsmen. An
apprentice or journeyman often worked in his employer's household, doing the same work and taking the same breaks, learning skills that would
eventually qualify him to set up his own business.[5]

The rapid expansion of capitalism in the first half of the nineteenth
century changed all this. In order to produce for a wider market, small farms
became more dependent on debt. Many went bankrupt. Farming became
less compatible with another trade, so that more people began to work full-
time at what had once been an adjunct occupation. Opportunities for inher-

iting a farm or becoming a master craftsman diminished, and workers faced the prospect of becoming permanent wage earners, expected to work for someone else all their lives rather than achieving self-employment.

Increasingly, employers moved workers out of their households and into central shops—later larger factories—where they could be supervised by a foreman or "boss," a word that was still new in the 1830s. The proportion of workers employed by others grew from 12 percent in 1800 to 40 percent in 1860. Even those lucky enough to remain self-employed had to change their personal priorities, family behaviors, marriage arrangements, and child-rearing practices in order to achieve the "independence" they so prized.[6]

Most people did not initially embrace this transformation wholeheartedly. Middle-class men enjoyed new economic opportunities but could not at first imagine how anarchy could be kept at bay when they were no longer at home to supervise wives, children, apprentices, and servants. Young girls who had once been servants or child-minders had more opportunities beyond the household, but also experienced a disorienting increase in personal responsibility for their behavior. Some were frightened by this; others loved it yet realized they would have to give up their independence upon marriage. Married women often felt isolated and useless as factories took over traditional tasks they had once done at home.

Working-class men liked the personal freedom they gained when they moved out of their masters' households, but resented the loss of traditional entitlements that had gone with the old system, such as sharing meals with the master of the house and being treated to drink breaks during the day. They also disliked the more rigid hours and work rules in the workshops and factories. New business cycles created unemployment, while increasing urbanization concentrated propertyless persons in squalid slums.

But the wage economy was here to stay, and families that tried to preserve the old household economy, keeping their members out of wage labor, were often the first to go bankrupt and lose their farms. People found themselves changing their behavior, against their original intentions, in ways that made them feel guilty or insecure. Historians believe that their anxiety provided much of the energy behind the religious revivals that swept the country during the period. While some people sought comfort in nostalgia for the old family economy and the ceremonies of patriarchal hierarchy, others showed those signs of personal distress that Skolnick noted. Per capita alcohol consumption reached an all-time high between 1800 and 1830.[7]

Gangs sprang up in poverty-stricken sections of the growing cities. From the 1830s to the 1860s, writes one specialist on gang violence, "hardly a week passed" when the Bowery Boys and the Dead Rabbits of New York

City didn't clash. Sometimes their battles "lasted two or three days, [with] endless melees of beating, maiming and murder. . . . Regiments of soldiers in full battle dress, marching through the streets to the scene of a gang melee, were not an uncommon sight."[8]

Male–female relations were also strained during this period of transition. As wives became more economically dependent on their husbands yet more responsible for daily domestic life, an undercurrent of anti-woman and antifamily sentiment found expression in stories such as the original Davy Crockett yarns. These were not the G-rated Disney versions but vulgar tales of adolescent rebellion against paternal control and female socialization. Davy Crockett ran away from his father, rejected education and steady work, drank heavily, provoked fights, committed cannibalism on Indians he killed, was obsessed with sexual imagery, and made fun of the emerging etiquette of refined womanhood. For their part, as women accepted a more secluded role at home, they increasingly viewed all men as potential Davy Crocketts—wild, brutish, and fundamentally "licentious." There is evidence that young women regarded marriage with new misgivings.[9]

These personal anxieties soon gave way to the second stage in Skolnick's scenario. Competing cultural and political movements offered different explanations and cure-alls for the problems associated with social change. Many involved scapegoating. Historians of the period, in fact, often refer to "the paranoid style" of the times. Conspiracy theories were rife: Catholics, Masons, bankers, slave owners, abolitionists, and foreigners were favorite targets. In the 1830s and 1840s, people whose prospects for self-employment were fading blamed Irish immigrants and free blacks for destroying the old apprentice system by working for too low wages. Nativist rallies turned into riots against Catholics; antiblack mobs burned down African-American houses. There were sixteen urban riots in America in 1834 and thirty-seven the following year. A pecking order also developed among some of the scapegoated groups. The Irish, originally considered a nonwhite race and ranked *lower* than slaves by many Protestant Americans, eventually "earned" their whiteness, in large part through antiblack activities.[10]

In "polite society," growing tensions between men and women accompanied the increased segregation of the sexes. Middle-class men channeled their gender hostilities into race and class prejudices. The contradictions of a new domestic ideology that desexualized "good" women but glorified their reproductive role were resolved by projecting sexuality onto African-American and working-class women, who were then considered fair game for exploitation. For their part, middle-class women transferred revulsion against the behavior of men in their own social milieu into campaigns against working-class taverns and "immigrant immorality."[11]

The middle of the nineteenth century ushered in the stage of restabilization. Disagreements over social and family issues did not end, but they proceeded from a common recognition that most men could not return to self-employment in the home or on the farm. The defeat of slavery in the Civil War ensured that the entire country would be run along capitalist lines. As it became clear that it was not possible to resurrect a family economy or preserve alternative systems such as slavery, the key social question became how to regulate relations between capital and labor. Once people realized they could not return to the colonial household economy, the debate over "the woman question" became whether to protect women's interests by secluding them in the family, away from the rough-and-tumble competition of the capitalist market and political party system, or to grant women the same independent legal and political existence that white men had acquired, so they could claim their interests as a right rather than a privilege.

It took decades for people to come to grips with the gigantic changes that "impersonal" social forces had wrought in their personal lives. Gradually, the laws, political institutions, economic practices, workplace norms, and cultural values suited to an agrarian economy based on household production and intense neighborly involvement in each other's affairs were overturned. New institutions elevated individual property rights over community norms, established the privacy of the nuclear family, and created professional police forces to hold personal rivalries and popular demonstrations in check. Family law and customs changed to increase women's domestic obligations and rights while lessening their involvement in the public economy. New cultural images of women as "angels in the house" replaced older ones of women as lusty yoke-mates of men. New norms of masculinity evolved, defining male authority in terms of breadwinning rather than personal control over the daily life of the household.

Lag and Adjustment in Contemporary Social Transformation

Today we are experiencing a socioeconomic transformation every bit as wrenching and far-reaching as that of the early nineteenth century—a total rearrangement of the links between families and the wider economy, along with a reorganization of work, gender roles, race relations, family structures, intergenerational expectations, personal rights, even our experience of time and space. The male breadwinner nuclear family system that was put together in the mid-nineteenth century to resolve that particular crisis of transition no longer meets the needs of today's families. Now, as then, clinging to old values and behaviors merely prolongs the period of transition and stress, preventing us from making needed adjustments in our lives and institutions.

For example, historian John Gillis reports that one way nineteenth-century families coped with the growing division between home and work was to develop new family rituals and holidays. When men had worked at home, mealtimes had seldom been private, or even very regular. Holidays had revolved around community festivals and visiting rather than home-cooked meals and private family celebrations. Leisurely dinner hours, Sunday family time, and nuclear family togetherness on holidays such as Christmas were invented in the mid-nineteenth century to alleviate women's concern that men's work outside the home made them strangers to the family and to ease men's anxiety that their domestic authority was being undercut by their absence.[12]

These new family rituals acquired tremendous emotional appeal because they asserted a symbolic unity of family activities and schedules that had ceased to prevail in reality. For this reason, they remain powerful symbols of a stable family life for most of us today. But such rituals could relieve stress only for so long as women were not employed outside the household and were able to devote vast quantities of time to preparing the meals and setting out the symbols of each occasion. They also depended on a woman's willingness to hide just how much work she was putting into the family's "days off."

This is why holidays today sometimes create more stress than they relieve, as working mothers try to reproduce rituals that developed in a time when wives had fewer obligations outside the home and had more kinswomen around to share the labor. Men and women need to create new family rituals that are compatible with today's family realities. In workshops I've conducted around the country, the people who seem most satisfied with their family relationships often mention the ways they have reworked older rituals and values.[13]

There are other signs that people are adjusting to new family realities and achieving some restabilization of personal life. Economist Elaine McCrate points out that the high point of divorce came in the 1970s, just when mothers had begun to work in massive numbers and before any new institutions or guidelines for working parents had developed. She suggests that part of the slowdown in divorce since 1980 may be explained by women's improved bargaining position in many marriages. Another encouraging finding is that men whose wives have worked for the longest periods of time are the ones who tend to do the most housework, suggesting that as couples get used to women's paid work, men do improve their participation at home.[14]

In the 1980s, sociologist Kathleen Gerson conducted in-depth interviews with 138 men to explore their responses to changing gender roles in their own personal lives. Some men, she found, had responded to the modern women's movement in a selfish way, welcoming women's new autonomy as an excuse for reducing their personal obligations. A second group had reacted as the "new consensus" recommends, by trying to reestablish their breadwinner role. But a third group had chosen a new path, combining autonomy with commitment in ways that led to the sharing of work and parenting between partners and an increase in the resources available to children. Their adoption of "mutual responsibilities as well as individual rights," Gerson found, produced more egalitarian and rewarding relationships than those based on the breadwinner role.[15]

Establishing new patterns is never easy. But in the long run change is healthier for relationships than resistance to change. One study in the 1980s found that men who had tried to adjust to their wives' expectations at home reported a decline in marital happiness in comparison to the past. But such "pro-feminist" men were "still *more* likely than their anti-feminist counterparts to describe themselves as 'very happy' in their marriage." Other research shows that husbands' dissatisfaction does not increase when they take on a larger share of housework, "possibly because the strain of additional work is counterbalanced by the gain in equity and fairness." The men in Gerson's study who took the new path were the ones who said they were most satisfied with their lives.[16]

Similarly, sharing child care and housework seems to help couples adjust to the stress of parenthood. Researchers studying new parents discovered that eighteen months after birth, 12.5 percent of the couples with whom they had not worked to reduce the diverging gender attitudes and experiences that new parents frequently fall into had separated or filed for divorce. *None* of the couples who had been helped to reduce their backsliding into divergent gender roles had split up.[17]

We have every reason to believe that new values about marriage and sex roles will make it easier for parents to sustain and enrich their relationships, especially when these values are reinforced by institutions such as flextime, parental leaves, and better child care facilities. But the advantage of working for new gender roles and family values is not only that it offers hope for saving many marriages. It also minimizes the damage to children when parental conflict and separation *do* occur.

Fathers with more egalitarian gender attitudes and a stronger identity as parents (that is, the fathers least likely to see themselves as domestic "junior partners") are the ones most likely to maintain contact with their children after a divorce, and even after remarriage. Terry Arendell's in-depth study of divorced fathers living in New York found that men with highly traditional gender-role attitudes tended to view divorce as a conflict with their wives that had to be settled either by "winning" or by disengaging. Only those who modified their traditional values about gender identity were able to continue relationships with their children after the divorce. And only those who developed new values of shared parenting were consistently able to put the children's well-being ahead of their feelings about the marriage itself.[18]

There is other evidence that people are adjusting to new realities. Recent groups of children who have experienced divorce are showing less severe reactions to it than earlier ones, possibly because the children feel less stigmatized, possibly because more parents are learning to divorce without intense acrimony. Twenty years ago, adult children from divorced homes were far more likely to divorce than those from nondivorced families. Today the differences are minor.[19]

The campaign to revive a "cultural script" in which lifelong marriage is "the primary institutional expression of commitment and obligation to others" is not only impractical; it is also an obstacle to developing new values that can stabilize many marriages and minimize the consequences of divorces that do occur. The "marriage script" propagates the notion that men's obligations to children are a package deal, contingent on living in the same household and having access to the services or support of the children's mother. This enables men who give up or lose any part of the package to feel justified in shirking *all* responsibility.[20]

For many children, the "package deal" has never been more than an empty box whose attractive wrapper allowed outsiders to assume the children were well cared for even when they were not. The last thing our society needs is another excuse for ignoring our collective responsibility for children: "As long as they have two married parents, we don't have to worry about them." Tragic mistakes have been made when courts have assumed that the person with the closest legal and biological ties to a child is most likely to take responsibility for that child's well-being. So the end of the package deal is potentially good for many children.[21]

The notion that marriage is the primary way parents provide for children also lets divorced and unmarried individuals off the hook. This mindset is a major reason that the rise of divorce has reduced the parental resources available to children. When a marriage ends, all too many men (and some women) feel justified in walking away from their child-rearing obligations. "Defining the family on the basis of the adults' legal relationship to each other," comment two family studies researchers, "discourages the continued interaction of parents and extended kin with children after parental divorce."[22]

And when legal relations were never established, there is nothing in the married-couple "cultural script" that encourages unmarried parents and their kin to recognize obligations to children whose demands, like their identities, the script defines as "illegitimate." How does it help children have access to more parental resources to discriminate against unmarried couples in housing, zoning, and taxes, as Gallagher and others propose? How does it help unmarried fathers fulfill their responsibilities to insist that fathering is an all-or-nothing proposition, hardly possible at all if the man isn't married to the mother of his child?

Recent movies and books have made a cliché out of the wry observation that children (and relationships) don't come with operating instructions. That's not really true. A very powerful set of operating instructions is in place in our society. It's just that most of those instructions are out of date, or they apply to only one of the many family models now on the road.

For 150 years, the married-couple nuclear family based on male bread-winning and female domesticity has been the main set of instructions for how we should organize adult sexual relationships, raise children, and meet interpersonal obligations. But trying to operate today's diverse families by yesterday's monolithic rules now causes more problems than it solves.

Our society urgently needs to create some larger, more inclusive package deal, where obligations to children (and the benefits of access to children) are not determined solely by biological relatedness, coresidence, parents' marital status, or notions of exclusive possession to "rights" in a child. We must start by acknowledging that every adult has a stake in every child. *Of course* parents have special responsibilities for their children, but those responsibilities exist independently of the relationship between the parents.

In some cases, such a value system may encourage parents, married or unmarried, to stay together for the sake of their children. But in other cases, it will mean that adults continue to meet responsibilities to their children after they split up, or if they have always lived in separate households. For this reason, we need to acknowledge and encourage the strong, enduring relationships that may exist between children and individuals *outside* the household. Many legal scholars suggest that we start from the standpoint of children's rights to an ongoing relationship with such individuals, rather than from the standpoint of competing adult rights in the child.[23]

Some theorists argue that it is important to retain the concept of the nuclear family to categorize a legally and emotionally privileged set of relationships, but that our definition of a family must be based on people's actual behaviors and feelings, not on abstract rules about who can be counted as family and who cannot. Others suggest that we stop talking about obligation in terms of "the family" and instead focus on "close relationships"—

strong interdependencies that persist over a long period. It may be that we could sidestep some of the emotional issues around defining family if we ceased using legal marriage and nuclear blood ties as our main way of distributing access to health insurance, parental leaves, job protection, and reimbursement for caretaking activities. As Katha Pollitt asks, "Why should access to health care be a byproduct of a legalized sexual connection, gay or straight? Wouldn't it make more sense to give everyone his or her own health insurance?"[24]

Economic, social, and demographic changes over the past 100 years have made it increasingly difficult to rely on marriage and the nuclear family to organize either the daily work of caregiving or the general tasks of redistribution to dependents. We must find a way to take some of the burden off an institution that can no longer go it alone. In the political realm, as economist Nancy Folbre puts it, we need to see that "children, like the environment, are a public good." In the interpersonal realm, as four child abuse researchers from the University of Maryland argue, we must reverse our usual pattern of ignoring families until a horrendous abuse case leads us to turn on the parents. They suggest replacing the after-the-fact notion of "parental culpability" with a before-the-fact notion of "shared responsibility, including parents, families, communities, and society."[25]

Is this too much to ask of human nature? I don't think so. There are certainly historical precedents demonstrating that people are capable of seeing children as a valued social good, not simply as the private luxury or burden of their own parents. Among traditional Hawaiians, for example, it was common to offer a child to a relative or friend in a *hanai* arrangement. The word comes from a verb meaning "to feed." Hanai adoptions did not normally come about because of parental disinterest or abandonment, nor did they cut the child off from the biological family of origin. They were ways of expanding the circle of close ties between adults and children. Instead of assuming that the love between hanai children and their adoptive parents would be less intense than a close blood tie, Hawaiians were sometimes said to favor hanai children over natural ones, and the ideal hanai relationship was seen as a model that biological relatives might strive to emulate.[26]

To some degree, hanai adoptions continue to be practiced in contemporary Hawaii. Some of the most interesting students I worked with when I taught at the University of Hawaii in Hilo had been raised as hanai children, and they felt no sense of neglect by their biological parents. I was also struck by the matter-of-fact way Hawaiian children assumed a right to adult aid and support, often phrasing their requests in honorary family terms. "Will you help me with this, auntie?" I would be asked by a child who needed assistance, a request that immediately drew me into the child's circle of protectors.

"In some African tribes," reports anthropologist Barbara Myerhoff, "all the elderly are loaned a child for warmth and companionship at night." In many Native American and African-American communities, the definition of family has traditionally included those who nurture and help to support a child, regardless of household residence or degree of biological relatedness. In Caribbean societies, children often move freely among several households, without transferring or losing their connections to adult caretakers. Multiple parenting is a longstanding tradition among the Pueblo and Navajo peoples in the United States, as well as populations in Ghana, the West Indies, and Polynesia. Psychology researcher Margaret Crosbie-Burnett and social work professor Edith Lewis argue that the adoption of such child-focused family norms would help contemporary American families deal more successfully with divorce or remarriage.[27]

The best expression of a truly child-centered social ethic was put forward during what may have been the first debate over family values ever held on the shores of this continent. When Jesuit missionaries from France encountered the Montagnais–Naskapi Indians during their sixteenth- and seventeenth-century explorations of the New World, they were impressed by the generosity and egalitarianism of the group, but found the native peoples sorely lacking in what the Jesuits defined as family values. The Indians failed to discipline their children severely enough for the tastes of the missionaries, and they allowed women too much personal independence.

Accordingly, the Jesuits set out to institutionalize the married-couple nuclear family, based on "correct" roles for husband and wife. They could not understand why Indian men were so reluctant to assume their authority as "heads of family." After many frustrating attempts to convince them, one Jesuit recorded in his journal that he pulled out his strongest argument against allowing wives so much liberty. If you do not keep your women at home, he explained to one Indian, you will never know for certain which of the children your wife bears actually belong to you. But the man was horrified rather than impressed by the Jesuit's logic. "Thou hast no sense," the Naskapi replied. "You French people love only your own children; but we love all the children of our tribe." This is one traditional value that doesn't get much attention in today's political and cultural debates.[28]

Some people I talk with seem to think that only "primitive" groups can feel such sentiments. Perhaps, they suggest, these feelings inevitably die out as societies get more complex and individuals develop more options to pursue their separate interests. Certainly, a greater variety of responses becomes possible, including many antisocial ones. But it's not inevitable that people will abandon commitments just because there is more "freedom and money sloshing around." As Francesca Cancian has noted, nontraditional gender and family roles can reflect an individualistic, self-interested orientation. But they can also express a truly interdependent value system, far more mutualistic than the traditional notion that in every relationship one party needs to be dominant and the other dependent.[29]

Nor is it necessarily true that people who remain single or childless will neglect their obligation to the next generation. In the 1920s, only 60 percent of women college graduates in America were married; 75 percent of women professionals were single. But these were the women most likely to found settlement houses, nurseries, and health clinics for children. Two historians who have studied the period suggest that such women were "making a choice between 'social housekeeping'—a commitment to lifelong professional work based on women's unique contribution to social service—and the pursuit of private housekeeping within the institution of marriage." Women no longer need to make this either/or choice, but it is possible to remain childless and still remain involved with the younger generation. As one contemporary childless woman wrote in a 1993 article: "We may not fit the traditional definition of family . . . but we aunts, uncles, teachers, counselors, neighbors, coaches, friends, big brothers and sisters are special kinds of family members to America's children."[30]

I too support a "values revolution" in America's attitudes toward children, although in a very different direction from the retreat to narrow blood ties recommended by the "new consensus" proponents. But values, like plants, need good soil, decent locations, and frequent applications of water and fertilizer if they are to put down roots deep enough to last. That's why it's never enough to try to change values in the abstract. It is essential to simultaneously change the social and economic context in which we conduct our lives.

Even with new values and institutions, there is no guarantee that all Americans will make responsible choices. But since choice is here to stay, we need to develop a range of ways to bolster caregiving, whether in or out of marriage, and also to provide a social safety net for children or other individuals whose families fail to meet their needs. As Gerson puts it, "the challenge is to build social institutions that support the best aspects of change . . . and discourage the worst."[31]

This is not a simple challenge. Making marital roles more equal requires us to restructure an institution that was built on the assumption that wives would not only love and honor but also *obey* their husbands. Developing child care, schooling, and work arrangements that fit the realities of working mothers runs into opposition from businesses who have gotten in the habit of assuming every employee has a wife. Forging new social obligations contradicts the all-or-nothing opposition between freedom and commitment that has so long been characteristic of America's frontier mentality—the idea that if you get in trouble, you can't count on help from outside the family, but, on the other hand, you can always pack up and move on.

Adapting to today's new family realities is challenge enough for any generation to meet, and it's no wonder that people have experienced serious lag and adjustment problems. But on top of this we are now living through an extremely stressful and disorienting set of socioeconomic transformations requiring even more far-reaching responses. Tragically, the reaction of our political and economic leaders to these challenges has been classic second stage: denial and scapegoating.

7

Looking for Someone to Blame: Families and Economic Change

According to economist and *Newsweek* columnist Robert J. Samuelson, "the paradox of our time" is that American families "are feeling bad about doing well." And by traditional measures of economic well-being, it *is* hard to understand why so many people feel that they are losing ground. After all, per capita income has risen steadily over the past few decades; recoveries from recessions have been robust; the stock market has been doing very well indeed. Between 1992 and 1995, following a recession in 1990–1991, the economy's leading indicators "showed strength rarely seen since the 1950s."

Homes are larger than ever. Almost every household in the country has a phone and a television. The number of college graduates has quadrupled since 1945. An "explosion of new products" has made life easier for millions of Americans, Samuelson argues, pointing to "the profusion of VCRs, personal computers, cable TV, microwave ovens." Between 1970 and 1990 alone, air traffic tripled, while the economy created 18 million new jobs and expanded the value of its output by nearly 30 percent.[1]

Business leaders and investors are upbeat. "The strength of this economy is not widely understood," says the president of CSX Corporation's railroad division, which hauled more freight in 1994 than at any time in ten years, with less than half the number of employees as before. "Frankly, I don't see any vulnerability." Alvin and Heidi Toffler, the well-known futurists, believe that the technological breakthroughs behind such gains in productivity are good for workers as well as capitalists. "Companies are hurrying to empower employees," they write.[2]

Samuelson and others admit that the rapid churning of what some observers have called "turbo-capitalism" creates casualties for families and individuals. But this, they say, is the price a free market system has always had to pay for its dynamism. Computer billionaire Bill Gates declares: "I've thought about the difficulties and find that, on balance, I'm confident and optimistic." "Men and women are worried that their own jobs will become obsolete, . . . that their children will get into industries that will cease to exist, or that economic upheaval will create wholesale unemployment, especially among older workers. These are legitimate concerns. Entire professions and industries will fade. But new ones will flourish. . . . The net result is that more gets done, raising the standard of living in the long run."[3]

This is historical perspective with a vengeance: Even if your family goes down the tube, others will prosper. Why aren't other Americans equally philosophical about the risks of this new stage of capitalism? According to Samuelson, it's because we've been led astray by "alarmist hype." Former political consultant turned columnist William Safire thinks that fear of downsizing is simply "the media angst-du-jour" and that Americans are afflicted with "opsiphobia—fear of prosperity." Or as journalist Michael Elliott puts it: "Americans whine."[4]

Elliott and Samuelson believe that people developed inflated expectations in the postwar years. "Much of Americans' contemporary . . . unhappiness stems from their failure to understand how damn lucky they once were," says Elliott. Samuelson argues that Americans unrealistically assumed that prosperity and security could continue to increase indefinitely at the same high rate they did in the 1950s and 1960s. Columnist George Will speculates that affluence has made us so bored we have to *invent* anxieties: "Progress produced leisure, abundance and security from predators. All this is boring to brains formed by and for hazardous circumstances."[5]

After years of talking with families who work tag-team shifts in order to care for their children, make hard choices between medical insurance and college savings, and think it's a big splurge to take modest vacations, I'm hard-pressed to believe these commentators are quite so naive as they sound. How can an employer who has cut his workforce in half not see any vulnerability in the economy? How can the journalists whose salaries and speaking fees have soared over the past two decades tell families who've been losing ground that pay cuts or layoffs can be a blessing in disguise?

Most middle-income families I talk with know that the postwar prosperity was exceptional and are uncomfortably aware that there's a grain of truth somewhere in the notion that we've been spoiled. People who recount their economic worries almost always say guiltily, "but maybe I expected too much." "I haven't changed the carpet or bought new furniture in thirteen years," one woman told me, after describing the family tensions that resulted from her husband's fear of threatened pay and benefit cuts at work, "but I guess we don't really *need* the microwave or the second car. So I tell him not to worry; we can make do."

But this isn't really the point. Cutting back on consumer goods and curbing expectations will not bring back the jobs being lost to technological change and management reorganization. Learning new skills and embracing the new technology is not enough either. It is the most modern, innovative industries that are shedding employees the fastest. That is why it is perfectly natural for people to feel "the most acute job insecurity since the Depression," and to be anxious about their families' future prospects even when they are not yet personally threatened by job loss or economic want.[6]

One of the most destabilizing trends for family life and family values is that the link between economic growth and majority living standards has been badly weakened, if not snapped. There's a growing sense that the old rules don't work anymore, that the expected connections between hard work, economic progress, and individual rewards no longer hold. We used to be told that rising sales and profits meant more employment and rising wages. Now the stock market falls when wages inch up even a little and soars when companies announce layoffs. "I used to believe that prosperity at the top would 'trickle down' through the middle to the bottom," one man told me. "Now it seems to suck everything up."

This isn't alarmist hype. It's an accurate description of an alarming new reality. According to economist Lester Thurow, writing in the *New York Times,* no country in the world, without undergoing a military defeat or an internal revolution, has ever experienced such a sharp redistribution of earnings as the United States has seen in the last generation.[7]

We're not just facing a temporary downturn. We're seeing a long-term reversal of trends that had previously made the risks and casualties of the market system seem worthwhile to many. Between 1947 and 1973, the median paycheck more than doubled, with the bottom 20 percent of the population receiving the biggest gains. But between 1973 and 1996, median earnings fell by 15 percent, with the bottom 20 percent experiencing the greatest loss.[8]

In past business cycles, competition and technological innovation periodically led to overproduction, causing businesses to cut back or fail, with ripple effects on unemployment. Later there would be a revival of

investment, production, and jobs; as unemployment fell, workers could organize to win higher wages. While poverty was persistent and harsh for
many groups, poverty rates fell when businesses recovered and employment rose. Though there were always important exceptions and pervasive
inequities, John F. Kennedy was partly right in arguing that "a rising tide
lifts all boats."

In the 1980s, however, the correlation between rising employment,
gross national product, and living standards broke down. The tide of economic growth, economists Sheldon Danziger and Peter Gottschalk conclude, "no longer lifts all boats. We see the recent period as one in which
the large yachts, moored in the safe harbors, rose with the tide, while the
small boats ran aground." The notion that we can "grow our way out" of
the economic problems facing so many families is now obsolete.[9]

The Economic Trends That Count for Most American Families

The economic stresses facing Americans are not just a matter of blocked aspirations, although blocked aspirations surely need to be taken seriously. It
is true that per capita income (the total after-tax income of the entire country divided by the number of people in the country) is up by almost 40 percent since 1973. But there are two problems with using this measure to
figure out what's happening to most families.

First, with the entry of wives and mothers into the labor force, more
people are working. So it's possible for per capita income to increase even
while individual wages fall. Real wages (the amount a worker can actually
buy with a paycheck) have been declining for most Americans since 1973.
Most families now need two earners, working longer hours, to maintain the
family living standard that could be provided by one earner in the 1950s
and 1960s.

Second, the average income you get by lumping the highest salaries,
bonuses, and fees together with the lowest can produce a very different figure than the *typical* income brought home by the majority of workers.
While 20 million households stayed enough ahead of inflation from 1991 to
1993 to keep the national average steady, 78 million households lost
ground.[10]

When we separate the exceptionally high wages that have been going to
some superstars from the incomes most ordinary families earn, we get a
clearer idea of the problem. According to the Bureau of Labor Statistics, between 1973 and 1993 weekly earnings of nonsupervisory workers (adjusted
for inflation) fell from $315.38 per week to $254.87, a decline of more than 19

percent. Economist David Gordon has developed a slightly different guide-post, called "real spendable hourly earnings," and reached a similar conclusion. By Gordon's calculations, the amount left in an average worker's pocket from his or her hourly wage, after taking out income taxes and Social Security taxes and adjusting for inflation, has fallen by nearly 1 percent a year since the early 1970s.[11]

And these figures understate how much of the burden of economic decline has been borne by young families or by young people who increasingly cannot *afford* family life. According to economists Andrew Sum, Neal Fogg, and Robert Taggert, "a young man under 25 years of age employed full time in 1994 earned 31 percent less per week than what his same-aged counterpart earned in 1973." This has meant a greatly lengthened period of what these researchers term "economic adolescence," the period when young adults are working full-time but not earning enough to support a family, or even, in many cases, to be fully self-sufficient.[12]

Another factor contributing to the American family's sense of being on shaky ground is the rise in job insecurity. Corporations have sought cheap labor overseas or in nonunionized sectors of the country, or they have reorganized by laying off full-time workers and replacing them with temps. A 1996 poll by the *New York Times* found that "nearly three-quarters of all households have had a close encounter with layoffs since 1980. . . . In one-third of all households, a family member has lost a job, and nearly 40 percent more know a relative, friend or neighbor who was laid off."[13]

Permanent jobs with full benefits are harder to find. As *Time* magazine has reported, the predictable job ladders of the 1950s and 1960s have been sawed off: "Companies are portable, workers are throwaway." Temporary jobs expanded by 211 percent between 1970 and 1990, compared with 54 percent for all employment. Manpower Inc., an employment agency for temps, is now the country's largest employer.[14]

Layoffs subject most families to a bit more hardship than Safire's airy "media angst-du-jour" remark implies. One in ten American adults told the *New York Times* that a lost job in their household had precipitated a major crisis in their lives. The time an unemployed worker spends looking for a new job has been increasing, while the chances of finding a job with comparable pay or benefits have fallen. The Labor Department reports that the average laid-off worker who found a new job took a 20 percent cut in pay.[15]

Not everyone has fallen behind. Between 1968 and 1994, the share of total income going to the top 20 percent of American households increased from 40.5 percent to 46.9 percent, while the share going to the bottom 80 percent fell. The inequalities behind the averages are even more dramatic when we look at who benefited from the aggregate economic growth that so impresses many economists. Between 1983 and 1989, reports economist Edward Wolfe, "the top 20 percent of wealth holders received 99 percent of the total gain in marketable wealth, while the bottom 80 percent of the population got only 1 percent." The *increase* alone in the income of the richest 2.5 million Americans between 1980 and 1990 equaled the *total* income received by the poorest 50 million Americans in 1990.[16]

When the rich get richer and the poor get poorer, it averages out to very little change on paper. In the real world, though, it's destabilizing and demoralizing. As a recent study concluded: "The factory workers' children who graduate from high school in the mid-1990s cannot expect to receive the kind of wages and benefits their fathers earned when they graduated from high school and were hired by large manufacturing firms in the early 1970s. And the corporate managers' children who graduate from college today can no longer expect the secure employment and opportunities for promotion that their fathers enjoyed." Before 1989, 60 percent of young men turning 30 had been able to attain a middle-class income; only 42 percent have succeeded in doing so since then.[17]

Doing better than your parents used to be the very hallmark of American identity. Such progress, far more than the total amount of goods or income that an individual had, was the traditional definition of success and measure of pride in our national achievements. The reversal of this expectation of generational mobility—what many researchers have called a U-turn in economic trends—erodes national confidence and social trust.[18]

As Lester Thurow remarks: "These are uncharted waters for American democracy." Since 1929, when accurate records began to be kept, never has America combined falling real wages for a majority of its workforce with rising per-capita gross domestic product. Not since the late 1920s, before the introduction of the progressive income tax, has the share of wealth held by the top 1 percent of the population reached such high levels, almost double what it was in the mid-1970s. "In effect," says Thurow, "we are conducting an enormous social and political experiment—something like putting a pressure cooker on the stove over a full flame and waiting to see how long it takes to explode."[19]

From Denial to Scapegoating: The Search for What Went Wrong

Faced with the gap between official measures of prosperity and people's own experience, it is no wonder that we have been seeing an increase in signs of individual psychological distress. As economist Edward Luttwak writes, "more disruptive change has been inflicted on working lives and entire industries than the connective tissue of many families and communities has been able to withstand."[20]

Insecure working conditions, low pay, long hours, and lack of control over work have been found to be significantly associated with increases in smoking, alcohol or drug use, accident proneness, and displacement of anger onto family members. Researchers in the 1970s found that the rate of physical abuse to children in homes with an employed husband was 14 percent; in homes with an unemployed husband, it rose to 22 percent. Many child abuse specialists believe that increases in abuse reporting in the 1980s were similarly correlated with increases in unemployment.[21]

Community relationships and social solidarities have also been strained. Political scientist Robert Putnam argues that there has been a disturbing decline in civic participation since the World War II era. His suggestion that television is the main culprit has stimulated considerable debate. But commentators generally reject the idea that the economic trends of the past twenty-five years have been a factor, because the decline in social trust has been most rapid among the affluent, whose gains, it is reasoned, ought to make them feel especially secure.[22]

Certainly, television blows crime stories out of proportion to their actual occurrence, creating exaggerated fears of danger. But often, exaggerated fears are also projections of anxiety or guilt about changing social relationships, and this applies *especially* to those who are doing well when others around them are slipping. For example, many historians believe that the witchcraft hysteria of seventeenth-century England originated among families who were abandoning older neighborhood networks to participate in the more individualistic market society that was then emerging. When such people turned down a loan or favor requested by a poorer neighbor, refused to let someone glean their fields, or sold something at market price rather than giving another village member a special break, they anticipated that their neighbors would be resentful. If something bad happened to them soon afterward, they assumed they had been bewitched by the resentful person.[23]

A similar psychological dynamic may be occurring among affluent or even merely comfortable Americans. Uneasily aware that social resentments are building, those who are doing okay are frightened that they may be arbitrarily singled out to bear the brunt of someone's class or racial rage. Perhaps this is why people are so fascinated, in a horrified way, by the statistically rare tragedies where privileged members of the community fall victim to random violence perpetrated by someone from a walk of life that they would never normally encounter.

No one is immune to this kind of fear, which is why, sooner or later, everyone pays the price for extreme social inequality. But if affluent Americans are becoming less trusting, the people falling behind in the redistribution of work and income are especially angered and frustrated by what they see around them.

When people endure seemingly inexplicable setbacks at the same time as they see other people doing better than ever, they find it easy to believe that someone has upset the natural order of things—and that someone needs to be punished. Today as in the past there are plenty of individuals willing to point the finger at possible candidates. Politicians have been especially active in nominating scapegoats. Indeed, as folksinger Utah Phillips once remarked, politics seems to be mostly about who controls the blame flow.

Channeling the Blame Flow

I got a good example of how people are sorting through competing explanations for their problems when I appeared on a call-in talk show in my hometown in December 1995. Usually the pace of such shows is too fast to allow a sustained dialogue with callers, but that day calls were light and a small-town sense of civility prevailed, so I got to pursue the subject of "what's gone wrong" in considerable depth, with a regular caller to the show named Helen. The topic, as the host introduced it, was "why American families are in trouble," and Helen started her call, as so many people around the country do, by expressing her anger at welfare cheats.

I used to respond to such remarks by reeling off the facts about how little welfare recipients really get, how few of them have large numbers of children, how many of them have disabilities, and how many of the rest move off welfare for work as soon as they are able. But this time I held back, because over the last few years I've come to understand a pattern well known to researchers in psychology: When presented with information that contradicts a fact people think they already know, people initially harden their position. Mixed evidence tends to reinforce the original belief rather than destabilize it.[24]

Another reason I didn't immediately trot out a lot of welfare facts and figures was because I've also learned that attacking welfare is sometimes the only way people have to convey their very legitimate concerns about the growing gap between work and rewards in America. Families who are working longer hours or requiring two full-time workers just to stay even understandably suspect that if they're working this hard and still not getting their fair share of the national income growth, someone else must be getting *more* than their share of income for *less* than their share of work. Even though many people are indignant about the huge bonuses paid to corporate CEOs, Wall Street speculators, sports figures, and media stars, it's not surprising that they tend to be especially suspicious of welfare recipients.[25]

For one thing, that's the direction in which politicians and conservative think tanks like to point us. As a result, 48 percent of Americans think welfare accounts for 20–50 percent of the federal budget, when in fact all welfare programs taken together make up only 5 percent of federal spending. For another, few people know how much the big earners really make: Most polls show that they typically underestimate those earnings by a factor of three or four. The people who control the media discussion of such issues are some of the biggest winners in the new economy, and they are as uncomfortable talking about their salaries as an earlier generation used to be talking about their sex lives.[26]

So people on welfare are an easy target, even though most Americans realize that it's not the poor, on welfare or off, who are raking in the difference between the total economic growth and the share going to middle- and lower-income families. In their new book, *The Winner-Take-All Society,* economists Robert Frank and Philip J. Cook argue that a major change in the distribution of rewards has occurred as traditional limits to the free market economy have broken down. As the subtitle of their book puts it: "More and More Americans Compete for Ever Fewer and Bigger Prizes, Encouraging Economic Waste, Income Inequality, and an Impoverished Cultural Life."[27]

Increasingly, people who begin with a relatively small edge, either of luck, capital, or skill, can rake in a higher and higher share of rewards. Investors with a lot of money to start with can make gigantic extra gains in today's stock markets, even if their judgment is actually quite mediocre. Superstar athletes, attorneys, or singers who are perhaps 5 percent more talented or popular than the next runner-up can get 1,000 percent more in salaries or contracts. This tendency is reinforced by technological changes that allow superstars to dominate the media more completely. If you can watch the best gymnast in the world on TV, why pay to see the runners-up, who in past times might have gotten a comfortable share of the market?[28]

So instead of directly contradicting Helen's assumptions about welfare families, I told her that I too had strong feelings about people getting money when they won't work. My father's favorite biblical phrase used to be "if any would not work, neither should he eat." As a former union organizer, that was my dad's critique of Wall Street speculators, stockholders, and financiers. Still, the principle applies to everyone, and I agreed with Helen that people who can work ought to do so. She agreed with me, in turn, that you have to make sure there *is* work before you get too tough on the eating question.

And that's just what government and business have refused to do. Most people want to work. But as of 1990 there were six adults in poverty for every available job paying above-poverty wages. Two researchers in a New York inner-city community recently found that there were fourteen applicants for every minimum-wage job opening at a fast-food restaurant. The real dirty little secret about welfare is that it's cheaper to write checks than to invest in creating jobs. In fact, today's welfare system was expanded as a substitute for the Full Employment Act proposed by the United Auto Workers and supported by several senators back in the 1940s. Welfare serves as a safety valve for an economy that *cannot handle* full employment. Indeed, because of the oversupply of workers in comparison to jobs, even if we *could* move every welfare recipient into the full-time job market, the ironic effect would be to increase the downward pressure on wages for all low-income workers.[29]

Helen had a friend who worked at a supermarket and had seen a woman buy steak with food stamps, then turn around and sell it for cash. Now maybe—Helen and I agreed on this—that woman was feeding a drug habit instead of her kid, and that's a terrible thing. But I pointed out that there might be more to it than that. A recent in-depth study in Chicago found that the typical single mother with one child got $399 per month in government assistance, counting her food stamps. In most cases, a family's rent and utilities alone came to $37 more than its welfare check. Even the lucky few who also received a government housing subsidy were constantly strapped for cash: They had only $160 a month left, after paying for housing, to meet all other expenses, from clothes to school supplies to transportation. The result was that almost all of them "cheated" by working off the books, and many of them traded food stamps for cash to buy family necessities that weren't covered by the stamps.[30]

At this point another caller joined the conversation to remind us about government subsidies to corporations—what one researcher has called the other AFDC program: Aid for Dependent Corporations. Corporate subsidies and tax breaks cost the Treasury $1,388 per person per year—more than three times what we spend on all child nutrition, food stamp, and welfare programs.[31]

Okay, Helen said, then how about government? Isn't too much government the problem? I agreed that American government has been very bureaucratic in dealing with the problems of the poor. Indeed, there has been a long historical pattern in the United States where government programs have done more to create middle-class career paths for functionaries than to actually help low-income families. But this, I argued, isn't necessarily because government by itself is the problem: It's who runs government and with what priorities. Contemporary priorities are evident in budget cuts that are often penny-wise and pound-foolish, eating into investments we need for future solvency. It's as if a family stopped its house payments and raided the kids' college fund in order to continue eating out every night.

While government has been very generous in promoting Campbell Soup and Gallo wine abroad, for example, the average level of government income assistance to low-income people in the United States is the second lowest of all the countries examined in a recent international survey. The U.S. government does less to smooth out inequality and to promote economic mobility than almost any other advanced industrial nation.[32]

On the other hand, our government has done some things remarkably well, and when I asked Helen to imagine what life would be like in her rural home on the outskirts of Tumwater, Washington, without government, she quickly came up with some examples of where government had been very effective—the rural electrification program that her grandparents had marveled at, the parks system, the highway system, and improvements in air and water quality since the passage of the Clean Water Act in 1972. We also talked about the fact that the Centers for Disease Control and Prevention is a world leader in protection against outbreaks of infection.[33]

The hunt was still on for someone to blame, though, and next we moved to the question of whether blacks were taking jobs from white men. At this point the host added Bob, another caller, to the conversation. Bob's answer to "what went wrong" was that women and blacks were now oppressing white men. He also claimed that the main social crisis tearing families apart was an adolescent drug epidemic spawned by black ghetto culture.

Bob was a lot less reasonable than Helen, but I could see why he might have received the wrong impression about what was happening to African Americans while he and his friends at a local factory were losing health benefits and facing layoffs. After all, movies and ads have recently gone to great lengths to show diversity, with the ironic consequence that blacks and women are now highly overrepresented in the *images* of professions and income levels in which they remain highly *underrepresented* in reality. A small proportion of minorities and white women have made striking (and highly visible) employment gains, but most still work in traditionally lower-paid, less secure jobs.[34]

Bob talked about the humiliation some of his friends felt when they were laid off and their wives continued to work. I could also understand these feelings, considering how men are still raised to equate their self-worth with their earning skills. And in recent recessions, it is true, women have faced fewer layoffs than men, reversing a long-time pattern. But this situation is due to the decline of high-paying industries in which men were traditionally concentrated, not because women have been taking jobs away from men.[35]

It was harder to be patient with Bob's misinterpretation of African-American employment trends. Study after study has found that white job applicants continue to be disproportionately chosen over equally qualified black ones, despite isolated incidents of affirmative action preference. Although African Americans made employment and wage gains during the 1970s, these were stalled during the 1980s, and working-class black men lost ground. Nearly a third of all black men who worked in durable goods manufacturing lost their jobs between 1979 and 1984. In the five cities of the Midwest where such jobs were concentrated, fully 50 percent of male African-American production workers were laid off. The commercial and industrial strips of the inner cities, which once employed thousands of residents, have been abandoned and left to rot.[36]

As for drugs, one of the best-kept secrets in this country is that the typical drug addict is a 40-year-old white man, not a teenage African American. A 40-year-old is fifteen times more likely to die from drug abuse than a youth of high-school age. If you're looking for villains here, the Vietnam War, together with its sorry economic aftermath for veterans, makes one good candidate. Men who served in Vietnam are two and a half times more likely to die from drug abuse than men the same age who did not. But, of course, joblessness makes drug dealing or use very visible, and it's easy to target young African Americans. When Los Angeles police decided to crack down on drug dealing around schools, reports the *Los Angeles Times*, "officers were placed at predominantly minority schools, despite federal studies showing more drug use among white youths." Naturally, nearly all those arrested were blacks and Latinos, feeding a stereotype that has been repeatedly proven false, that minorities are more likely to use drugs than whites.[37]

I didn't make much headway on this issue with Bob, who eventually hung up in disgust, but Helen stayed in there, and I guess I convinced her that inner-city African Americans were not responsible for the problems facing families in her community, because finally there was a short silence. "Well, then," she asked, "whose neck *should* I wring?"

Whose Neck Should We Wring?

Helen's question threw me for a loop. There are certainly some legitimate targets for anger out there, and more plausible suspects than welfare recipients or inner-city kids when it comes to assigning blame for the economic setbacks of working families. For example, Pat Buchanan's belated discovery that corporate CEOs have been raking in cash while laying off employees has helped direct people's attention to important inequities in the way work is organized and rewarded.

In the 1960s, the average chief executive officer of a large corporation earned forty-one times as much as the average factory worker (a difference already four times higher than that found in Japan or Germany). A three-year study of the 300 largest companies in the United States found that the spread had widened dramatically by the early 1990s—and it's still increasing. In 1992, the CEO earned 145 times more than the average employee; by 1993, it was 170 times as much; by 1994, it was 187 times as much. An update in 1996 showed that the figure was still rising as of 1995, with CEOs earning more than 200 times as much as the average worker. And some of the biggest pay gains went to CEOs who had recently mandated massive layoffs.[38]

Buchanan blames our problems on loss of jobs overseas, and the early phases of industrial reorganization did involve the export of many high-paid jobs to lower-paid workers overseas. But in the most recent phase, many of those low-wage jobs have been reimported and assigned to small businesses unlikely to face government regulation or union organizing drives and more easily controlled by giant corporations. High-tech, white-collar workers have now begun to face the same global competition that their blue-collar counterparts faced earlier, as computer and phone links enable corporations to pay educated locals in other parts of the world to do the same jobs at a fraction of the costs. However, there are signs that these jobs too will eventually be reassigned at home, only for much lower wages. In fact, several studies have found that companies engaged in "downsizing" often hire new workers as fast as they lay off old ones—but they take on less experienced workers at lower salaries or hire people back as "independent contractors" and temps, thereby avoiding paying benefits.[39]

While conservatives overestimate the effect of foreign competition and gloss over problems in the small businesses that have sprung up at home, liberals often offer an equally superficial analysis—that our workers simply need better skills in order to keep up with today's technology. However, as economist David Howell points out, there has been no significant increase in the proportion of high-skill jobs during the past few years. And real wages have declined among youths whose reading skills and high school graduation rates have been *improving* for the past twenty years. The main reason for this situation has been the success of employers in undermining traditional wage-setting institutions, such as unions and government minimum wage standards, as well as in substituting temporary and part-time workers for full-time, permanent workers entitled to some modicum of job security and benefits.[40]

But the issue goes deeper than corporate greed or individual villainy.

What we are seeing is a breakdown of America's implicit postwar wage bargain with the working class, in which corporations ensured labor stability by expanding employment, rewarding productivity increases with wage rises, and investing in jobs and infrastructure, while government subsidized home ownership and higher education for young families. A long-term shift from manufacturing to service production has led to the erosion of high-paid union jobs and traditional blue-collar routes to economic security. Employment has increasingly polarized into a minority of high-paying careers, such as those in information or entertainment, and a majority of jobs that have lost the security and benefits promised in the postwar era.

For all the rhetoric about private enterprise during the cold war era, the economy of the 1950s and 1960s set many limits on pure competition. Regulated industries could count on predictable profits and were thus not under pressure to set internal pay schedules by the most minute calculations of profit or to immediately shed any part of the operation that was making lower than average returns. Corporations were more likely to stay in the same communities, and they therefore had to weigh the advantages of short-term cost-cutting measures against their need for a reliable, steady, and motivated workforce. Today, by contrast, as one CEO summed up contemporary corporate values: "You can't be emotionally bound to any particular asset."[41]

"We were the lucky ones," says Martin Sooby, age 67, who moved into Levittown in 1954, the day after he got married. Raised in the poverty-stricken coal country of Pennsylvania for the first nine years of his life, Sooby spent the next ten in a Philadelphia orphanage. He joined the army at age 19 and served in Germany for the next six years. Sooby is a good example of the way that expanding economic opportunities and government assistance programs such as veterans' benefits can help people rise above difficult family backgrounds. Sooby overcame his hard childhood to establish a stable marriage and a satisfying life, but he now worries that his own children and grandchildren, despite more auspicious beginnings, will not be so lucky. "We hit the seam just right," he explains. "When we came back from the war, it was a question of supply and demand. The factories were all booming, and they needed our labor." In addition, veterans' benefits assured him a low down payment and manageable interest rates on a new home. Sooby's grandchildren do indeed face a more difficult future.[42]

The destruction of older limits on the working of pure competition also explains much of the cultural and moral crisis that many Americans feel today. For all the talk about the antifamily values of movie stars and rap singers, the simple truth is that the free market is what's behind the collapse of television's family hour. Sex and violence sell consumer goods better than more thought-provoking subjects. The people who watch such shows

may not represent the entire range of the audience; they may even be a minority. But they are the ones most likely to buy advertised products. The
deregulation of television allows news and entertainment channels to compete for the most profitable audience segment by ratcheting up the kind of
images and action most likely to catch the attention of a consumer surfing
through the channels. Madison Avenue advertisers have done far more to
coarsen popular culture and break down our sense of "a shared civic life"
than any of the obscure artists that are periodically profiled as examples of
America's moral decay.[43]

Blaming the Family for Economic Decline

The fallback position for those in denial about the socioeconomic transformation we are experiencing is to admit that many families are in economic
stress but to blame their plight on divorce and unwed motherhood.
Lawrence Mead of New York University argues that economic inequalities
stemming from differences in wages and employment patterns "are now
trivial in comparison to those stemming from family structure." David
Blankenhorn claims that the "primary fault line" dividing privileged and
nonprivileged Americans is no longer "race, religion, class, education, or
gender" but family structure. Every major newspaper in the country has
published editorials and opinion pieces along these lines. This "new consensus" produces a delightfully simple, inexpensive solution to the economic
ills of America's families. From Republican Dan Quayle to the Democratic
Party's Progressive Policy Institute, we hear the same words: "Marriage is
the best anti-poverty program for children."[44]

Now I am as horrified as anyone by irresponsible parents who yield to
the temptations of our winner-take-all society and abandon their family
obligations. But we are kidding ourselves if we think the solution to the
economic difficulties of America's children lies in getting their parents back
together. Single-parent families, it is true, are five to six times more likely to
be poor than two-parent ones. But correlations are not the same as causes.
The association between poverty and single parenthood has several different sources, suggesting that the battle to end child poverty needs to be
fought on a number of different fronts.

One reason that single-parent families are more liable to be poor than
two-parent families is because falling real wages have made it increasingly
difficult for one earner to support a family. More than one-third of all *two-
parent* families with children would be poor if both parents didn't work. In
this case, the higher poverty rates of one-parent families are not caused by
divorce or unwed motherhood per se but by the growing need for more

than one income per household. Thus a good part of the gap between two-parent and one-parent families, which is much higher today than it was in the past, is the consequence rather than the cause of economic decline.[45]

Another reason that one-parent families are likely to be poor is because the vast majority of single-parent heads of household are women, who continue to be paid far less than men. One study conducted during the highest period of divorce rates found that if women were paid the same as similarly qualified men, the number of poor families would be cut in half.[46]

Many single-parent families fall into poverty, at least temporarily, because of unfair property divisions or inadequate enforcement of child support after a divorce. Although the figures were exaggerated in past studies, the fact remains that women, especially women with children, usually lose income after a divorce. The most recent data show a 27 percent drop in women's standard of living in the first year after divorce and a 10 percent increase in that of men. In 1995, only 56 percent of custodial mothers were awarded child support, and only half of these received the full amount they were due.[47]

In these examples, the solution to poverty in single-parent families does not lie in getting parents back together again but in raising real wages, equalizing the pay of men and women, and making child support and maintenance provisions more fair. In many cases, though, parents who don't earn enough to support two households *could* adequately support one. In such circumstances, it may be technically correct to say that marriage is the solution to child poverty. But even here, things are not always so simple.

Sometimes, for example, the causal arrow points in the opposite direction. Poor parents are twice as likely to divorce as more affluent ones, and job loss also increases divorce even among nonpoor families. Sociologist Scott South calculates that every time the unemployment rate rises by 1 percent, approximately 10,000 extra divorces occur. Jobless individuals are two to three times less likely to marry in the first place. And regardless of their individual values or personal characteristics, teens who live in areas of high unemployment and inferior schools are five to seven times more likely to become unwed parents than more fortunately situated teens.[48]

In the majority of cases, it is poverty and social deprivation that cause unwed motherhood, not the other way around. The fall in real wages and employment prospects for youth after 1970 *preceded* the rise in teen childbearing, which started after 1975 and accelerated in the 1980s. Indeed, reports researcher Mike Males, "the correlation between childhood poverty and later teenage childbearing is so strong that during the 1969–1993 period, the teen birth rate could be calculated with 90 percent accuracy from the previous decade's child poverty rate." According to a two-year study conducted by the Alan Guttmacher Institute, 38 percent of America's 15- to 19-year-old youths were poor in 1994. But of the one in forty teens who became an unwed parent, 85 percent were poor.[49]

Of course causal relationships seldom flow entirely in one direction. Single parenthood can worsen poverty, educational failure, and low earnings capacity, creating a downward spiral. And I certainly wouldn't deny that values regarding marriage have changed, so that more men and women refuse to get married than in the past. But it's also true, as one poverty researcher has put it, that "almost no one volunteers for roles and duties they cannot fulfill." The fact is that fewer and fewer young men from low-income communities can *afford* to get married, or can be regarded by women as suitable marriage partners.[50]

Today the real wages of a young male high school graduate are lower than those earned by a comparable worker back in 1963. Between 1972 and 1994 the percentage of men aged 25 to 34 with incomes *below* the poverty level for a family of four increased from 14 percent to 32 percent. When you realize that almost a third of all young men do not earn more than $15,141 a year, which is the figure defined as poverty level for a family of four in 1994, it's easier to understand why many young men are not rushing to get married, and why many young women don't bother to pursue them. By 1993, nearly half the African-American and Latino men aged 25 to 34 did not earn enough to support a family of four.[51]

For African-American families in particular, the notion that family structure has replaced class and race as the main cause of poverty is absurd. The head of the U.S. Census Department Bureau of Marriage and Family Statistics estimates that at least one-half to three-fourths—perhaps more—of the black–white differential in childhood poverty would remain even if *all* children in African-American families had two parents present in the home. Nor do other family and cultural variations explain the high rates of African-American poverty: Youth poverty rates for African Americans have grown steadily over a period during which black teenage birth rates have dropped and high school graduation rates and test scores have risen.[52]

The most recent and thorough review of the research on the links between poverty and family structure was issued by the Tufts University Center on Hunger, Poverty and Nutrition in 1995. After reviewing seventy-three separate scholarly studies of the subject, the researchers concluded that "single-parent families are not a primary cause of the overall growth of poverty." Rather, poverty is increasing because of declines in employment, wages, and job training opportunities—"far-reaching changes in the economy . . . which hurt both poor and non-poor Americans." Most poverty, in other words, comes from our changing earnings structure, not our changing family structure.[53]

Obviously, single parenthood and family instability intensify preexisting financial insecurity, throwing some people into economic distress and increasing the magnitude of poverty for those already impoverished. And equally obviously, those exceptional individuals who can construct a stable two-parent family in the absence of a stable community or a stable job will usually benefit from doing so. But marriage will not resolve the crisis of child well-being in our country. According to Donald Hernandez, chief of the U.S. Census Department Bureau of Marriage and Family Statistics, even if we could reunite every child in America with both biological parents—and any look at abuse statistics tells you that's certainly not in the best interest of every child—two-thirds of the children who are poor today would *still* be poor.[54]

8

How Ignoring Historical and Societal Change Puts Kids at Risk

E ven before recent economic setbacks, long-term historical processes had already undermined the ability of families to raise the next generation without outside assistance. Children used to be economic assets to a family, and the costs of raising them to an age where they could contribute to family subsistence were quite small. Industrialization gradually increased the expense of raising, educating, or training children and decreased their returns to the family, whether nuclear or extended. The cost of caring for all family dependencies rose as it became more difficult to integrate caregiving with the locations and rhythms of modern workplaces.[1]

After the turn of the century, the abolition of child labor, positive though it was, further increased the costs of raising children. Marital desertion became a growing problem, since fathers were less likely to seek child custody or maintain contact once the economic benefits of children had fallen. At the same time, more and more elderly Americans were ending up in almshouses. States passed laws requiring adult children to support their parents and absent fathers to support their children but found them hard to enforce. Private charities were unable to come anywhere near meeting the needs of children or the elderly, and local institutions could no longer cope with the concentrations of poverty that occurred in urban areas.[2]

As early as the mid-nineteenth century, new public institutions, such as schools, had become essential supplements to family child rearing in all classes, and government had begun to recognize its responsibility to invest in programs to ensure safe and adequate supplies of food, clean air, water, housing, and sanitation facilities. In the early twentieth century, the federal government gradually took over many other functions that had formerly been provided by extended families and voluntary societies, establishing pensions, disability funds, insurance programs, and supplemental cash assistance for families. Government also performed a number of new functions, such as helping to protect family members from abuse. Some of the services government provided were inadequate, while others were unnecessarily intrusive. But I know of no serious historian who doesn't believe that children of all classes were better off as a result of government's expanded role.[3]

The growth of public schooling and government assistance programs for families reflected society's recognition that the rising cost of children made it essential for the task of raising and educating future workers to be shared by all members of society, not just dumped onto parents. The federal government expanded the education system and instituted maternity and child nutrition programs in the early 1900s. During the 1930s, the Civilian Conservation Corps and the National Youth Administration were formed to meet what was agreed to be a societal, not just a parental, responsibility to find work for youths. In the 1940s, the government organized child care centers for women war-production workers. In the 1950s and 1960s, state and federal governments expanded their housing subsidies for families and began providing much more extensive higher education and job programs for young people.

Passing the Buck on Child Support

But in the economic and social climate that has prevailed since the mid-1970s, the long historical expansion of support systems for child raising has been reversed. Governments and corporations have transferred more and more of the costs of raising, educating, and training children back onto parents. As politicians and employers have demonstrated growing indifference to the needs of the next generation, these attitudes have spread throughout society, with nonparents pushing the costs of the next generation onto parents and many parents engaging in their own cost-shifting behaviors.[4]

Spending on education, child and maternal health, and the infrastructure for future generations has not kept up with needs for the past twenty years. Government has developed, economist Sylvia Hewlett observes, "a mindset . . . that is extraordinarily careless of children." As public policy analyst Iris Marion Young argues, "American society has been severely damaged by three decades of private and public disinvestment in basic manufacturing, new and rehabilitated housing, bridges and rail lines, public education, adult retraining, and social services such as preventive health care and libraries." Yet parents are increasingly expected, on their own, "to fill these gaping holes in the American dream."[5]

The extent to which America has shifted the costs of raising children back onto parents can be seen in the extraordinary retreat from the expansion of public education—a child-centered reform in which the United States once led the world. A 1989 study by the Educational Writers Association found that a quarter of the country's school buildings were inadequate, obsolete, or downright dangerous. A 1994 survey found that conditions had continued to deteriorate, and the 1997 budget does not provide enough money to make a dent in the problem. Researchers report a direct correlation between poor physical conditions in schools and poor test scores.[6]

Teachers' salaries, expenditures per pupil, and other indicators of school quality (including the physical plant) significantly affect the employment prospects and wages of high school graduates. Yet unlike other nations, American schools are financed at the local rather than the federal level. If parents do not live in affluent communities with a high enough proportion of neighbors willing to vote for school bonds, they have few ways of assuring a quality education other than to enroll their children in private schools. And voters, many of them parents who believe they already "did their bit" by raising their own children, are becoming less and less willing to subsidize schools for "other" people's kids. School bond failures are way up in comparison with earlier decades. At the same time, the property tax cuts of the 1970s and 1980s greatly decreased the resources available to schools.

Child advocate and educational researcher Jonathon Kozol reports that New York City spends half as much per student as surrounding suburbs. In 1992, the country's forty-seven largest urban school districts spent nearly *$900 less on each student* than did their suburban counterparts—even though the urban schools were far more likely to have students needing special services. There are also substantial variations *within* school districts. Poorer neighborhoods, which often contain more children, receive much lower public subsidies than affluent ones.[7]

International comparisons reveal that education is simply not a national priority in the United States the way it is in many countries. We have a piecemeal, incoherent system that fails to train teachers thoroughly, keep track of student progress in a consistent way, or ensure equality of access. Things are no better in the work world. Only 1 percent of the funding employers devote to training goes toward raising basic skills, those most needed by young entry-level workers. Both publicly and privately funded education is heavily skewed against the apprenticeship programs and vocational training needed by youngsters whose parents cannot afford to send them to college. Government spending on employment and training programs, in inflation-adjusted dollars, is today only one-third of what it was in 1980. At the same time, the cost of higher education has soared, while loans and scholarships have been cut back.[8]

Housing policies provide another example of government disinvestment in future generations. In the 1970s, government was financing about 400,000 new apartments a year. In 1996, Congress cut the number of new families who can expect rent subsidies or vouchers to zero.[9]

Economists and political scientists debate where this disinvestment in the next generation began and why it has spread so widely in the United States. Part of the problem is that the economic and political changes of the past few decades have increasingly put families with children at a disadvantage. The pressures of a fast-paced, winner-take-all economy handicap parents in comparison to nonparents, because parents have less time to produce income and more demands on them for redistribution than nonparents.

Under a system such as Social Security, furthermore, economist Nancy Folbre argues, nonparents can actually become "free riders" on parents. By now, most people realize that retirees get much more from Social Security than they actually put in. It is future workers, raised by parents at their personal expense, who create the Social Security funds on which all aging workers will later draw, even if they did not invest in rearing any of those future workers. Thus nonparents can benefit from other people's children without contributing to the costs of raising them.[10]

These trends have been exacerbated by what economist Robert Reich calls the "secession of the successful." Increasingly, affluent parents as well as nonparents have withdrawn funding from "public institutions shared by all and dedicated their savings to their own private services"—from exclusive schools and recreational facilities to private security for their walled-off neighborhoods. Government disinvestment widens the cycle, leaving middle-class families scrambling to buy privately what they can no longer count on receiving from public institutions, and needing to cut other expenses to make ends meet. In a tax system where voters have no say about whether expensive bombers get built, but plenty of chances to take out their frustrations in local school levies, children increasingly lose out in the contest for resources.[11]

In other words, long-term economic processes have gradually undermined Americans' consciousness of intergenerational obligations, while short-term economic setbacks have encouraged them to seize on quick-fix ways to keep more of their shrinking paychecks. Politicians have opportunistically encouraged people to rob the next generation. In confrontations over scarce resources or contested priorities, children, after all, are not an organized lobbying group.

The historical rise in the private costs of rearing children, combined with recent public disinvestment in social capital, forms the background to what economist Joan Acker calls "a growing crisis of distribution" in modern industrial societies. In this crisis, it is not only children in single-parent families who have lost ground. There has been a decline in the economic and social resources available to children of *all* families except those in the top 20 percent of the income hierarchy.[12]

The Impact of Economic Inequality on Families

Cutbacks in social support systems, economic decline for working families, growing poverty for the unemployed or marginally employed, and highly visible affluence for the top 20 percent, along with the dazzling increase in consumer goods and services, all combine to make family life more difficult and social solidarity more elusive for everyone. The main countertrend to the job and wage setbacks in the United States since the mid-1970s has been a tremendous expansion of the consumer economy in fields that compete with family life and social ties, providing youth of all classes with fleeting and sometimes dangerous compensation for their exclusion from meaningful participation in work, civic life, and public space.

I spoke a year or so ago near Lakewood, California, a town made famous by the Spur Posse, a group of high school athletes who developed a point system for sexual conquests. One of the women at my talk had a son who attended the same school as the Spur Posse youths, and she made a memorable comment about the life that faces so many young people in this city of middle-class homes but increasingly lower-class jobs. "A lot of these kids," she said, "have way too little future, but way too much *now*."[13]

For many families, of course, the *now* is already bleak, and it is naive to think that parents can always protect their children from the impact of economic loss. Researchers find that the risk of violent behavior is nearly six times higher among people who are laid off from their jobs than among their employed counterparts, regardless of whether or not the individuals had a prior history of psychiatric disorder or alcohol abuse. A study of 350 white families in rural Iowa found that declining income, unstable work, or family debt in 1989 were linked to significantly higher levels of aggression in middle-school children two years later. These youths were more likely to beat someone up, deface property, set fires, and use weapons against others than youths who had not experienced economic stress.[14]

One of the main ways that children are hurt by unemployment and income loss, in middle- and upper-income families as well as low-income ones, is through the increase in stress and depression that their parents experience. When parents are distracted or irritated with each other because of financial or job worries, they tend to be less supportive of their children. Too preoccupied to reinforce—or even notice—their children's considerate behavior, parents become overly sensitive to disruptive behavior because it adds to their feelings of stress. Their attempts to nip "bad" behavior in the bud increase hostile exchanges with their children. With their own emotional resources overtaxed, parents find it hard to summon the patience for negotiation, tact, and complex reasoning. Instead, they issue orders, followed by physical punishment when immediate obedience is not forthcoming. Parents may see children's resistance as yet another challenge to their authority and self-esteem, which are already threatened by economic setbacks having nothing to do with the kids.[15]

Often, parents are not aware that they have fallen into these patterns. When researchers ask parents who have been laid off about the effects on their families, few report problems. Some even tell researchers it's great to have the extra time with their kids. Children's accounts, however, almost invariably mention increased conflict and tension with parents. Observers' comparisons of interactions between employed and unemployed parents and their children suggest that the kids' perceptions are more accurate than the parents'. Without other adult mentors or social support systems in the community, kids often bear the brunt of their parents' economic stress.[16]

Most of the effect of economic loss on children is channeled through changes in parenting practices, but economic insecurity also reduces kids' confidence in their parents and thereby increases their vulnerability to peer pressure. They become depressed and less motivated, and their lowered aspirations often have long-range consequences for their future.[17]

I got a vivid illustration of this a year or so ago when, after we had read studies of these family processes in class, one of my male students broke down crying. Embarrassed, he came to my office later and told me that he had transferred to the state college where I teach after two years at a community college and a year of full-time work. He had been raised to think he would go directly to a major university from high school. But his father had lost a well-paying job in the early 1980s, and by the time he found another, the family had gone through most of its savings.

My student told me how much he had resented his parents' inability to send him to the college of his choice. He had begun hanging out with a crowd that reinforced his growing contempt for his parents and their seemingly ineffectual response to the family crisis. During his last two years of high school he had defied rules, frequently staying out all night, binging on alcohol, and letting his grades slip. There were shouting matches with his father, tearful recriminations from his mother.

Recently he and his parents had begun to mend their fences, but this was the first time, he said, he had really thought about how much pain his contempt had added to their lives. "I couldn't get past my father yelling at me and insulting me," he said. "I couldn't see how he must have been hurting. And when my mom cried, it just made me feel more like going out and getting stoned."

The effects of economic loss on children seem to be more pronounced for boys than for girls. In contrast to the cycles of anger and disrespect between sons and fathers triggered by economic hardship, mothers in deprived families often gain regard for their daughters' opinions, allowing them to participate more in family decisions. There are also gender differences in the ways that economic loss affects parenting. Both fathers and mothers are likely to respond to economic stress with inconsistent and harsh parenting, but men are more likely to explode at their children.[18]

When marital conflict is part of the equation, things get even worse. Fathers tend to react to children in an increasingly hostile, arbitrary manner, while children tend "to question the father's authority and form coalitions with the mother against the father." A strong marital relationship can temper these reactions, but economic loss has been found to produce dramatic declines in marital quality and supportiveness. Furthermore, whereas support from husbands lessens the impact of economic hardship on women's parenting practices, support from wives does not always have the same effect on fathers. Even with highly supportive wives, men under economic stress are far more likely to be explosive, inconsistent parents.[19]

Individuals with exceptionally good interpersonal skills can and do survive economic stress without such severe reactions, but those from less than ideal backgrounds, who in better conditions often overcome their personal weaknesses, may find the gains they have made over the years wiped away. For example, the Iowa study found that parents who had grown up in troubled families had fewer people skills and less self-confidence as adults. They were therefore "less capable of eliciting social support from others" to help them "withstand the psychological onslaught of economic disadvantage." As the social safety net has unraveled, such individuals and their children increasingly fall by the wayside.[20]

The Effects of Poverty on Families and Children

Here's what Robert Rector of the Heritage Foundation has to say about the relationship between economic trends and family issues: "Is poverty harmful for children? I think not. Your bank account does not indicate the type of home you have."[21]

Do Rector and his counterparts have any idea of the terrible binds faced by unemployed or impoverished Americans, or of the havoc that poverty wreaks on families? I think not. Consider the fact that the number of underweight infants seen at hospitals rises sharply in the three months after the coldest snap of winter, in what Dr. Deborah Frank calls the "heat-or-eat" choice that many poor families have to make.[22]

Actually, the size of people's bank account has a lot to do with what type of home they can provide, which in turn has a tremendous impact on children's health and well-being. For example, poor children are especially likely to live in older homes where drinking water still flows through lead pipes and where there hasn't been a new paint job since 1978—the last year lead-based paint was used. It's estimated that 64 million homes contain lead-based paint. More than 1.7 million American children suffer from lead poisoning, the Environmental Protection Agency reported in 1996.[23]

Children who have been exposed to lead are seven times less likely to graduate from high school, six times more likely to have a reading disability, and six times more likely to engage in violence than other children, regardless of their family background. A four-year study of more than 800 boys in Pittsburgh, released February 7, 1996, showed that boys with higher lead levels were more likely than other boys to engage in antisocial acts, regardless of their parents' marital status or intelligence, and aside from any differences in income, medical problems, race, or ethnicity. Another study that followed 987 African-American children from birth to age 22 found that a history of lead poisoning was "the strongest predictor of disciplinary problems in junior high school boys and the third strongest predictor of both juvenile and adult offenses."[24]

Rector also claims that "the biggest dietary problem of people living in poverty is obesity, not hunger." Many poor adults *are* obese, since empty calories cost less than fruits or fish, but for kids, this is simply false. Children in poverty are not more overweight than other children, but they are two to three times more likely to suffer from stunted growth. Columnist George Will says of the urban poor, "theirs is a poverty of inner resources." Yes, indeed—like nutrients. In 1992, an estimated 12 million American children had diets whose nutrient levels were significantly below the recommended allowances established by the National Academy of Sciences. Iron deficiency anemia affects nearly a quarter of America's impoverished children, and this condition is associated with long-term intellectual impairment. An article in the *American Journal of Epidemiology* concludes that "differences in nutritional status between poor and nonpoor children remain large even when controls for other characteristics associated with poverty, such as low maternal educational attainment, single-parent family structure, young maternal age, low maternal academic ability, and minority racial identification, are included."[25]

Poverty exerts direct effects on children's health and mental functioning even in the most solid families, with completely devoted and competent parents. But poverty, like job and income loss in general, also strains marital relationships and parent–child interactions. With nowhere to turn, increasingly cut off from social support or hope for help from public agencies, desperate parents sometimes behave in desperate ways.

Contrary to much of the discussion in the family values camp, most of the parenting problems in impoverished families have to do with harsh, punitive discipline rather than permissiveness. But poverty can distract parents from effective follow-through on discipline. A study of children raised during the Great Depression of the 1930s found that poverty interfered with parental control over youths, making delinquency more likely "regardless of the children's initial temperament, the parents' own tendencies toward crime or deviance or mental instability, marital status and other factors." It's interesting to note that the two peaks in murder rates in the twentieth century occurred in 1933 and 1993. Yet whereas researchers easily recognize the social roots of violence in the Great Depression, many persist in denying the social and economic causes of today's troubled family and neighborhood relationships.[26]

Exceptionally competent parents, of course, can protect their children from many risks. Considering how many children from deprived backgrounds manage to get through school, avoid criminal involvement, and find jobs, it's clear that there are some very competent and caring parents in poverty-stricken communities. Indeed, when you look at the effort it takes in such communities to keep children fed and physically safe, not to mention finding them warm clothes to wear and a quiet place to study, you have to admire the heroism that so many parents show. But if we made heroism a requirement for raising children, how many of us would have been issued the children with which we've been blessed? And even heroes can lose a child to lead poisoning, asthma, violence, or the bad breaks that occur so much more often in impoverished neighborhoods than in affluent communities.[27]

Impoverished families in urban areas are especially vulnerable today because changes in the nature and location of jobs over the past two decades mean that urban poverty has come to play an unprecedented role in society. Once urban poverty was a harsh but temporary way of forcing rural migrants to accept the demands and rhythms of industrial work in the city, as well as providing a cheap labor pool to hold down wages. Today, however, it permanently channels people out of the labor market—and, increasingly, out of any claim to common humanity with those who venture into the city to eat, shop, or work downtown and then retreat to their suburban homes at night.[28]

The proportion of poor people who live in areas where at least 40 percent of the other residents are also poor has more than doubled since the mid-1970s. And the chance of escaping poverty has declined. "In the 1970s, 37 out of 100 people who were poor moved out of poverty within a year; by the 1980s that figure was only 23 out of 100."[29]

The length of time spent in poverty has a powerful impact on children's well-being. Simple annual comparisons of income levels do not adequately measure the degree of disadvantage experienced by children who live for years at a time in areas of concentrated poverty. Persistent poverty during the first five years of life, for example, leaves children with an IQ deficit of more than nine points, regardless of family structure, race, ethnic group, or maternal education. Several studies have shown that the corrosive effect of chronic poverty outweighs the impact of individual life events and family histories on people's depression levels and coping skills.[30]

It is no wonder, then, that the odds of extreme behavioral problems are more than twice as high for poor children as for nonpoor ones. The most careful studies suggest that poverty, economic insecurity, and the effects of neglected neighborhoods pose stronger risks to children than growing up in single-parent families, and are better predictors of low educational achievement or serious difficulties with the law. A child's chance of experiencing a poor home environment goes up in association with a number of different factors, including single parenthood, large numbers of siblings, and low maternal education, but the largest effects are almost invariably found to be family and neighborhood poverty rather than family structure.[31]

Poor children are twice as likely to drop out of high school as other children. Mothers in one-parent families that are poor are no more likely to be abusive than mothers in two-parent families that are poor, but poor mothers—single or married—are significantly more likely to be abusive than mothers with incomes above the poverty line. For men, single fatherhood by itself does have an independent effect on abuse rates, but poverty has a stronger impact. Poor single fathers are three times as likely as nonpoor single fathers to abuse their children, and four times as likely as nonpoor fathers in a two-parent family.[32]

Poverty, Family Form, and Crime: What Sociological Studies Can and Cannot Tell Us

You've undoubtedly heard studies quoted that contradict the findings presented here, especially when it comes to explaining antisocial behavior. Many researchers claim that even after controlling for income, single parenthood is the major cause of crime and violence. Barbara Dafoe Whitehead of the Institute for American Values, who wrote the "Dan Quayle Was Right" article in 1993, is often cited on this point. According to Whitehead, "more than 70 percent of all juveniles in state reform institutions come from fatherless homes." Mayors, police, and social workers, she claims, "consistently point to family breakup as the most important source of rising rates of crime." In the eight months after Whitehead's article appeared, I almost never gave a lecture without being drawn aside at the end by a single mother, often with the article in hand and the quote circled, asking me fearfully if I thought that her situation would really cause her child to end up in trouble with the law. Whitehead had clearly reached a mass audience and touched a raw nerve.[33]

But the studies are not nearly so unanimous as Whitehead suggests. According to a 1993 report of the National Academy of Sciences, for example, "personal and neighborhood income are the strongest predictors of violent crime." A recent summary of research on gangs, issued by the U.S. Department of Justice, concluded that single-parent families do not on their own predict gang membership. Martin Sanchez Jankowski spent ten years hanging out with gangs to write an ethnographic account of their activities. He found that there were "as many gang members from homes where the nuclear family was intact as there were from families where the father was absent" and "as many members who claimed close relationships with their families as those who denied them." Of course, many gangs are concentrated in neighborhoods that have high rates of single-parent families, so they will have a higher than average number of kids from one-parent families, but not necessarily disproportionate for their community.[34]

Cause and effect in human behavior are seldom simple. If single parenthood "caused" crime and violence, then Sweden and Denmark ought to have higher rates than the United States, instead of rates that are dramatically lower. Indeed, research in other countries does not find the same association between single-parent families and adolescent risk-taking behaviors that so much American research notes, which suggests that something more complicated is going on.[35]

Even in the American studies, there is good reason to doubt how powerful the reported "associations" really are. Researchers who say they have "controlled" for other variables often overlook the dynamics of class. Controlling for income, for example, does not take into account the broader patterns of a person's life. College students frequently have very low incomes, but their social status and future prospects are generally greater than someone who pulls down a higher wage working at a low-skill, dead-end job. An African-American family with the same income as a white family is likely to have less than half as many total family assets. Nor are all poverty incomes alike. The deeper and more long-lasting poverty is, the worse its effects. Yet many studies do not distinguish between current income and long-term economic status.[36]

A few years ago, there was a short-lived fad for public officials or reporters to try living on a welfare mother's budget or a poverty-level income for a month. The conclusion was usually: "It's very hard, but it can be done." Every time I glanced at such a magazine article or heard a news story about such an experiment on the radio, I knew I could expect a visit from an African-American friend of mine who had spent her first twenty-two years in a housing project in the San Francisco Bay Area. As the only professor she had access to, it was my job to brew the coffee and let her vent.

"Did they have their teeth unstraightened or their grammar undone, so everyone would know they were the bottom of the barrel?" she would demand. "Did they first wear their car down to its last legs so that a tire or part would be sure to go and they'd have to choose between paying the rent and making it to a job interview? Did they throw out all the staples in their kitchen before they started cooking on a food-stamp allotment? Did they let their kids get mugged a couple of times and then, just to teach them that life is hard, make sure they also got shoved up against a nearby building by the cops every few days?"

My friend's outbursts were sometimes emotionally draining for us both, but they certainly reinforced in me a healthy skepticism about what you can and can't capture in a study of the separate "factors" affecting youthful behavior. Most statistics also do not control for bias in police and court records or reports of outside observers. When researchers have asked young people themselves how much delinquency they engage in, "family structure was unrelated to the seriousness of the offense." But school officials, juvenile authorities, and police are more likely to record behaviors committed by children from single-parent families and more likely to take measures against those kids.[37]

Youths from single-parent families are certainly overrepresented among the prison population. Part of the reason is that the majority of people in prison come from impoverished, desperate neighborhoods where there are high proportions of single-parent families that generally are a result, not a cause, of the community's problems. Another part of the story is legal bias. "When a white middle-class youth is arrested for a non-violent offense," writes former Judge Lois Forer, "the juvenile court usually 'adjusts' the offense. The boy has no record. In the inner city, youths are routinely adjudicated delinquent. Later this record counts heavily against them." Public defenders consistently tell me that they have a much slimmer chance of getting a youngster off with probation if the child has one parent than if he has two, regardless of the nature of the crime committed.[38]

Criminologist William Chambliss has spent several years, along with his students, riding with the Rapid Deployment Unit of the Washington, D.C., Metropolitan Police. He points out that "the intensive surveillance of black neighborhoods" leads to arrest and sentencing disparities that actually help *create* the single-parent families that "pro-family" spokespeople tell us are the source of crime.[39]

To deny that one-parent families are the cause of crime and violence is not to say there aren't some potentially dangerous interactions that occur between family structure, economic stress, parenting behaviors, and child outcomes. This is especially true in neighborhoods whose men have been marginalized by economic change. But crime and violence generally result only from the interaction and mutual reinforcement of *several* different factors, not from family factors alone.

One study found that on its own a high concentration of poverty in a neighborhood is not always linked to predelinquent childhood behaviors. Nor is a high level of residential turnover. But if the two factors exist together they do produce significant antisocial behavior. Similarly, "economic deprivation combined with a lack of social support creates an especially dangerous situation for children." The more risk factors at play, the more likely children are to get into trouble. One study found that more than half of adolescent delinquents "grew up with five or more separate risk factors."[40]

Children in inner-city African-American communities, for example, have risk factors piled on top of each other. Chronic joblessness, extreme segregation, economic and political abandonment of the cities, and the resultant discouragement, researcher Phillip Bowman argues, have made the transition from adolescence to adulthood an acute challenge for impoverished African Americans.[41]

Columnist George Will has a simple formula to explain their problems: "What is called the race crisis is a class problem arising from dysfunctional families and destructive behaviors." He's got it partly right. Many family forms and behaviors that are commonly attributed to race are in fact responses to class position. But race and racism help explain why African Americans and Latinos are concentrated in the industries and regions where economic setbacks have been the most devastating, and why minorities have accumulated so few assets over the years, leaving them especially vulnerable to unemployment and income loss. And the evidence suggests that the rest of Will's statement is almost exactly backward. America's class problem is a major *cause* of dysfunctional families and destructive behaviors, especially among impoverished racial groups on whom government and society have turned their backs.[42]

In many inner-city communities, long-term poverty combines with lack of social support, dilapidated schools, overcrowded classrooms, and the sense that the rest of society doesn't care to create chronic despair in children, punctuated by bouts of rage. Herb Schreier, chief of psychiatry at Children's Hospital in Oakland, California, described to me how some of the kids in an African-American and Asian high school there went on a rampage after the fire that swept through Berkeley and Oakland in 1991. When teachers talked with the students later, it turned out that they were infuriated by the outpouring of public sympathy and aid that victims of the fire had received. How could they have reacted so disgracefully to such a heartwarming response? Almost exactly two years earlier the Cypress Expressway had collapsed in the great Bay Area earthquake. The rubble was still sitting in their neighborhood, and this devastated community had received no such aid and sympathy. "No one cares about *us*," the kids said. "No one ever does anything about us."

No wonder such youths become alienated. They have watched their parents get fired after diligently trudging off to a menial job for twenty years. They have seen building after building on their block abandoned. And when some kids have the perfectly normal response of throwing stones at a vacant building, the broken windows and boards stay unrepaired. Everything in their environment is ugly except the images on TV. And don't think they don't notice: One of the first proposals the notorious Bloods and Crips gangs made to the city of L.A. after the riots in 1992 was that the city place flowerboxes on their street corners. It hasn't happened yet. Meanwhile, mired in poverty but surrounded by images of affluence, is it any wonder that young people look for some other way to get a piece of the American dream?[43]

Joe Marshall, cofounder of the Omega Boys Club, works with youth in an impoverished San Francisco neighborhood very similar to that in which he grew up. He remarks that there are not more hard-core "bad guys" today, but there are fewer alternatives to throwing in your lot with them. In his youth, he recalls, poverty was widespread, but at least there were jobs that gave young people work experience, spending money, and a sense of dignity. Even with high unemployment rates and low wages, the hope that these jobs provided kept most people working or looking for work. Kids who fell for the lure of easy money or the street life used to see it as a bad choice they had made. "Don't turn out like me," they would tell younger boys. "Run on home now." Today, with fewer and fewer alternatives almost every year, the "bad guys" play a different role.[44]

Not every social ill in America, of course, is caused by economic deprivation. Conservatives are quite right to say that poverty alone does not explain the alienation and fragmentation so prevalent today, or the terrible turmoil in so many families. But the shattering of older social expectations, along with the evolution of rich and poor into two separate universes, explains much of it. And the abandonment of the social safety net explains even more. As Jerome Skolnick put it in his 1994 presidential address to the American Society of Criminology, "Unemployment is a risk factor for crime. Patterned unemployment through time, and across racial and ethnic divisions, is a cause." Especially, criminologist Gilbert Geiss points out, when unemployment and poverty rub shoulders with "a society of affluence, in which your self-esteem is tied to failure to achieve that affluence."[45]

It is time to abandon denial, self-righteousness, and scapegoating and to deal directly with the moral issues raised by these economic changes and by the last few decades of disinvestment in the younger generation. The question that gets lost in the debate over marital stability, parental responsibility, and personal character is whether we as a nation are willing to foster long-term commitments in economic and social life, whether we as a people have the character to defer immediate gratification in order to invest in the future of our communities. At heart, this is not a family crisis but a social crisis.

The worst effect of today's family values crusade is that by blaming our problems on the breakdown of the traditional family it fails to recognize the strengths of today's diverse families—strengths we can mobilize to help *solve* our social problems. We need to reject the false notion that there is one perfect family form that automatically protects its members from outside forces, while other family forms or values automatically put them at risk. *All* families are at risk when they're left to face new challenges on their own. All families have the potential to rise above their weaknesses when they get support and encouragement from others.

When you read life histories of children from impoverished neighborhoods, the first point that strikes you is the stunning number of obstacles they face, the hundreds of tiny curves where it's possible to fall off a path much narrower and higher than any that more privileged children have to tread. But the second point is how eager most parents are to do right by their children.

Similarly, when I talk with families undergoing major changes in their marital roles, family forms, or work relations, I am constantly amazed by their resilience and creativity. What they need is social and moral support to meet their challenges and hone their strengths. What they don't need is to be subjected to a family values exam in which they are graded on the basis of some standardized form that was codified a century ago.

9

Working with What We've Got: The Strengths and Vulnerabilities of Today's Families

W ith 50 percent of American children living in something other than a married-couple family with both biological parents present, and with the tremendous variety of male and female responsibilities in today's different families, the time for abstract pronouncements about good or bad family structures and correct or incorrect parental roles is past. How a family functions is more important than its structure or its formal roles.

There are some principles of family functioning that, at a general level, seem to work well for every kind of family. Family researchers and psychologists, for example, distinguish three general styles of parenting, not all of which are equally effective.

Authoritarian parenting is restrictive, controlling, and more concerned with the adults' needs for order and obedience than with the children's developmental tasks. Lines of communication run from the top down, with little give-and-take in family discussions or decisions. Negotiation with children is seen as a violation of correct parent–child boundaries. Discipline often takes the form of punishment rather than figuring out ways to ensure that the child accepts the logical consequences of his or her acts. Parents hold the child to high standards, but they are not responsive to the child's needs and desires.

Permissive parents, by contrast, are responsive but undemanding, indulgent of their children's impulsive behaviors and almost always willing to negotiate or renegotiate a decision. They are often highly affectionate, but such parents are sometimes hard for a child to read because it's never clear when "no" really means no—or when a "yes" will be regretted.

Midway between these two extremes are authoritative parents, who are responsive and demanding at the same time. They set limits based on an understanding of what age-appropriate boundaries their child needs, but they also take their child's point of view into account when making decisions and are willing to negotiate new rules. Parents remain warm and emotionally supportive even when they are enforcing consequences. As their children age, they increasingly hold them accountable for their acts rather than restricting their behavior in advance. As one researcher describes such parents, they are accepting, democratic, but also firm.[1]

Antisocial behavior and poor school performance in young people is associated with both extremes. The permissive pattern of placing few demands on children does little to increase their self-confidence and competence, while inadequate monitoring is a problem for adolescents because it opens the door to involvement in undesirable activities. But coercive parenting can be even worse, as it may draw parent and child into a cycle of rebellion and hostility that culminates in the adolescent's premature break with the family or the parents' rejection of the child. The child's break only hardens his or her self-image as an alienated troublemaker, and parental rejection is "the most powerful predictor" of subsequent violence.[2]

Authoritative parenting, on the other hand, in every family structure and at all income levels, tends to produce close parent–child relations and self-confident, competent children. Of course, it's all very well to know that in the abstract, but it's harder in practice to be authoritative when many of us aren't sure what the "right" answers are in today's society, where the logical consequences of acts are different than they were a generation or two ago and where the line between monitoring, restricting, and overindulging seems very blurred.

I don't know many parents, in any kind of family, who are confident that they've got it right. General proclamations that "intact" families are most likely to function well, while one-parent families and stepfamilies are more likely to fail, are no more helpful to intact families trying to cope with their particular situations than they are to other kinds of families. What parents need today is more concrete research about how different families can create processes that work for their individual situations.

Knowing the form of a family tells us very little about the communication and problem solving that goes on within it, the child-rearing practices that hold sway, or most of the other important variables that determine effective child raising. Different family structures may produce different stress points or pose distinctive challenges, but ultimately every family form provides its members with some resources or strengths to build on and some vulnerabilities or danger points to avoid.

Take the breadwinner–homemaker model. In an economy where work, home, and school are in different locations, this family potentially provides kids with more maternal time, supervision, and homework help. The mother has more chances to meet with teachers, help out in school, and chauffeur children to extracurricular activities. The parents don't have to scramble to rearrange schedules when a child gets sick or needs extra attention.

Male breadwinner families seem to be especially beneficial to the health and happiness of men, so long as they can live up to their provider roles. Yet the pressures of being the sole provider may distance a father from his kids, while these families often isolate the mother and lower her self-esteem. Homemakers with young children, for example, tend to be more depressed than other groups of women. Furthermore, such families may have a tough time adjusting to rapid economic change. Parents with strong values about male breadwinning are *more* likely than other parents to experience conflict and severe distress if the father faces economic setbacks or the mother has to find a job.[3]

Two-earner families have less family time together, and they are more likely to quarrel over housework, sometimes to the point of rupture. Yet Arlie Hochschild found that "sharing the second shift improved a marriage *regardless* of what ideas either [spouse] had about men's and women's roles. Whether they were traditional or egalitarian, couples were happier when the men did more housework and childcare." Furthermore, families with a working mother are more likely to raise children who respect women—no small advantage in a world where women are rapidly becoming the majority of the workforce and old-fashioned notions about women are a potent cause of workplace hostilities.[4]

Neither of these family types seems to have a clear advantage over the other when it comes to raising children successfully, but different dynamics are at work in each. The best predictor of secure mother–child attachment in a dual-earner family is the mother's satisfaction with child care arrangements, while in a male breadwinner family it is the mother's personal coping skills.[5]

Both types of two-parent families have the advantage that more than one adult is available to the child. Parents can back each other up in discipline, compensate for each other's weaknesses, spell each other in tasks or time, and model healthy conflict resolution. On the other hand, many two-parent families have the illusion that a father's presence provides them with some magic psychological shield, which may lead the mother to avoid confronting damaging paternal behavior rather than risk a split. And as we've seen, a conflicted marriage can actually be worse for a child than a divorce.

Researchers from the Fatherhood Project at the Families and Work Institute in New York point out that "it is presence, not absence, that often lies at the heart of troubled families. It is common for family members to be in the same room and be oblivious to each other's thoughts and feelings." As Harvard psychologist Samuel Osherson puts it, "Sometimes a father or mother can be in the same room as a child, but emotionally already have walked out the door."[6]

Even harmonious couples and hands-on parents need to beware of certain pitfalls. Thinking their family self-sufficient, they may not expose their children to experiences and values that differ from their own. Such families occasionally foster an inward orientation that hinders a child from striking out in new directions or learning to appreciate difference in others. I was raised in neighborhoods where all adults felt free to act parentally toward children, and I have noticed that when I continue this tradition by commenting on something dangerous or hurtful that local children are doing, it is often youths from two-parent families who are the *most* hostile in their response: "You can't tell me that; you're not my mom."

Collaborative two-parent families certainly benefit children. But it *is* possible for single parents to find effective substitutes for the second parent. Occasionally, in fact, the need for more than one adult can be satisfied best by adding someone *other* than the father or a lover. In a random sample of Baltimore schoolchildren during their first two years of school, researchers found that family structure had no consistent effects on grades, with only one exception: "African American children in single-mother families where other adults are present got higher marks in reading at the beginning of first grade than did their counterparts in mother-only *or* mother–father families."[7]

It's worth noting that the two-parent advantage also applies to gay and lesbian couples, a point that gets lost in many debates over same-sex marriage, adoption, and custody issues. This is not a question that can be sidestepped by forbidding artificial insemination to unwed mothers or prohibiting homosexuals from adopting. Ninety-nine percent of children being raised in gay or lesbian families were born within marriage and live with a parent who came out after a divorce.[8]

Julie Schwartz Gottman, codirector of the Seattle Marital and Family Institute, compared three groups of adult women: one raised by divorced mothers who had stayed single, another by mothers who had divorced and remarried, and a third group raised by divorced mothers in lesbian couples. Using eighteen different scales of social adjustment, she found no significant differences among the groups, but there was a tendency for the daughters of heterosexual remarried women *and* of lesbian couples to exhibit more independence and leadership qualities than daughters of women who divorced and remained single.[9]

Gottman's finding of normal adjustment in children of gay and lesbian families, with a slight advantage for those whose parents had partners, has been confirmed by a considerable body of research. Children raised by gay and lesbian parents seem to be as well adjusted, on average, as children raised by heterosexual parents, with the same range of variation within each group. Dr. Charlotte Patterson found in her research with 4- to 9-year-old children that there were only two significant differences between children of lesbian and heterosexual parents: Children of lesbian mothers were more likely to report feelings of anger and fear than children of heterosexual mothers, but also more likely to report positive feelings such as contentment and a general sense of well-being. Researchers suspect this may be because they are more open than average about communicating feelings, good and bad.[10]

Children in gay and lesbian families face the disadvantage of negative feedback from outside the family, especially in early adolescence, but many such families have important countervailing strengths. Lesbian couples, for example, have greater parenting awareness skills, on average, than heterosexual parents. They are also more likely to share child care and housework equitably, a trait associated with higher parental satisfaction and child well-being in *all* types of families. Finally, and contrary to what stereotype might lead one to expect, lesbian mothers, in comparison to heterosexual single mothers, "have more congenial relations with ex-spouses and include men more regularly in their children's lives." When I talk with such mothers and the fathers of their children, they suggest that this is because sexual jealousy is not part of the ex-spouse dynamic. One man told me, "if she'd left me for another man, I'd have gone ballistic. But I can't compete with a woman and don't want to."[11]

Many people are concerned that lesbian or gay parents will "recruit" children to their sexual orientation. *Any* parent who proselytizes about sexuality has a problem—whether it's a father of a Spur Posse rapist bragging about the "virile specimens" he's sired or a homosexual parent urging a child to experiment with same-sex relations. But unlike the documented cases of fathers who encourage sons to "prove" their heterosexual masculinity, there is no evidence of gay and lesbian parents doing anything comparable with their children. The largest survey to date of adult sons of gay fathers found that more than 90 percent were heterosexual, no matter how long a time they had lived with their fathers. Similarly, comparisons of women raised by lesbian and heterosexual mothers show no differences in their gender identity or sexual orientation.[12]

What the research clearly reveals is that it is not helpful to children for gay or lesbian parents to hide their homosexuality. When children learn this information in adolescence or in custody disputes, it is harder for them to accept it than when they are given the information at a younger age and allowed to assimilate it gradually.[13]

The biggest problem for children of gay and lesbian parents is hostility or ridicule from the outside world. Yet youngsters whose parents are open and supportive seem to learn effective ways of coping—and it's worth remembering that in the long run it is not necessarily bad for adolescents to have something that sets them apart from peers. Being popular and successful in adolescence sometimes forestalls later growth, as youngsters peak too early and have difficulty moving on to new values and challenges. By contrast, painful adolescent experiences can contribute to a young person's future maturity and problem-solving abilities. This factor is also important to consider in evaluating how family changes such as divorce and remarriage affect children over the long haul.[14]

Single-Parent Families: Strengths and Weaknesses

Single-parent families have only one parent in the home to provide financial and emotional resources. When one adult is sad or angry, the whole house is upset. It also takes single-parent families longer than two-parent ones to recover from economic reverses. These are serious handicaps. Yet anthropologists point out that, "when combined with an extended network of concerned kin, the one-parent family often can tender more emotional support and offer more options to family members than an isolated nuclear family." In some situations, children of a single mother may get more attention and assistance from the mother's kin, for a greater total amount of support, than children whose mother moves away from her family to be with her husband.[15]

An African-American colleague of mine tells me that his single mother's lack of a stable marriage gave her the flexibility to link him up with a huge network of kin and close family friends. She sent him to live with whatever friends or relatives were employed or had contacts with successful men in the black community. He thus gained access to mentoring that his own irregularly employed (though never entirely absent) father could not provide. Today, my friend argues, the cutbacks in social programs, growth of unemployment, and increasing isolation of poor inner-city blacks from job networks make single motherhood much more problematic. Yet the community collapse that makes single motherhood harder also increases its likelihood, and heaping more blame on single mothers does not help.

As my friend's example suggests, single-parent families do not necessarily lack male role models. At lectures and workshops I've conducted, I have often been surprised by the vehemence with which many mothers in female-headed families deny that they are single parents. In many cases they appreciate the parenting that the nonresidential father contributes and want it to be recognized as a legitimate form of fathering. Research confirms their instincts. When nonresidential fathers behave as parents, rather than friends or entertainers, they can have a significant impact on children's development. "Fathers do not need to live with their child" to engage in monitoring, support, and other authoritative parenting practices, say researchers who have conducted an intensive study of rural Iowa families. It is also possible to involve never-married fathers with their children on a regular basis, and several innovative programs have had encouraging success in doing so.[16]

Still, there are certainly daily pressures on single parents that even the most supportive nonresidential parents cannot relieve. Adults in single-parent families, on average, spend less time supervising homework than adults in two-parent families, which can hold back a child's academic progress. Because they are often pressed for time, single parents are less likely than married ones to attend open-house nights at school, extracurricular activities, school programs, and parent–teacher association meetings. Yet such activities have been shown to be more effective than monitoring homework in promoting academic achievement. A teacher who has met a parent, for example, is more likely to work with the family in helping a child get past any temporary academic or behavior difficulties.[17]

Single parents spend more time talking with their children than married parents do, a behavior that can lead to accelerated academic and emotional maturity so long as the parent takes care not to confide too much anger or distress. (Ironically, children of mothers who have made a conscious choice for singlehood and do not go through the intense bitterness of a failed relationship have a potential advantage here. On the other hand, mothers in divorced families spend more time than either currently married or never-married women working on homework projects with their children.) Single parents are also more likely than two-parent families to praise good grades, which tends to produce higher academic performance.

But single parents are more likely to get upset and angry when their children receive bad grades, a reaction that is associated with defiance and a further decline in grades.[18]

Adolescents in single-parent families face fewer pressures to conform to traditional gender roles. They tend to have greater maturity, autonomy, and self-confidence than teens in two-parent families. Depending on the dynamics of the family, this can lead either to more potentially dangerous risk taking *or* to more breadth and depth of thinking—or to both.

In some conditions, one researcher suggests, the lack of other domestic responsibilities and competing ties can make a single person a good candidate for a foster parent. Single adoptive or foster parents "may be particularly suitable for certain children who need more undivided attention."[19]

It's important to develop a balanced assessment of the strengths as well as the weaknesses in single-parent families because, despite periodic claims that our society glorifies single motherhood, one of the biggest problems for single-parent families is the persistent bias they face. In one study, teachers were shown a videotape of a child engaging in a variety of actions. The teachers consistently rated the child's actions much more negatively when they were told that he or she came from a single-parent family than when they believed the child came from an intact home. Children in one-parent families do just about as well as those in two-parent families on standardized tests, but they are rated much more negatively on subjective measures of achievement, such as teachers' evaluations or deportment ratings.[20]

The problems of single parenthood tend to be greatest among groups whose cultural values most emphasize two-parent families and paternal authority, and least among those who have a history of tolerance and support for single mothers. Sara McLanahan and Gary Sandefur found that family disruption is most likely to produce negative effects among Hispanics and least likely to do so among blacks, with whites falling in between. Living in a middle-income neighborhood has a strong positive effect for children from black single-parent homes, but children in white single-parent homes face a *greater* risk of rejection by peers when they live in middle-income neighborhoods than when they live in low-income neighborhoods.[21]

As these examples suggest, generalizations about family form and functioning are also complicated by many other factors. Variables such as the race, class, or ethnicity of the family have different impacts on children depending on their age, gender, individual temperament, and interaction with siblings. Higher proportions of boys than girls have trouble adjusting to divorce; higher proportions of girls have trouble adjusting to remarriage. In some cases, parenting styles that are destructive for white children are helpful to youths who must learn to deal with racial prejudice. Girls are disadvantaged by having many siblings, because they are often made to do too much caretaking. But they gain an advantage from having brothers because fathers are more likely to get involved with all their children when they have sons.[22]

The sex of the custodial parent has no clear relationship to the effectiveness of single-parent families. Some research in the early 1980s suggested that adolescents did better when living with the same-sex parent, but a 1992 study was unable to replicate this finding. There are, however, different dynamics in single-mother and single-father families. The greatest cause of stress for custodial single mothers is money. For custodial fathers, relations with the nonresidential mother are the biggest problem. Single fathers seem to monitor their children less effectively than single mothers. But when single mothers come into conflict with their boys, they tend to have longer, more drawn-out disputes, with increasing frustration on both sides.[23]

This problem is sometimes interpreted as a case of boys "needing a father's guidance," but the research doesn't bear this out. Stories I hear from single mothers and their children suggest that one of the reasons single mothers and adolescent boys often come into conflict is precisely because they have been so intimate in the past and are therefore more ambivalent about the normal process of adolescent disengagement. The boys seem threatened by the ties they still feel, and may find it necessary to assert their independence or supposed indifference all the more loudly. Mothers tell me that, in the absence of a partner, the child's normal adolescent withdrawal inspires a greater sense of loss, and that they must guard against a tendency to express their pain as anger and resentment.

In order to maintain communication, some mothers engage in a behavior that works very well with adult males, but has the effect of further frightening their sons: Mom redoubles her efforts to demonstrate, in words and body language, an intense interest in everything her child tells her. The mother feels as if she is demonstrating her attention and respect, which she knows from experience is very flattering to an adult male. The teenager, however, already acutely self-conscious about being the object of attention, feels as if he is being subjected to the third degree. Many single mothers tell me that they have had to adopt a masculine technique that used to annoy them when they were married: diffusing emotional intensity by conducting conversations while in the process of doing something else—playing cards or watching television, for example.

One of the difficulties for single parents of either sex is setting clear limits and preserving generational boundaries. In a two-parent family, the parent looks to the other parent for confirmation: "Johnny doesn't do very well when he stays up late, so let's make bedtime 9 P.M., okay?" In a single-parent family, the natural need for confirmation often comes out this way: "Johnny, you don't do very well when you stay up late, so let's make your bedtime 9 P.M., okay?" For years, Johnny will happily reply, "okay." But by the time he reaches early adolescence, he is likely to start saying no, leaving the parent in the awkward position of either backing down or having to rephrase as a command something that had been posed as a request. And adolescence is a little late to *start* issuing parental commands.

In workshops I've conducted with single parents, when I ask them what their advice would be for others, they almost invariably say that it would be to set limits *before* they are needed, when the children are still in the cooperative, intimate mode that so many single-parent families establish with their young children. In general, single parents need to beware of the temptation to become best friends or totally democratic collaborators with their children, whereas two-parent families need to beware of confining consultation to the adults.[24]

Different family forms also have different stress points over time. The maximum period of stress for two-parent families is generally the first few years after the birth of a child, sometimes because the husband resents his wife's transfer of time, energy, and services to the infant, sometimes because the wife resents the father's lack of such transfer, often because of tensions over the redivision of domestic roles. Considerable anecdotal evidence indicates that unwed mothers with flexible jobs and financial security actually experience *less* stress than couples during the early months, because the mother does not have to balance two relationships and two other sets of needs.[25]

The maximum stress for single-parent families usually occurs in the early teen years, as youngsters begin to demand more freedom from parental control. It's easier to wear a parent down when she or he has no ally to reinforce resistance to a child's insistence that "everybody else's parents let them." Thus single parents are apt to relinquish parental decision-making rights too early, which encourages negative forms of behavior in their children. However, it is by no means inevitable that single parents will fall into this trap. Studies that control for family process have found that single parenthood is *not* related to early teen sexual behavior, but *rules* about dating are. It is sometimes harder to establish and enforce such rules when one is alone, though, which is why it is often helpful for single parents to have another adult join the household for a while or to become regularly involved in family routines.[26]

The stresses of single parenthood can be a challenge to effective child rearing. But as psychologist Bonnie R. Strickland puts it, "well-adjusted children of both sexes can be reared in families of varying configurations." The most critical ingredient in such families is how well the main caregiver functions. And those who care about the future of children ought to be supporting a wide range of social policies and programs to make sure that children's caregivers, whether they live singly or with a partner, have the resources they need to function well.[27]

Remarriage and Stepfamilies

The contradictory data on stepfamilies also illustrate the problem with sweeping generalizations about family structure. While remarriage tends to reduce stresses associated with economic insecurity, some studies suggest that children in stepfamilies, taken as a whole, have the same added risks for emotional problems as do children in one-parent families; they are actually *more* likely to repeat a grade than children whose mothers have never married. Yet most stepfamilies work quite well. In a recent long-term, ongoing government study, 80 percent of children in stepfamilies were judged to be doing well psychologically—not a whole lot worse than the 90 percent in intact biological families. The large majority of stepparents and children in one national survey rated their households as "relaxed" and "close," while less than one-third described their households as "tense" or "disorganized." Sibling conflict, found in all types of families, was only slightly more frequent in families with stepfathers.[28]

The trouble with generalizing about stepfamilies is that they are even more complicated and varied than other family types because there are so many possible routes to forming them. Kay Pasley and Marilyn Ihinger-Tallman have identified nine "structurally distinct" types of remarried families, depending on the custody and visitation arrangements of each partner, the presence of children from the new marriage, and whether there are children from one or both of the remarried parents' former families. The challenges of blending a new family mount with the complexity of the combinations that are being put together.[29]

There seem to be two pieces of advice we can confidently give to parents considering remarriage. The first is *not* to marry just to find a mother or father for your child. While remarriage may be helpful for single-parent families experiencing economic distress, those with adequate financial resources may find that their children's adjustment and academic performance are initially set back. Many children take longer to adjust to remarriage than to divorce, especially when they are teens.[30]

But the second piece of advice is not to be scared off. Most stepfamilies do well, and a good relationship with a stepparent does appear to strengthen a child's emotional life and academic achievement.[31]

Although stepfamilies create new stresses and adaptive challenges, write researchers Mavis Hetherington and James Bray, they "also offer opportunities for personal growth and more harmonious, fulfilling family and personal relationships." Children gain access to several different role models, get the chance to see their parents in a happier personal situation than in the past, and can benefit from the flexibility they learn in coping with new roles and relations.[32]

The most important thing to grasp about stepfamilies is that they require people to put aside traditional assumptions about how a family evolves and functions. Since the parent–child relationships predate the marriage, each parent and child brings a history of already formed family values, rules, rituals, and habits to the new household. This situation can lead to conflict and misunderstanding. Research does not support the stereotype that children in stepfamilies normally suffer from conflicting loyalties, but there is often considerable ambiguity about parenting roles and boundaries. For adolescents, the situation can be particularly tense. Their understandable resentment of the newcomer may cause their age-appropriate distancing from the biological parent to proceed too rapidly.[33]

Another major challenge to stepfamilies lies in the fact that traditional gender roles often conflict with the new family structure. As therapists Monica McGoldrick and Betty Carter put it, "if the old rules that called for women to rear children and men to earn and manage the financing are not working well in first-marriage families, which they are not, they have absolutely no chance at all in a system where some of the children are strangers to the wife, and where some of the finances include sources of income and expenditure that are not in the husband's power to control"—for example, alimony or child support.[34]

For stepfamilies to meet the needs of both adults and children, they have to create a new family "culture" that reworks older patterns into some kind of coherent whole, allowing members to mourn losses from the previous families without cutting off those relationships. The main barriers to doing this include leftover conflict from previous marriages, unrealistic expectations about instant bonding within the new family, and attempts to reproduce traditional nuclear family norms.[35]

As Lawrence Ganong and Marilyn Coleman point out, stepfamilies that try to function like a first-marriage nuclear family "must engage in massive denial and distortion of reality," pretending that former spouses, with their separate family histories, do not exist and cutting members off from important people or traditions in their life. This is not healthy. Nor is it realistic for the biological parent in the household to expect to have sole control over child-rearing decisions. Thus stepfamilies need to have "more permeable boundaries" than nuclear families usually maintain. And a stepparent–stepchild relationship probably *should* be less emotionally close than a parent–child relationship.[36]

Old-fashioned gender roles pose another problem for stepfamilies. *Stepmother* families have more conflicts, many specialists believe, because both women and men often expect the wife to shoulder responsibility for child care and for the general emotional well-being of the family. A stepmother may therefore try to solve problems between her husband and his children or the children and their biological mother, which sets the stepmother up to be the villain for both the children and the ex-wife. In stepfather families, a woman having trouble with her children may push her new husband to assume a disciplinary role far too early in the marriage, which tends to set back or even derail his developing relationship with the children.[37]

Therapists recommend that stepfamilies be encouraged to see the problems they face as a consequence of their structural complexities, not of ill will or personal inadequacy. Indeed, many of the difficulties may actually be a result of previous strengths in earlier family arrangements—the woman's desire to make relationships work, for example, or the children's strong commitments to older ties and habits. Hetherington found that sons "who were high in self-esteem, assertiveness, and social competence before the remarriage" were most likely to start out being "acrimonious and negative toward stepfathers." In the long run, though, these boys were especially likely to accept and benefit from a stepfather's addition to the household. Boys who were close to their mothers in the single-parent family tend to resent the establishment of a strong marital alliance in the new stepfamily. Girls are more likely to welcome a close marital relationship, possibly because it serves as a buffer "against the threat of inappropriate intimacy between stepfathers and stepdaughters."[38]

Experts agree that stepfamilies need to develop new norms permitting parental collaboration across household boundaries. They need to facilitate interactions between children and extended kin on the noncustodial parent's side of the family. They must let go of romantic fantasies about being able to start over. They also have to become much more flexible about gender roles. The biological parent, whether male or female, should be the primary parent, which means that women must control their tendency to fix everybody's emotional problems and men must control theirs to leave emotional intimacy to women. A new stepfather should resist his wife's desire to have him relieve her of disciplinary duties; similarly, a new wife should resist a husband's pressure to take on maternal roles such as managing schedules, supervising housework, or even making sure the kids remember their lunches on the way to school.[39]

What seems to work best is for a stepparent to initially play the role of camp counselor, uncle, aunt, or even sitter—someone who exercises more adult authority than a friend but is less responsible for direction and discipline than a parent. Behaving supportively toward stepchildren is more effective than trying to exercise control, although stepparents should back up their partners' disciplinary decisions in a matter-of-fact manner and help to keep track of children's whereabouts. Stepparents of adolescents have to recognize that even under the best circumstances, resistance to them is likely to continue for some time. If stepparents understand this reaction as normal, they can control their own natural impulse to feel rejected and to back away.[40]

Parenting in stepfamilies requires a thick skin, a sensitive ear, and a highly developed sense of balance. A successful stepfamily has to tolerate ambiguous, flexible, and often somewhat distant relationships, without allowing any member to disengage entirely. It has to accept a closer relationship between biological parent and child than between stepparent and child without letting that closeness evolve into a parent–child coalition that undermines the united front of the marriage partners. And effective communication skills are even more important in stepfamilies than they are in other kinds of families.[41]

These tasks are challenging, which may be why stepfamilies take longer to come together as a unified team, are more vulnerable to disruption, and often experience renewed turmoil during adolescence. But Jan Lawton, director of the Stepfamily Project in Queensland, Australia, points out that while the divorce rate among remarried families is high in the first two years, it then slows down. After five years, second marriages are more stable than first ones. And researchers have found that even modest, short-term training in communication and problem solving can dramatically increase the stability of stepfamilies.[42]

Adapting to Diversity

Most work policies, school schedules, and even measures of "good" and "bad" adjustment have been developed to fit the characteristics of just one family form—the two-parent, primary breadwinner model. But what works for that kind of family often doesn't work for different family types. And what's a "sign of trouble" for a two-parent, always-married family isn't necessarily so for other families.[43]

A while ago I was talking with several teachers about how classroom expectations and patterns favor kids from some families over others when someone challenged the group to think of teaching techniques that play to the strengths of nontraditional families. A few months later, one teacher called me up to describe what she and her colleague had found. They had noticed that their timing of homework assignments was based on the schedules of families with one primary earner. Such families tend to get schoolwork done during the week so that they can engage in recreational activities over the weekend. By contrast, weeknights are the period of maximum stress for one-parent and dual-earner families, with weekends the time when they can catch up.[44] So the teachers changed two of their typical homework assignments in order to make it easier for single parents in particular to give their children's homework their full attention.

The new weekday reading assignment was for the child to read aloud to a parent while the parent was making dinner or running errands. It turned out that this assignment was actually easier for many single parents than it was for couples, who were eager to talk to each other at the end of the day. Furthermore, many single parents were able to praise their children far more enthusiastically and sincerely than were two-parent families that had to give up established rituals between husband and wife. "My mother really loves this," reported one youngster. "She says she used to get bored making dinner while I watched TV. I really make her feel better."

The teachers also found a math assignment that made a difference. They required students to accompany a parent to the store on the weekend and figure out the cost advantages of buying one brand over another. Again, they found, this assignment was easier for many single-parent families than for some two-parent ones, whose habit was to send one parent off for a quick shopping trip while the other took the kids to lessons or games. A number of children from two-parent families consistently failed to complete the homework, and within just a few weeks they were acting hostile and defiant about it. This assignment was also hard for stepfamilies, except in cases where a nonresidential parent had remained in contact with the teacher and could be approached to have the assignment explained. In these cases, the parent getting the child for a visit was delighted to have a parental activity to share with his or her child, and took extra care to do a good job.

Even with such a seemingly objective task as homework, then, one size clearly does not fit all. I'm not suggesting that changing our homework assignments is any panacea for the challenges facing today's families and teachers. But if even such a simple readjustment can have an impact, think how much we could accomplish if we stopped expecting nontraditional families to fail and started thinking creatively about how to help every family build on its resources and minimize its vulnerabilities.

What Today's Families Really Need

It's time to stop arguing about the relative merits of ideal family types and have a serious discussion about how to build the support systems that modern families need. Families require access to high-quality, well-regulated, affordable child care. The tax allowance for children should be expanded to keep up with the inflation that has occurred since it was first instituted. Parents need family-friendly work policies, including paid parental leaves.

For families under economic stress, job creation and job training have to go hand in hand. Stiffer child support enforcement must be supplemented with income support programs and/or realistic jobs programs for single mothers. A national health insurance system would mean that parents who lose their jobs or choose part-time work would not be risking their children's health, or their own. The Earned Income Tax credit, which supplements wages for those who can only find low-paying jobs, helped counteract some of the economic reverses for children from 1990 to 1995. Such measures should be expanded, not cut back, as is currently under way.

In the realm of socialization, programs on child development should be incorporated into high school classes, so that young people will begin to learn what parenting is all about. Supportive, well-structured schools can also make a tremendous difference for children from single-parent homes and from stepfamilies.[45]

Almost all high school students can benefit from community service programs, as long as these are not confined to "cleaning up after others." Young people consistently express a desire to help others in ways that draw on and at the same time enhance their personal skills. One teacher in the Oregon public schools tells me that he has had tremendous success with at-risk students by teaching them a few academic skills and then asking them to teach these skills to other students. The role reversal, he reports, does wonders not just for the tutors but for the dynamics of the entire classroom. In my own town, teachers at my neighborhood school used to take fourth and fifth graders to local preschools three times a week to read to the younger children. This worked especially well to motivate poor readers to improve.[46]

Many of the best programs are preventive, but we also know how to help families that are already in trouble. A history of poverty or even severe family problems does not doom a child or youth to failure. In study after study, two things stand out in the history of kids who rise above difficult backgrounds. Contrary to conservative rhetoric, neither has anything to do with labeling kids "bad," trying them as adults, shouting "three strikes and you're out," or reinstituting chain gangs in prison. But contrary to some liberal myths, neither does the answer lie in offering workshops on self-esteem or teaching kids to "celebrate yourself."

The first factor is getting a second chance to succeed at something the person failed at before—going back to school, being helped to pass a class (as opposed to being passed through it), having a chance to correct a wrong and make it right (as opposed to being either punished or excused), receiving concrete aid and an opportunity to reciprocate it. The second is the intervention of just one caring person from *outside* the family, not to moralize or even to motivate, but to roll up his or her sleeves and get involved in that person's life.[47]

Polarized debates over whether to set high standards *or* foster self-esteem miss the point: What works is the combination of high standards and concrete help to achieve them. The issue of whether to reward good behavior or punish bad is another false dichotomy. Sanctions and penalties are important in working with troubled families or individuals, but sanctions without incentives and penalties without rewards are a route to disaster.[48]

Last spring I got into a conversation about this issue with the man sitting next to me on a flight back from England. Gary described himself as a member of a typical traditional family. The sole breadwinner, he was proud that he'd been able to support his wife while she raised their three children and that this luxury had also allowed her to take classes in art and literature. In fact, our conversation started when he pointed out some interesting features of a cathedral that appeared in a travelogue we were halfheartedly watching. "My wife taught me that," he said. "I don't have time to look into those sorts of things, so my wife's the expert on that."

The conversation turned to his children and from there to the subject of "what's wrong with kids today." I told him a little about my reading on the effects of poverty on children and we talked about the stresses of modern life even for middle-class families. He was a good-hearted man, and he soon wanted to know what he could do. His wife had been thinking of volunteering in the local schools or at a low-income day care center. He'd be delighted to support her in that, he said, but did I think it would do any good?

So I told him about the research on the two factors that seem to foster resiliency in kids, and suddenly he said, with as much surprise as if he'd only just remembered, "Why, I can testify to that." It turns out that, despite his earlier insistence that irresponsible parents were the cause of all our social and individual problems, his own mother had been married five times. The only time he had ever completed a single year in the same school was when a sympathetic math teacher who thought he had some talent let him move in with his family.

After six months, the teacher couldn't stand Gary's behavior and kicked him out. But a few years later, the good memory of what it was like to have someone think you could make it inspired Gary to go back to school. (Years afterward, Gary tracked down his old high school teacher to say thanks. The man had thought until then that Gary was one of his failures.) Math turned out to be his best subject and Gary went on to college, majoring in engineering. "I did it under the National Defense Education Act," he said, "but, you're right, they don't have that anymore, do they?"

Gary is a textbook example of the ways that romanticization of the traditional family can make people forget the lessons of their own past. History and sociology, by contrast, help people get in touch with the real complexity of family life, both their own and others. They also demonstrate that personal interventions and social second chances do make a difference.

In *The Transcendent Child: Tales of Triumph Over the Past*, psychotherapist Lillian Rubin points to the recurring importance of mentors, sometimes in long-lasting relationships, sometimes in brief but important ones like that of Gary with his tenth-grade math teacher, in the lives of children who rise above difficult and painful pasts. Anthropologists William Kornblum and Terry Williams, tracking 900 children in urban and rural poverty areas, found that "the most significant" difference in whether a teen ended up on the streets or in a stable job was "the presence or absence of adult mentors." An evaluation of the impact of Big Brother/Big Sisters mentoring programs found that "the involvement of a Big Brother or Big Sister in a young person's life for a single year reduced first-time drug use by 46 percent . . . , cut school absenteeism by 52 percent, and lowered violent behavior by 33 percent. . . . The effects were sustained for both boys and girls and across races."[49]

The Fatherhood Project, a national research and education program on ways to increase men's involvement in parenting, has found that even men who have been previously "written off" as totally uninterested in their children "can and want to be reached." Training people to alter their expectations of other people's behaviors can be a big help all by itself. West Virginia increased paternity acknowledgment among unwed fathers from 15 to 60 percent in three years, partly by teaching maternity nurses to encourage men to establish paternity. Preschools have seen dramatic increases in fathers' involvement when they have trained staff to assume that men are interested in their children and wish to take responsibility for them. Similarly, James Comer has shown in his work with inner-city schools that even impoverished parents, highly distrustful of mainstream institutions, become actively involved in their children's education when brought into partnership with schools.[50]

But personal interventions have to be backed up with social services and concrete assistance for individuals or families in trouble. People working to involve low-income fathers with their children find that "a job component is key" to success. In programs that make a difference for at-risk kids, "the secret is intensity." Baltimore's Choice Program has caseworkers who check in with teens in the program "as often as five times a day." Successful job training programs provide trainees with daily telephone advice on the job and help for years afterward, even when (as is usual) they lose that first job.[51]

Such programs demand patience, respect, and flexibility. They also require staff to deal with the whole range of problems confronting their clients. Prenatal care programs that ignore a family's impending eviction, for example, are likely to fail. And preaching or lecturing is not enough. Boot camps and "Scared Straight" programs that don't provide youth and families with practical social skills are not successful. Indeed, they sometimes have long-range negative results. Job training and placement must be combined with mentoring, educational innovation, and help with practical problems such as finding housing.[52]

We also know what doesn't work: fragmentation of services; red tape; denial of flexibility and judgment calls to frontline workers; destroying successful programs by asking caseworkers to take on ever new problems and multiplying their case loads; paying entrepreneurial "experts" to identify families' "dysfunctions" instead of learning what their real needs and resources are; funding careers for bureaucrats or consultants rather than hiring people who will pitch in to help families cope with their daily challenges; or conversely, relying so strongly on people's natural resiliency that we overestimate what they can do without social support programs.[53]

Getting rid of what doesn't work and expanding the programs that do will not be cheap. There's no cut-rate way to make sure that people succeed at *real* tasks and reach *meaningful* goals. The Economic Policy Institute estimates that it would take $112 billion a year to bring our children's health, nutrition, and education up to the standards that now exist in Europe. The Milton S. Eisenhower Foundation and Family Service America recommend appropriating $150 billion for children, youth, and families over the next ten years and another $150 billion for coordinated housing, security, and infrastructure over the same period.[54]

Still, America is not exactly broke. The U.S. government spends well over a *trillion* dollars a year on programs of various sorts, including advertising campaigns for American corporations and subsidies to agricultural landowners. In 1996, Congress decided it could afford to offer corporations and individuals $229 billion in tax cuts over the next seven years. Military spending alone still comes to almost $300 billion a year, despite the end of the cold war.[55]

Reporter Sam Roberts comments that, according to Census Bureau calculations in 1990, we could have lifted every poor family in America out of poverty for less than what we "spent in forty-three days in 1991 on the Persian Gulf War." If we taxed the richest 1 percent of Americans at the same rates they paid under President Eisenhower in 1954, they would have paid an additional $73 billion in taxes in 1993. Two researchers who have recently documented how much the government gives to corporations and the rich in income transfers and tax subsidies claim that a 26 percent cut in this spending would balance the budget.[56]

Here is one case, then, where the problem really *isn't* "the economy, stupid." The issue is not whether we have the money to help America's families but whether we have the values to do so.

The good news is that most Americans *do* support programs to assist children and families. For example, 79 percent of respondents to a November 1995 *Business Week* survey said that they believed government should protect vulnerable members of society by providing social benefits and guaranteeing minimum living standards. In a recent poll, 45 percent of Americans wanted the federal government to "actively create new programs for children's safety and improve the quality of health care and education opportunities that they receive," while another 25 percent favored *expanding* existing programs to ensure basic coverage.[57]

The bad news is that people do not actively demand such programs because they have been demoralized by a massive campaign to convince us that it does no good to even make the effort, because nothing works. Yet the evidence is clear that schools, social programs, and caring individuals can compensate for stressful environments and troubled families.

A twenty-one-year study of low-income families conducted by the Frank Porter Graham Child Development Center at the University of North Carolina found that a high-quality preschool program created substantial academic and IQ gains that lasted well into the teenage years. The Perry Preschool Project works with low-income families, almost half of them from single-parent homes: Graduates of this program were twice as likely as nongraduates to be employed or involved in further training by the age of 19. Their arrest rates were 40 percent lower and their teen pregnancy rates 42 percent lower than the control group's. Similarly, in a home visitation program for impoverished single teen mothers, those who received nurse visits had 75 percent fewer verified cases of child abuse than mothers in a group that did not receive visits. They punished their children less often and they also had 43 percent fewer subsequent pregnancies.[58]

The problem with the campaign to restore the traditional family is that it keeps people so busy grieving for a misremembered past that they cannot identify such possibilities in the present, far less plan effectively for the future. Yet contrary to the new consensus, the biggest lesson of the past is that there are no solutions there.

The most serious issues facing American families and youth today are shocking not in comparison to where we *used* to be but in comparison to where we *ought* to be. Child poverty rates are actually lower now than in the "golden age" of the 1950s, but the United States ranks last among eighteen western industrial nations in the percentage of children who live in poverty. Infant mortality has fallen sharply since the 1950s, but twenty-two other developed countries have lower rates than we do. High school graduation rates are higher than ever before; illiteracy is one-fifth what it was in 1940; the average proficiency of 13-year-olds in math, science, and writing was greater in 1992 than in the 1970s. But our scores have not kept pace with gains made by other industrial nations.[59]

We will not solve these problems by looking backward. It's time, as anthropologist Jennifer James puts it, to start "thinking in the future tense."[60] I like to look at it as adding dimension to the line the family values crusaders try to draw between "good" families and "bad." When you work on a flat surface, a line is a line, and the longer you make it, the further apart the two ends get. But once you start working in three dimensions, you can bend that line to form a sphere. When that happens, the longer you extend your line, the more your circle can encompass. Isn't it time to stop drawing dividing lines between families and start bringing as many of them as possible into our sphere of social support?

Acknowledgments

I first would like to thank the hundreds of individuals who wrote or called me after reading my last book or hearing my views on radio, television, or a public panel. Their questions, comments, and personal stories gave me a new outlook on many family issues. Without the willingness of these people to share their concerns, tell their histories, and, often, to participate in extended interviews, I never could have written this book.

I also would like to thank Gay Salisbury, Marketing Manager at Basic Books, for encouraging me to use the stories and insights I gained from these experiences to write about family research in a new way, paying more attention to the impact of historical trends and socioeconomic changes on the daily life of contemporary families. My editor at Basic Books, Gail Winston, kept me focused on whom I was writing for and why. She helped me reconceptualize several chapters at critical points, and made valiant efforts to curb my tendency to stuff every paragraph with too many facts, figures, and references. Her editorial assistant, Stephanie Snow, also offered astute suggestions and comments.

My debts to other scholars are immense, and I have tried to acknowledge them in my notes. I'm grateful to Paul Amato for his cogent comments on the chapter about divorce; Bradley Miller and Peta Henderson for their close readings of chapter 1; and the many family researchers and therapists who allowed me to pick their brains and bibliographies. My colleague Chuck Nisbet generously shared articles and references that he found on the internet.

Jacyn Rebekah Piper, my research assistant, tracked down citations, using her computer skills to find articles I never could have dug up on my own. Between us, we severely taxed the resources of the entire library staff at The Evergreen State College, yet they consistently went out of their way to make this research possible. My special thanks to Bill Bruner, Ernestine Kimbro, Lee Lyttle, Rich Edwards, Linda Fraidenberg, Randy Stilson, and Frank Motley. Pam Udovich kindly rearranged many weekends and evenings to decipher my scrawled changes, correct and print successive drafts, and help verify citations.

The Evergreen State College granted me a leave to complete the book, even though it meant an inconvenient rearrangement of teaching assignments. All my colleagues at TESC have been unstinting in their support, and my experience doing interdisciplinary team teaching with them has greatly broadened my perspective as a family historian.

Finally, of course, this book would not be possible without the support of my family. My husband, Will Reissner, did everything from building me bookshelves to editing the manuscript. My son Kris chided me when I sounded too academic and took time from his busy high school schedule to cook dinner and calm me down when I got too wound up. My sister, Sharron, helped out in ways too numerous to mention. My stepfather, stepsiblings, and in-laws in the Waddington and Shelley clans contradicted every unflattering stereotype ever leveled against these types of family members. And while my mother's Alzheimer's disease means that she can no longer read or comment on my work, I continue to draw on a backlog of her encouragement and support that will last a lifetime.

Notes

Introduction

1. These points are developed at more length in *The Way We Never Were: American Families and the Nostalgia Trap* (New York: Basic Books, 1992).

2. Watson quoted in Richard Gelles, *Contemporary Families: A Sociological View* (Thousand Oaks, Calif.: Sage, 1995), p. 487; Amatai Etzioni, "The Family: Is It Obsolete?" *Journal of Current Social Issues* 14 (1977), p. 4.

3. Elizabeth Kolbert, "Public Opinion Polls Swerve with the Turn of a Phrase," *New York Times*, June 5, 1995, p. A1.

4. *New York Times*, May 19, 1992, p. A1; *Washington Post National Weekly Edition*, May 11–17, 1992, p. 11; *Olympian*, September 29, 1991, and May 21, 1992; *Liberal Opinion Week*, August 31, 1992; Margaret Carlson, "All Eyes on Hillary," *Time*, September 14, 1992, p. 32; "Evangelist's Feminist Warning Becomes Campaign Issue," *Phoenix Gazette*, Sept. 5, 1992; *U.S. News & World Report*, October 19, 1992, p. 56.

5. David Rosenbaum and Steve Lohr, "With a Stable Economy, Clinton Hopes for Credit," *New York Times*, August 3, 1996; Daniel Patrick Moynihan, "A Landmark for Families," *New York Times*, November 16, 1992; Barbara Dafoe Whitehead, "Dan Quayle Was Right," *Atlantic Monthly*, April 1993; David Popenoe, "The Controversial Truth: Two Parents Are Better," *New York Times*, December 26, 1992; Dan Quayle, "Murphy Brown Revisited," *Washington Post National Weekly Edition*, December 20–26, 1993; Ronald Brownstein, "The Politics of Values: Candidates Find Common Ground," *Los Angeles Times*, August 1, 1994; Dan Quayle and Diane Medved, *The American Family: Discovering the Values That Make Us Strong* (New York: HarperCollins, 1996), p. 2.

6. *U.S. News & World Report,* August 1, 1994, p. 27; *Chicago Tribune,* editorial, March 25, 1993; David Broder, "Quayle: Right on the Family," *Washington Post,* March 24, 1993; *Wall Street Journal,* October 29, 1993; Joan Beck, "Teen Pregnancy Issue Bipartisan," *Oregonian,* March 31, 1994; David Broder, "Illegitimacy: An Unprecedented National Catastrophe," *Washington Post,* June 22, 1994; Richard Whitmire, Lacking a Father's Touch," *Olympian,* October 27, 1994, p. A6; Charmaine Yoest, "Fount of Virtue, Spring of Wealth: How the Strong Family Sustains a Prosperous Society," *The World & I,* August 1994, p. 372.

7. Marshall Fine, "Family Values," *Olympian,* May 25, 1996, p. D1; Don Oldenburg, "Visions of Their Family Values," *Washington Post,* July 7, 1992, p. C5.

8. "Family News from Dr. Dobson," *Focus on the Family,* 11 (November 1996), p. 1; Gertrude Himmelfarb, *The De-Moralization of Society: From Victorian Virtues to Modern Values* (New York: Knopf, 1995); Gertrude Himmelfarb, "Clinton and Congress: The Victorians Get a Bad Rap," *New York Times,* January 9, 1995.

9. Jean Porter, "The Moral Life According to William Bennett," *Christian Century,* October 5, 1994, p. 898.

10. "Can We Talk? The Marriage Strategy," *Mirabella,* March 1995, p. 84.

Chapter 1

Getting Past the Sound Bites

1. Mike Males, *The Scapegoat Generation: America's War on Adolescents* (Monroe, Me.: Common Courage Press, 1996), pp. 229–238; Paul Holinger, *Suicide and Homicide Among Adolescents* (New York: Guilford, 1994), p. 37.

2. Kirk Astroth, "Beyond Ephebiphobia: Problem Adults or Problem Youths?" *Phi Delta Kappan,* January 1993, p. 413.

3. Kenneth Maton, "Meaningful Involvement in Instrumental Activity and Well-Being: Studies of Older Adolescents and At Risk Urban Teen-Agers," *American Journal of Community Psychology* 18 (1990), p. 297; David Hamburg, *Today's Children: Creating a Future for a Generation in Crisis* (New York: Times Books, 1992), p. 201.

4. Jeffrey Maddrick, *The End of Affluence: The Causes and Consequences of America's Economic Dilemma* (New York: Random House, 1995), pp. 109–112; Laurence Steinberg, "The Logic of Adolescence," in Peter Edelman and Joyce Ladner, eds., *Adolescence and Poverty: Challenge for the 1990s* (Washington, D.C.: Center for National Policy Press), p. 30.

5. L. J. Stone and J. Church, *Childhood and Adolescence: A Psychology of the Growing Person* (New York: Random House, 1968), p. 447 (emphasis added).

6. Elena Nightingale and Lisa Wolverton, "Adolescent Rolelessness in Modern Society," Working Paper, Carnegie Council on Adolescent Development, September 1988, p. 5; "Sex and America's Teenagers," Alan Guttmacher Institute, New York, N.Y., 1994, p. 21.

7. Steinberg, "The Logic of Adolescence," p. 30.

8. Kristin Luker, *Dubious Conceptions: The Politics of Teenage Pregnancy* (Cambridge, Mass.: Harvard University Press, 1996), p. 27.

9. Ellen Greenberger and Laurence Steinberg, *When Teenagers Work: The Psy-*

chological and Social Costs of Adolescent Employment (New York: Basic Books, 1986), pp. 58–65.

10. Thomas Wartenberg, "The Situated Concept of Social Power," *Social Theory and Practice* 14 (1988).

11. Judith Bruce, Cynthia Lloyd, and Ann Leonard, with Patrice Engle and Niev Duffy, *Families in Focus: New Perspectives on Mothers, Fathers, and Children* (New York: The Population Council, 1995), p. 29; Heidi Hartmann, "The Family as the Locus of Gender, Class and Political Struggle: The Example of Housework," *Signs* 6 (1981).

12. John Gray, *Men Are from Mars, Women Are from Venus* (New York: HarperCollins, 1992).

13. Karen Peterson, "A Global Ambassador Between the Sexes," *USA Today,* March 28, 1994, pp. 1D and 2D; Gray, *Men Are from Mars,* p. 265.

14. Gray, *Men Are from Mars,* pp. 180–184, 199–202. On unequal bargaining power, see Amartya Sen, "Economics and the Family," *Asian Development Review* 1 (1983).

15. Betty Carter, *Love, Honor, and Negotiate: Making Your Marriage Work* (New York: Pocket Books, 1996). As Andrew Greeley points out in "The Declining Morale of Women" (*Sociology and Social Research* 73, 1989), women's morale in marriage has declined far more significantly than men's. Unless their frustrations with the marriage bargain are addressed more directly, not just placated, men and women *could* end up on different planets.

16. The images are taken from Robert Bly's *Iron John: A Book About Men* (Reading, Mass.: Addison-Wesley, 1990). For a critique, see R. W. Connell, "Drumming Up the Wrong Tree," *Tikkun* 7 (1992).

17. Julie Brines, "Economic Dependency, Gender, and the Division of Labor at Home," *American Journal of Sociology* 100 (1994), p. 683; Gregory Lehne, "Homophobia Among Men: Supporting and Defining the Male Role," in Michael Kimmel and Michael Messner, eds., *Men's Lives* (New York: Macmillan, 1989), pp. 416–429.

18. Carol Gilligan, Nona Lyons, and Trudy Hanmer, *Making Connections: The Relational World of Adolescent Girls at Emma Willard School* (Cambridge, Mass.: Harvard University Press, 1990); Peggy Orenstein, *School Girls: Young Women, Self-Esteem, and the Confidence Gap* (New York: Doubleday, 1994); Carol Gilligan and Lynn Mickel Brown, *Meeting at the Crossroads: Women's Psychology and Girls' Development* (Cambridge, Mass.: Harvard University Press, 1992); Myra and David Sadker, *Failing at Fairness: How American Schools Cheat Girls* (New York: Scribners and Sons, 1994); *How Schools Shortchange Girls: The AAUW Report: A Study of Major Findings on Girls and Education* (Washington, D.C.: AAUW Educational Foundation, 1992); Mark Kann, "The Costs of Being on Top," *Journal of the National Association for Women Deans* 49 (1986); Eugene August, "Real Men Don't: Anti-Male Bias in English," in Melita Schaum and Connie Flanagan, eds., *Gender Images: Readings for Composition* (Boston: Houghton Mifflin, 1992), pp. 131–141.

19. Philip A. Cowan, Carolyn Pape Cowan, and Patricia K. Kerig, "Mothers, Fathers, Sons, and Daughters: Gender Differences in Family Formation and Parenting Styles," in Philip Cowan et al., eds., *Family, Self, and Society: Toward a New Agenda for Family Research* (Hillsdale, N.J.: Lawrence Erlbaum, 1993), p. 190.

20. This useful concept is explained more fully in a book looking at the complex ways that class, gender, ethnicity, marital status, job experiences, and regional history interact to structure (but not determine) the lives of working mothers. See Louise Lamphere, Patricia Zavella, and Felipe Gonzales, with Peter Evans, *Sunbelt Working Mothers: Reconciling Family and Factory* (Ithaca, N.Y.: Cornell University Press, 1993), p. 4 and passim.

21. See, for example, Melvin Oliver and Thomas Shapiro, *Black Wealth/White Wealth: A New Perspective on Racial Inequality* (New York: Routledge, 1995).

22. Betty Carter, "Focusing Your Wide-Angle Lens," *Family Therapy Networker*, November/December 1995, p. 31. The examples in this and the next two paragraphs are drawn from Vince Bielski, "Our Magnificent Obsession," *Family Therapy Networker*, March/April 1996, pp. 31, 33.

23. Marianne Walters, "The Codependent Cinderella Who Loves Too Much . . . Fights Back," *Family Therapy Networker*, July/August 1990, p. 57. For an ethnographic case study of the tensions impoverished African Americans face between behaviors that are important for social solidarity and those that are important for individual mobility, see Carol Stack, *All Our Kin: Strategies for Survival in a Black Community* (New York: Harper and Row, 1974).

24. John Snarey, *How Fathers Care for the Next Generation: A Four-Decade Study* (Cambridge, Mass.: Harvard University Press, 1993), p. 329.

25. Daniel Goleman, *Emotional Intelligence* (New York: Bantam, 1995).

26. *New York Times*, December 12, 1994, p. A8; September 12, 1995, p. A1.

27. *New York Times*, March 7 and 10, 1996, pp. A1, E1; *Olympian*, March 7, 1996, p. A4.

28. *New York Times*, July 14, 1993, p. A1.

29. Shirley Zimmerman, "Family Trends: What Implications for Family Policy?" *Family Relations* 41 (1992), p. 423; S. Philip Morgan, "Late Nineteenth- and Early Twentieth-Century Childlessness," *American Journal of Sociology* 97 (1991), p. 800.

30. Alfred Blumstein, "Youth, Violence, Guns, and the Illicit Drug Industry," *Journal of Criminal Law and Criminology* 86 (1995), and personal interview, March 1996; Clifford Krauss, "Now How Low Can Crime Go?" *New York Times*, January 28, 1996.

31. See, for example, Arnold Hirsch, *Making the Second Ghetto: Race & Housing in Chicago, 1940–1960* (New York: Cambridge University Press, 1985).

32. Edward Walsh, "It's the Automatic Weapons, Stupid," *Washington Post National Weekly Edition*, December 6–12, 1993, p. 37.

33. Mike Males, *Scapegoat Generation*, p. 107.

34. Sam Roberts, *Who We Are: A Portrait of America Based on the Latest U.S. Census* (New York: Random House, 1993), p. 54; Steven Rawlings, *Household and Family Characteristics: March 1993* (Washington, D.C.: Bureau of the Census, June 1994); "California Unwed Mother Tally Includes Many Married Moms," *New York Times*, May 5, 1996.

35. Gregory Acs, "Do Welfare Benefits Promote Out-of-Wedlock Childbearing?" Urban Institute, Washington, D.C., 1996, p. 1; *Olympian*, March 30, 1995, p. D8; Andrew Cherlin, *Marriage, Divorce, Remarriage* (Cambridge, Mass.: Harvard University Press, 1981), pp. 53–65; Peter Li, "Labour Reproduction and the Family Under

Advanced Capitalism," *Journal of Comparative Family Studies* 24 (1993), pp. 367–386; Steve Rawlings and Arlene Saluter, *Household and Family Characteristics: March 1994*, Current Population Reports Series P20–483 (Washington, D.C.: Bureau of the Census, U.S. Department of Commerce, September 1995), pp. v–vxii; Sam Roberts, *Who We Are: A Portrait of America Based on the Latest U.S. Census* (New York: Times Books, 1995), p. 50; Margaret Usdansky, "Single Motherhood: Stereotypes vs. Statistics," *New York Times*, February 11, 1996, p. 4; Daphne Spain and Suzanne Bianchi, *Balancing Act: Motherhood, Marriage, and Employment Among American Women* (New York: Russell Sage, 1996), p. 7; Rebecca Blank et al., "A Primer on Welfare Reform," in R. Kent Weaver and William T. Dickens, eds., *Looking Before We Leap: Social Science and Welfare Reform* (Washington, D.C.: Brookings Institution, 1995), p. 28.

36. In 1990, a researcher spent 50 days in TV newsrooms in several large urban centers. He found that 56 percent of the stories were "inaccurate or misleading," usually because of oversimplification but often because, in order to cut costs, they accepted film footage from public relations firms or from other TV stations. John McManus, "Local TV News: Not A Pretty Picture," *Columbia Journalism Review* 29 (1990).

37. David Popenoe, *Life Without Father: Compelling New Evidence That Fatherhood and Marriage Are Indispensable for the Good of Children and Society* (New York: The Free Press, 1996), p. 194; David Popenoe, "American Family Decline, 1960–1990," *Journal of Marriage and the Family* 55 (1993), p. 539; Rector quoted in "Study Group Says Marriage Dying," *Honolulu Advertiser*, March 29, 1996, p. E6; "Marriage in America: A Report to the Nation," Council on Families in America, New York, N.Y., March 1995, p. 4.

38. David Popenoe, "The American Family Crisis," *National Forum* 75 (1995), p. 19; Charles Murray, "The Partial Restoration of Traditional Society," *Public Interest*, Fall 1995; Paul Starr, "Restoration Fever," *American Prospect*, March–April 1996, p. 6.

39. "100 Years of Marriage and Divorce Statistics, United States, 1867–1967," U.S. Department of Health, Education and Welfare, Series 21, #24, December 1973, pp. 7–8; Roberts, *Who We Are* (1993 ed.), pp. 35–50; Edward Kain, *The Myth of Family Decline: Understanding Families in a World of Rapid Social Change* (Lexington, Mass.: D. C. Heath, 1990), p. 74; *U.S. News & World Report*, March 25, 1996, p. 12; Morgan, "Late Nineteenth- and Early Twentieth-Century Childlessness," p. 800; Rayna Rapp and Ellen Ross, "The Twenties' Backlash: Compulsory Heterosexuality, the Consumer Family, and the Waging of Feminism," in Amy Swerdlow and Hanna Lessinger, eds., *Class, Race, Sex: The Dynamics of Control* (Boston: G. K. Hall, 1983), p. 94.

40. Michael Haines, "Long-term Marriage Patterns in the United States from Colonial Times to the Present," *History of the Family* 1 (1996), pp. 17, 27.

41. The information here and in the rest of this chapter, unless otherwise noted, comes from Rawlings and Saluter, *Household and Family Characteristics*, pp. xviii–ix; Arthur Norton and Louisa Miller, *Marriage, Divorce, and Remarriage in the 1990s*, Current Population Reports Series P23–180 (Washington, D.C.: Bureau of the Census, October 1992); Richard Gelles, *Contemporary Families: A Sociological View* (Thousand Oaks, Calif.: Sage, 1995), pp. 116–120, 176; Kingsley Davis, "Wives and Work: A Theory of the Sex Role Revolution and Its Consequences," in Sanford

Dornbusch and Myra Strober, eds., *Feminism, Children, and the New Families* (New York: Guilford, 1988), p. 67; Roberts, *Who We Are* (1995 ed.), pp. 32–64; Shirley Zimmerman, "Family Trends: What Implications for Family Policy?" *Family Relations* 41 (1992), p. 424; Usdansky, "Single Motherhood," p. 4; *New York Times,* August 30, 1994, p. A9; *New York Times,* March 10, 1996, p. A11, and March 17, 1996, p. A8; *Statistical Abstracts of the United States* (Washington, D.C.: Bureau of the Census, 1992); McLanahan and Casper, "Growing Diversity and Inequality in the American Family," in Reynolds Farley, ed., *State of the Union: America in the 1990s* (New York: Russell Sage, 1995). David Popenoe is quoted by Karen Peterson, "The Fallout of Divorce," *Olympian,* April 1, 1995; new estimates on the percent of marriages ending in divorce come from Norton and Miller, *Marriage, Divorce, and Remarriage in the 1990s,* p. 5.

42. Norton and Miller, *Marriage, Divorce, and Remarriage in the 1990s,* p. 2; Roderick Phillips, *Untying the Knot: A Short History of Divorce* (Cambridge: Cambridge University Press, 1991), p. 117; Arlene Skolnick, *Embattled Paradise: The American Family in an Age of Uncertainty* (New York: Basic Books, 1991), p. 156.

43. Valerie Oppenheimer, "Women's Economic Independence and Men's Career Maturity—Their Impact on Marriage Formation in the 1980s," *Mathematical Social Sciences* 30 (1995), pp. 95–96; Valerie Oppenheimer, "Women's Rising Employment and the Future of the Family in Industrial Societies," *Population and Development Review* 20 (1994), pp. 293–342; Valerie Oppenheimer, "Life-Cycle Jobs and the Transition to Adult Occupational Careers," *Population Index* 54 (1988), p. 517; Valerie Oppenheimer, "A Theory of Marriage Timing," *American Journal of Sociology* 94 (1988), pp. 563–591; Elaine Tyler May, *Homeward Bound: American Families in the Cold War Era* (New York: Basic Books, 1988), p. 202; Mirra Komarovsky, *Blue-Collar Marriage* (New Haven, Conn.: Yale University Press, 1962).

Chapter 2

What We Really Miss About the 1950s

1. Steven Thomma, "Nostalgia for '50s Surfaces," *Philadelphia Inquirer,* Feb. 4, 1996.

2. Frank Levy, *Dollars and Dreams: The Changing American Income Distribution* (New York: Russell Sage, 1987), p. 6; Frank Levy, "Incomes and Income Inequality," in Reynolds Farley, ed., *State of the Union: America in the 1990s,* vol. 1 (New York: Russell Sage, 1995), pp. 1–57; Richard May and Kathryn Porter, "Poverty and Income Trends, 1994," Washington, D.C.: Center on Budget and Policy Priorities, March 1996; Rob Nelson and Jon Cowan, "Buster Power," *USA Weekend,* October 14–16, 1994, p. 10.

3. Judith Wallerstein and Sandra Blakeslee, *The Good Marriage: How and Why Love Lasts* (Boston: Houghton Mifflin, 1995), p. 15.

4. Donald Hernandez, *America's Children: Resources from Family, Government and the Economy* (New York: Russell Sage, 1993), pp. 99, 102; James Morone, "The Corrosive Politics of Virtue," *American Prospect* 26 (May–June 1996), p. 37; "Study Finds U.S. No. 1 in Violence," *Olympian,* November 13, 1992. See also Stephen Mintz and Susan Kellogg, *Domestic Revolutions: A Social History of American Family Life* (New York: The Free Press, 1988).

5. William Tuttle, Jr., *"Daddy's Gone to War": The Second World War in the Lives of America's Children* (New York: Oxford University Press, 1993).

6. "Marriage and Divorce," *March of Time*, film series 14 (1948).

7. Arlene Skolnick and Stacey Rosencrantz, "The New Crusade for the Old Family," *American Prospect*, Summer 1994, p. 65; Hernandez, *America's Children*, pp. 128–132; Andrew Cherlin, "Changing Family and Household: Contemporary Lessons from Historical Research," *Annual Review of Sociology* 9 (1983), pp. 54–58; Sam Roberts, *Who We Are: A Portrait of America Based on the Latest Census* (New York: Times Books, 1995), p. 45.

8. Levy, "Incomes and Income Inequality," p. 20; Arthur Norton and Louisa Miller, *Marriage, Divorce, and Remarriage in the 1990s*, Current Population Reports Series P23–180 (Washington, D.C.: Bureau of the Census, October 1992); Roberts, *Who We Are* (1995 ed.), pp. 50–53.

9. Dennis Hogan and Daniel Lichter, "Children and Youth: Living Arrangements and Welfare," in Farley, ed., *State of the Union*, vol. 2, p. 99; Richard Gelles, *Contemporary Families: A Sociological View* (Thousand Oaks, Calif.: Sage, 1995), p. 115; Hernandez, *America's Children*, p. 102. The fact that only a small percentage of children had mothers in the paid labor force, though a full 40 percent did not live in male breadwinner–female homemaker families, was because some children had mothers who worked, unpaid, in farms or family businesses, or fathers who were unemployed, or the children were not living with both parents.

10. Edward Strecker, *Their Mothers' Sons: The Psychiatrist Examines an American Problem* (Philadelphia: J. B. Lippincott, 1946), p. 209.

11. For discussion of the discontents, and often searing misery, that were considered normal in a "good-enough" marriage in the 1950s and 1960s, see Lillian Rubin, *Worlds of Pain: Life in the Working-Class Family* (New York: Basic Books, 1976); Mirra Komarovsky, *Blue Collar Marriage* (New Haven, Conn.: Vintage, 1962); Elaine Tyler May, *Homeward Bound: American Families in the Cold War Era* (New York: Basic Books, 1988).

12. See Robert Putnam, "The Strange Disappearance of Civic America," *American Prospect*, Winter 1996. For a glowing if somewhat lopsided picture of 1950s community solidarities, see Alan Ehrenhalt, *The Lost City: Discovering the Forgotten Virtues of Community in the Chicago of the 1950s* (New York: Basic Books, 1995). For a chilling account of communities uniting against perceived outsiders, in the same city, see Arnold Hirsch, *Making the Second Ghetto: Race and Housing in Chicago, 1940–1960* (Cambridge, Mass.: Harvard University Press, 1983). On homicide rates, see "Study Finds United States No. 1 in Violence," *Olympian*, November 13, 1992; *New York Times*, November 13, 1992, p. A9; and Douglas Lee Eckberg, "Estimates of Early Twentieth-Century U.S. Homicide Rates: An Econometric Forecasting Approach," *Demography* 32 (1995), p. 14. On lengthening commutes, see "It's Taking Longer to Get to Work," *Olympian*, December 6, 1995.

13. The figures in this and the following paragraph come from Levy, "Incomes and Income Inequality," pp. 1–57; May and Porter, "Poverty and Income Trends, 1994"; Reynolds Farley, *The New American Reality: Who We Are, How We Got Here, Where We Are Going* (New York: Russell Sage, 1996), pp. 83–85; Gelles, *Contemporary Families*, p. 115; David Grissmer, Sheila Nataraj Kirby, Mark Bender, and Stephanie

Williamson, *Student Achievement and the Changing American Family,* Rand Institute on Education and Training (Santa Monica, Calif.: Rand, 1994), p. 106.

14. William Chafe, *The Unfinished Journey: America Since World War II* (New York: Oxford University Press, 1986), pp. 113, 143; Marc Linder, "Eisenhower-Era Marxist-Confiscatory Taxation: Requiem for the Rhetoric of Rate Reduction for the Rich," *Tulane Law Review* 70 (1996), p. 917; Barry Bluestone and Teresa Ghilarducci, "Rewarding Work: Feasible Antipoverty Policy," *American Prospect* 28 (1996), p. 42; Theda Skocpol, "Delivering for Young Families," *American Prospect* 28 (1996), p. 67.

15. Joel Tarr, "The Evolution of the Urban Infrastructure in the Nineteenth and Twentieth Centuries," in Royce Hanson, ed., *Perspectives on Urban Infrastructure* (Washington, D.C.: National Academy Press, 1984); Mark Aldrich, *A History of Public Works Investment in the United States,* report prepared by the CPNSAD Research Corporation for the U.S. Department of Commerce, April 1980.

16. For more information on this government financing, see Kenneth Jackson, *Crabgrass Frontier: The Suburbanization of the United States* (New York: Oxford University Press, 1985); and *The Way We Never Were,* chapter 4.

17. John Cook and Laura Sherman, "Economic Security Among America's Poor: The Impact of State Welfare Waivers on Asset Accumulation," Center on Hunger, Poverty, and Nutrition Policy, Tufts University, May 1996.

18. Robert Kuttner, "The Incredible Shrinking American Paycheck," *Washington Post National Weekly Edition,* November 6–12, 1995, p. 23; Donald Bartlett and James Steele, *America: What Went Wrong?* (Kansas City: Andrews McMeel, 1992), p. 20.

19. Richard Barnet, "Lords of the Global Economy," *Nation,* December 19, 1994, p. 756; Clay Chandler, "U.S. Corporations: Good Citizens or Bad?" *Washington Post National Weekly Edition,* May 20–26, 1996, p. 16; Steven Pearlstein, "No More Mr. Nice Guy: Corporate America Has Done an About-Face in How It Pays and Treats Employees," *Washington Post National Weekly Edition,* December 18–24, 1995, p. 10; Robert Kuttner, "Ducking Class Warfare," *Washington Post National Weekly Edition,* March 11–17, 1996, p. 5; Henry Allen, "Ha! So Much for Loyalty," *Washington Post National Weekly Edition,* March 4–10, 1996, p. 11.

20. Ehrenhalt, *The Lost City,* pp. 11–12; Jeremy Rifken, *The End of Work: The Decline of the Global Labor Force and the Dawn of the Post-Market Era* (New York: G. P. Putnam's Sons, 1995), pp. 169, 170, 231; Juliet Schorr, *The Overworked American: The Unexpected Decline of Leisure* (New York: Basic Books, 1991).

21. For documentation that these problems existed, see chapter 2 of *The Way We Never Were.*

22. The poverty figures come from census data collected in *The State of America's Children Yearbook, 1996* (Washington, D.C.: Children's Defense Fund, 1996), p. 77. See also Hirsch, *Making the Second Ghetto;* Raymond Mohl, "Making the Second Ghetto in Metropolitan Miami, 1940–1960," *Journal of Urban History* 25 (1995), p. 396; Micaela di Leonardo, "Boys on the Hood," *Nation,* August 17–24, 1992, p. 180; Jackson, *Crabgrass Frontier,* pp. 226–227.

23. Susan Douglas, *Where the Girls Are: Growing Up Female with the Mass Media* (New York: Times Books, 1994), pp. 25, 37.

24. *The State of America's Children Yearbook, 1966,* p. 77; May and Porter,

"Poverty and Income Trends: 1994," p. 23; Sara McLanahan et al., *Losing Ground: A Critique*, University of Wisconsin Institute for Research on Poverty, Special Report No. 38, 1985.

25. For studies of how both middle-class and working-class women in the 1950s quickly departed from, or never quite accepted, the predominant image of women, see Joanne Meyerowitz, ed., *Not June Cleaver: Women and Gender in Postwar America, 1945–1960* (Philadelphia: Temple University Press, 1994).

26. Lynn Karoly, "The Trend in Inequality Among Families, Individuals, and Workers in the United States: A Twenty-Five Year Perspective," in Sheldon Danziger and Peter Gottschalk, eds., *Rising Inequality in America* (New York: Russell Sage, 1993), pp. 48, 77–78; Michael Bernstein and David Adler, eds., *Understanding American Economic Decline* (New York: Cambridge University Press, 1994); Geoffrey Holtz, *Welcome to the Jungle: The Why Behind "Generation X"* (New York: St. Martin's Press, 1995), p. 167; "Widening Wage Inequality," *Urban Institute Policy and Research Report*, Winter/Spring 1995, p. 4.

27. Gordon Berlin and Andrew Sum, *Toward a More Perfect Union: Basic Skills, Poor Families, and Our Economic Future* (New York: Ford Foundation, 1988), pp. 5–6.

28. Kevin Phillips, "Down and Out: Can the Middle Class Rise Again?" *New York Times Magazine*, January 10, 1993, p. 32.

29. Karoly, "Trends in Income Inequality," p. 78. On the origins of egalitarian antitax sentiments in America, see James Huston, "The American Revolutionaries, the Political Economy of Aristocracy, and the American Concept of the Distribution of Wealth, 1765–1900," *American Historical Review* 98 (1993), p. 1084.

30. Kevin Phillips, *Boiling Point: Republicans, Democrats, and the Decline of Middle-Class Prosperity* (New York: Random House, 1993); "Making America's Economy Competitive Again" (Washington, D.C.: Rebuild America Coalition, 1992), p. 8; "Statement on Key Welfare Reform Issues: The Empirical Evidence," Tufts University Center on Hunger, Poverty, and Nutrition Policy, 1995, pp. 13–14; May and Porter, "Poverty and Income Trends: 1994," p. 87; Robert Pear, "Typical Relief Check Worth Half That of 1970," *New York Times*, November 27, 1996, p. A10.

31. Richard Easterlin, *Birth and Fortune: The Impact of Numbers on Personal Welfare* (Chicago: University of Chicago Press, 1987).

32. Farley, *The New American Reality*, p. 85.

33. Irene Browne, "The Baby Boom and Trends in Poverty, 1967–1987," *Social Forces* 73 (1995), pp. 1072, 1086.

Chapter 3

Why Working Mothers Are Here to Stay

1. Steve Rawlings and Arlene Saluter, *Household and Family Characteristics: March 1994*, Current Population Reports Series P20–483 (Washington, D.C.: Bureau of the Census, U.S. Department of Commerce, September 1995), pp. v–xvii; Richard Gelles, *Contemporary Families: A Sociological View* (Thousand Oaks, Calif.: Sage, 1995), pp. 116–120, 176; Kingsley Davis, "Wives and Work: A Theory of the Sex Role

Revolution and Its Consequences," in Sanford Dornbusch and Myra Strober, eds., *Feminism, Children, and the New Families* (New York: Guilford, 1988), p. 67.

2. David Popenoe, "Modern Marriage: Revising the Cultural Script," in David Popenoe, Jean Bethke Elshtain, and David Blankenhorn, eds., *Promises to Keep: Decline and Renewal of Marriage in America* (Lanham, Md.: Rowman and Littlefield, 1996), p. 254.

3. "Wanted: A Culture to Celebrate Fathers," *Christian Science Monitor*, November 3, 1994, p. 13.

4. "Marriage in America: A Report to the Nation," Council on Families in America, New York, N.Y., March 1995, pp. 4, 13, 17; David Blankenhorn, *Fatherless America: Confronting Our Most Urgent Social Problem* (New York: Basic Books, 1995), pp. 103, 111, 190; David Blankenhorn on *Morning Edition*, NPR transcript, April 15, 1996; David Popenoe, "The American Family Crisis," *National Forum* 75 (1995), p. 19; David Popenoe, *Life Without Father: Compelling New Evidence That Fatherhood and Marriage Are Indispensable for the Good of Children and Society* (New York: The Free Press, 1996), pp. 3–5, 150–151, 173–177, 183.

5. Blankenhorn, *Fatherless America*, pp. 25, 34; "The Marriage Strategy," *Mirabella*, March 1995, p. 90; Popenoe, *Life Without Father*, p. 12; David Broder, "Beware the Unattached Male," *Washington Post*, February 16, 1994.

6. Blankenhorn, *Fatherless America*, pp. 3–16, 116–123, 180.

7. "The Marriage Strategy," *Mirabella*, March 1995, p. 84; Blankenhorn, *Fatherless America*, pp. 117, 216; Maggie Gallagher, *Enemies of Eros* (Chicago: Bonus Books, 1989); Popenoe, *Life Without Father*, p. 197; Popenoe, "Modern Marriage," p. 264. For a more moderate discussion of sequencing, which led to the notorious "mommy track" debate a few years back, see Felice Schwartz, *Breaking with Tradition: Women, Management, and the New Facts of Life* (New York: Warner, 1992).

8. "Study Group Says Marriage Dying," *Honolulu Advertiser*, March 29, 1996; Dan Quayle and Diane Medved, *The American Family: Discovering the Values That Make Us Strong* (New York: HarperCollins, 1996), p. 207; Blankenhorn, quoting "a good family man," in *Fatherless America*, p. 216; Peggy O'Crawley, "Promise Keepers: Part Religion, Part Male-Bonding," *Hackensack New Jersey Sunday Record*, January 21, 1996.

9. Frances Dahlberg, ed., *Women the Gatherer* (New Haven, Conn.: Yale University Press, 1981); Richard Borshay Lee, *The Kung San: Men, Women, and Work in a Foraging Society* (New York: Cambridge University Press, 1979), pp. 269–271; George Silbauer, *Hunter and Habitat in the Central Kalahari Desert* (New York: Cambridge University Press, 1981), pp. 198–203.

10. For further development of the evidence and argument here, see my *Social Origins of Private Life: A History of American Families, 1600–1900* (London: Verso, 1988). See also Laurel Thacher Ulrich, *Good Wives: Image and Reality in the Lives of Women in Northern New England, 1650–1750* (New York: Knopf, 1983); Jeanne Boydston, *Home and Work: Housework, Wages, and the Ideology of Labor in the Early Republic* (New York: Oxford University Press, 1990).

11. Native-born women of color in the United States have always been more likely to work outside the home than white women, but they too tended to withdraw from paid employment when possible. Thus one study of Mexicanas and Chicanas

found that the Chicanas, who accepted dominant American notions about motherhood, were ambivalent about paid work, while the Mexicanas considered breadwinning an essential component of mothering, not a competitor to it. See Denise Segura, "Working at Motherhood: Chicana and Mexican Immigrant Mothers and Employment," in Evelyn Nakano Glenn, Grace Chang, and Linda Rennie Forcey, eds., *Mothering: Ideology, Experience, and Agency* (New York: Routledge, 1994), pp. 211–233.

12. Claudia Goldin, *Understanding the Gender Gap: An Economic History of American Women* (New York: Oxford University Press, 1990).

13. Edward Kain, *Myth of Family Decline: Understanding Families in a World of Rapid Social Change* (Lexington, Mass.: D. C. Heath, 1990), pp. 85–88, 98; Lynn Weiner, *From Working Girl to Working Mother: The Female Labor Force in the United States* (Chapel Hill: University of North Carolina Press, 1985), p. 84.

14. Donald Hernandez, *America's Children: Resources from Family, Government and the Economy* (New York: Russell Sage, 1993), pp. 98–142.

15. Andrew Cherlin, *Marriage, Divorce, Remarriage* (Cambridge, Mass.: Harvard University Press, 1981), pp. 50–56.

16. Tamar Lewin, "More Women Earn Half Their Household Income," *New York Times,* May 11, 1995; Coontz, *The Way We Never Were,* pp. 260, 266; "Public College Tuition Has Soared," *Olympian,* August 16, 1996, p. A10.

17. Lewin, "Study Says More Women Earn Half Their Household Income"; Aimee Dechter and Pamela Smock, "The Fading Breadwinner Role and the Economic Implications for Young Couples," Institute for Research on Poverty, Discussion Paper 1051–94, December 1994.

18. Daphne Spain and Suzanne Bianchi, *Balancing Act: Motherhood, Marriage, and Employment Among American Women* (New York: Russell Sage, 1996), pp. xv, 82, 193.

19. Lewin, "More Women Earn Half Their Household Income."

20. Louise Lamphere, Patricia Zavella, and Felipe Gonzales, with Peter Evans, *Sunbelt Working Mothers: Reconciling Family and Factory* (Ithaca, N.Y.: Cornell University Press, 1993); Lewin, "More Women Earn Half Their Household Income."

21. Phillip Blumstein and Pepper Schwartz, *American Couples: Money, Work, Sex* (New York: William Morrow, 1983); Gelles, *Contemporary Families,* p. 344.

22. Hernandez, *America's Children,* p. 396.

23. Joan Smith, "Transforming Households: Working-Class Women and Economic Crisis," *Social Problems* 34 (1987), pp. 425–427; Judith Bruce, Cynthia Lloyd, and Ann Leonard, with Patrice Engle and Niev Duffy, *Families in Focus: New Perspectives on Mothers, Fathers, and Children* (New York: The Population Council, 1995); Tamar Lewin, "The Decay of Families Is Global, Study Says," *New York Times,* May 30, 1996, p. A5.

24. Coontz, *The Social Origins of Private Life,* pp. 348–350; Smith, "Transforming Households," pp. 427–428.

25. Lamar Alexander, quoted in *Time,* February 26, 1996, pp. 11, 40.

26. Phyllis Moen, *Women's Two Roles: A Contemporary Dilemma* (New York: Auburn House, 1992), p. 133.

27. "Curfews and Common Sense," *New York Times,* June 11, 1996, p. A14.

28. R. Emerson Dobash and Russell P. Dobash, "Wives: The 'Appropriate' Victims of Marital Violence," *Victimology* 2 (1977–1978), pp. 426–432.

29. On cross-cultural patterns of mothering, see Glenn, Chang, and Forcey, *Mothering*; Maxine Baca Zinn and Bonnie Thornton Dill, eds., *Women of Color in U.S. Society* (Philadelphia: Temple University Press, 1994); Stephanie Coontz and Peta Henderson, eds., *Women's Work, Men's Property: The Origins of Gender and Class* (London: Verso, 1986). On colonial women's work and mothering, see Boydston, *Home and Work;* Ulrich, *Good Wives;* and Karin Calvert, *Children in the House* (Boston: Northeastern University Press, 1992).

30. John Gillis, "Bringing Up Father: British Paternal Identities, 1700 to Present," *Masculinities* 3 (1995), pp. 6, 16.

31. Mary Frances Berry, *The Politics of Parenthood: Child Care, Women's Rights, and the Myth of the Good Mother* (New York: Viking, 1993), pp. 46–50.

32. Gillis, "Bringing Up Father," p. 17; Michael Grossberg, *Governing the Hearth: Law and the Family in Nineteenth-Century America* (Chapel Hill: University of North Carolina Press, 1985). For a variation of the same process in the South, see Peter Bardaglio, *Reconstructing the Household: Families, Sex, and the Law in the Nineteenth-Century South* (Chapel Hill: University of North Carolina Press, 1995).

33. Rosalind Barnett and Caryl Rivers, *She Works/He Works: How Two-Income Families Are Happier, Healthier, and Better-off* (New York: HarperCollins, 1996), pp. 36, 59, 62; Tamar Lewin, "Workers of Both Sexes Make Trade-Offs for Family, Study Shows," *New York Times,* October 29, 1995, p. 14.

34. Barnett and Rivers, *She Works/He Works,* pp. 66, 82; Norma Radin, "Primary-Caregiving Fathers in Intact Families," in Adele Gottfried and Allen Gottfried, eds., *Redefining Families: Implications for Children's Development* (New York: Plenum, 1994), pp. 45–46.

35. Martha Moorehouse, "Work and Family Dynamics," in Philip A. Cowan, Carolyn Pape Cowan, and Patricia K. Kerig, eds., *Family, Self, and Society: Toward a New Agenda for Family Research* (Hillsdale, N.J.: Lawrence Erlbaum, 1993), p. 266; Adele Gottfried, Kay Brathurst, and Allan Gottfried, "The Role of Maternal and Dual-Earner Employment Status in Children's Development," in Gottfried and Gottfried, eds., *Redefining Families,* p. 92.

36. Subadra Seshadri, "Assessment of Nutrition and Health Situations: A Household-Level Perspective," in Romy Borooah et al., eds., *Capturing Complexity: An Interdisciplinary Look at Women, Households and Development* (Thousand Oaks, Calif.: Sage, 1994), p. 236; Bruce et al., *Families in Focus,* pp. 31–33.

37. Pepper Schwartz, "Some People with Multiple Roles Are Blessedly Stressed," *New York Times,* November 17, 1994. For a review of the research on employment and women's health, see Barnett and Rivers, *She Works/He Works.*

38. Jacqueline Lerner and Nancy Galambos, "The Influences of Maternal Employment Across Life: The New York Longitudinal Study," in Adele Gottfried and Alan Gottfried, eds., *Maternal Employment and Children's Development: Longitudinal Research* (New York: Plenum, 1988); Jacqueline Lerner, *Working Women and Their Families* (Thousand Oaks, Calif.: Sage, 1994), pp. 45–46. See also note 24.

39. Theodore Greenstein, "Are the 'Most Advantaged' Children Truly Disadvantaged by Early Maternal Employment?" *Journal of Family Issues* 16 (1995); Diane

Scott-Jones, "Family Influences on Cognitive Development and School Achievement," *Review of Research in Education* 11 (1984), p. 276; Lois Hoffman, "Maternal Employment and the Young Child," in Marion Perlmutter, ed., *The Minnesota Symposia on Child Psychology*, vol. 17 (Hillsdale, N.J.: Lawrence Erlbaum, 1984); Anita Shreve, *Remaking Motherhood: How Working Mothers Are Shaping Our Children's Future* (New York: Viking, 1987), pp. 82, 100–104; Harriet Mischel and Robert Fuhr, "Maternal Employment: Its Psychological Effects on Children and Their Families," in Sanford Dornbusch and Myra Strober, eds., *Feminism, Children, and the New Families* (New York: Guilford, 1988), pp. 200–201; Jacqueline Lerner, *Working Women*, p. 39; Lerner and Galambos, "The Influences of Maternal Employment Across Life."

40. Lerner, *Working Women and Their Families*; David W. Grissmer, Sheila Nataraj Kirby, Mark Berends, and Stephanie Williamson, *Student Achievement and the Changing American Family* (Santa Monica, Calif.: Rand Institute on Education and Training, 1994), p. 74; Lois Hoffman, "Effects of Maternal Employment in the Two-Parent Family," *American Psychologist* 44 (1989), pp. 283–292; Kristen Moore and Isabel Sawhill, "Implications of Women's Employment for Home and Family Life," in Patricia Voydanoff, ed., *Work and Family* (Palo Alto, Calif.: Mayfield, 1984), pp. 153–171; Toby Parcel and Elizabeth Menaghan, "Maternal Working Conditions and Children's Verbal Facilities," *Social Psychology Quarterly* 53 (1990); Cynthia Epstein, "Toward a Family Policy: Changes in Mothers' Lives," in Andrew Cherlin, ed., *The Changing American Family and Public Policy* (Washington, D.C.: The Urban Institute Press, 1988), pp. 178–180; Barbara Heynes and Sophia Catsambis, "Mothers' Employment and Children's Achievement: A Critique," *Sociology of Education* 59 (1986), p. 109; Mischel and Fuhr, "Maternal Employment," pp. 195, 197, 202; Ellen Greenberger and Wendy Goldberg, "Work, Parenting, and the Socialization of Children," *Developmental Psychology* 25 (1989); Elizabeth Menaghan and Toby Parcel, "Determining Children's Home Environments: The Impact of Maternal Characteristics and Current Occupational and Family Conditions," *Journal of Marriage and the Family* 53 (1991), p. 427; Shreve, *Remaking Motherhood*, p. 143.

41. Sandra Scarr, *Mother Care/Other Care* (New York: Basic Books, 1994); Moorehouse, "Work and Family Dynamics," pp. 268, 275.

42. W. Keith Bryant and Cathleen Zick, "An Examination of Parent–Child Shared Time," *Journal of Marriage and the Family* 58 (1996), p. 236.

43. Jay Belsky, "Parental and Nonparental Child Care and Children's Socioemotional Development: A Decade in Review," in Alan Booth, ed., *Contemporary Families: Looking Forward, Looking Back* (Minneapolis: National Council on Family Relations, 1991), pp. 132–133; Jay Belsky, "Infant Day Care: A Cause for Concern?" *Zero to Three: Bulletin of the National Center for Clinical Infant Programs* (Washington, D.C.: U.S. Government Printing Office, 1986); Deborah Phillips et al., "Selective Review of Infant Day Care Research: A Cause for Concern!" *Zero to Three: Bulletin of the National Center for Clinical Infant Programs* (Washington, D.C.: U.S. Government Printing Office, 1987); Alison Clarke-Stewart, "Infant Day Care: Maligned or Malignant?" *American Psychologist* 44 (1989), pp. 268–269.

44. Susan Chira, "Study Says Babies in Child Care Keep Secure Bonds to Mothers," *New York Times*, April 21, 1996.

45. Alison Clarke-Stewart, *Daycare: The Developing Child* (Cambridge, Mass.:

Harvard University Press, 1982); David Hamburg, *Today's Children: Creating a Future for a Generation in Crisis* (New York: Times Books, 1992), p. 113; Charles Leroux and Cindy Schreuder, "Preschool Worth the Cost," *Chicago Tribune*, November 1, 1994; Dennis Kelly, "Preschool Has Lasting Effects," *USA Today*, April 22, 1993; Susan Faludi, "The Kids Are All Right," *Utne Reader*, May/June 1993, p. 68; Richard Whitmire, "Child Experts Defend Value of Head Start," *Olympian*, February 2, 1996; Frances Campbell and Craig Ramey, "Effects of Early Intervention on Academic Achievement: A Follow-up Study of Children from Low-Income Families," *Child Development* 65 (1994).

46. Randolph Schmid, "More Parents Rely on Day Care," *Olympian*, April 24, 1996, p. A6.

47. Ellen Galinsky, Carollee Howes, Susan Kontos, and Marybeth Shinn, "Public Policy Report: The Study of Children in Family Child Care and Relative Care—Key Findings and Policy Recommendations," *Young Children*, November 1994, p. 60; Deborah Phillips and Anne Bridgeman, eds., *New Findings on Children, Families, and Self-Sufficiency* (Washington, D.C.: National Academy Press, 1995), pp. 17–19; The Children's Foundation, *1995 Child Day Care Licensing Study* (Washington, D.C.: The Children's Foundation, 1995); Sandra Scarr, Deborah Phillips, and Kathleen McCartney, "Facts, Fantasies and the Future of Child Care in the United States," *Psychological Science* 1 (1990); Carnegie Corporation of New York, *Starting Points: Meeting the Needs of Our Youngest Children* (New York: Carnegie Corporation of New York, 1994); Belsky, "Parental and Nonparental Child Care"; Margaret O'Brien Caughy, Janet DiPietro, and Donna Strobino, "Day-Care Participation as a Protective Factor in the Cognitive Development of Low-Income Children," *Child Development* 65 (1994), p. 467; Susan Chira, "Working-Class Parents Face Shortage of Day Care Centers," *New York Times*, September 14, 1993, p. A13.

48. National Research Council Institute of Medicine, *Child Care for Low-Income Families: Summary of Two Workshops* (Washington, D.C.: National Academy Press, 1995), p. 1; Hyman Rodman, David Pratto, and Rosemary Nelson, "Child Care Arrangements and Children's Functioning: A Comparison of Self-Care and Adult-Care Children," *Developmental Psychology* 21 (1985); Lerner, *Working Women and Their Families*, p. 89.

49. Constance Hays, "Increasing Shift Work Challenges Child Care," *New York Times*, June 8, 1995, p. B5; Karen Fox Folk and Unae Yi, "Piecing Together Child Care with Multiple Arrangements: Crazy Quilt or Preferred Pattern for Employed Parents of Preschool Children?" *Journal of Marriage and the Family* 56 (1994); *Child Care Consumer Education Brief*, National Center for Children in Poverty, August 1993; Deborah Phillips, Miriam Voran, Ellen Kisker, Carollee Howes, and Marey Whitebook, "Child Care for Children in Poverty: Opportunity or Inequity?" *Child Development* 65 (1994), p. 489; Phillips and Bridgeman, *New Findings on Children*, pp. 17–19.

50. Julia Wrigley, *Other People's Children* (New York: Basic Books, 1995).

51. Ellen Galinsky, J. T. Bond, and D. A. Friedman, *The Changing American Workforce: Highlights of the National Study* (New York: Families and Work Institute, 1993); Arlie Hochschild with Anne Machung, *The Second Shift: Working Parents and the Revolution at Home* (New York: Viking, 1989), pp. 3–4; Martin O'Connell, *Where's Papa? Fathers' Roles in Child Care*, Policy Reports No. 20 (Washington,

D.C.: Population Reference Bureau, 1993); Andrew Greeley, "The Declining Morale of Women," *Sociology and Social Research* 73 (1989), p. 53; Karen Czapanskiy, "Volunteers and Draftees: The Struggle for Parental Equality," *UCLA Law Review* 38 (1992), p. 1457; David Demo and Alan Acock, "Family Diversity and the Division of Domestic Labor: How Much Have Things Really Changed?" *Family Relations* 42 (1993), p. 331.

52. Hochschild, *The Second Shift;* Daphne Spain and Suzanne Bianchi, *Balancing Act: Marriage, Motherhood, and Employment Among American Women* (New York: Russell Sage, 1996), p. 169.

53. Spain and Bianchi, *Balancing Act,* pp. 169–171; Julie Brines, "Economic Dependency, Gender, and the Division of Labor at Home," *American Journal of Sociology* 100 (1994).

54. Karen Peterson, "Dads Aren't Using Family Leave, " *USA Today,* April 1, 1995.

55. Bruce et al., *Families in Focus,* pp. 55–56.

56. Blankenhorn, *Fatherless America,* p. 101. For similar recommendations by other family values crusaders, see the references cited in notes 2, 3, 4, and 7.

57. Spain and Bianchi, *Balancing Act,* pp. 173, 176, 191.

58. Barnett and Rivers, *She Works/He Works,* pp. 32–37, 98–99, 110–111, 115, 125.

59. Philip A. Cowan, Carolyn Pape Cowan, and Patricia Kerig, "Mothers, Fathers, Sons, and Daughters: Gender Differences in Family Formation and Parenting Style," in Cowan et al., eds., *Family, Self, and Society*; Ellen D. Nannis and Philip A. Cowan, eds., *Developmental Psychopathology and Its Treatment* (San Francisco: Jossey-Bass, 1988); Carolyn Pape Cowan and Philip A. Cowan, *When Partners Become Parents: The Big Life Change for Couples* (New York: Basic Books, 1992); Betty Carter and Joan Peters, *Love, Honor and Negotiate: Making Your Marriage Work* (New York: Pocket Books, 1996), pp. 4, 9, 15.

60. Blankenhorn, *Fatherless America,* p. 112.

61. Barnett and Rivers, *She Works/He Works,* p. 56.

62. Sheila Kamerman, "Gender Role and Family Structure Changes in the Advanced Industrialized West: Implications for Social Policy," in Katherine McFate, Roger Lawson, and William Julius Wilson, eds., *Poverty, Inequality, and the Future of Social Policy* (New York: Russell Sage, 1995); Spain and Bianchi, *Balancing Act,* p. 168; Ronald Angel and Jacqueline Angel, *Painful Inheritance: Health and the New Generation of Fatherless Families* (Madison: University of Wisconsin, 1993), p. 44; Valerie Polakow, *Lives on the Edge: Single Mothers and Their Children in the Other America* (Chicago: University of Chicago Press, 1993), p. 166.

63. On the need for better regulations, see Helen Blank, *Protecting Our Children: State and Federal Policies for Exempt Child Care Settings* (Washington, D.C.: Children's Defense Fund, January 1994). On companies with good policies, see the annual reports of *Working Mother* magazine on the 100 best companies for working mothers. On what we know about how to provide good child care see: Sandra Scarr, Marlene Eisenberg, and Kirby Deater-Deckard, "Measurement of Quality in Child Care Centers," *Early Childhood Research Quarterly* 9 (1994); Mary Larner and Nina Chaudry, "Promoting Professionalism Through Family Day Care Networks," National Center for Children in Poverty, Columbia University School of Public

Health, August 1993; Gina Adams and Jodi Sandfort, *First Steps, Promising Futures: State Prekindergarten Initiatives in the Early 1990s* (Washington, D.C.: Children's Defense Fund, 1994).

64. Adam Smith, *An Inquiry into the Nature and Causes of the Wealth of Nations,* vol. 2, Edwin Cannan, ed. (Chicago: University of Chicago Press, 1976), p. 244.

65. Sheila Kamerman and Alfred Kahn, *A Welcome for Every Child: Care, Education, and Family Support for Infants and Toddlers in Europe* (Arlington, Va.: Zero to Three/National Center for Clinical Infant Programs, 1994); Sheila Kamerman and Alfred Kahn, *Starting Right: How America Neglects Its Youngest Children and What We Can Do About It* (New York: Oxford University Press, 1995); Sandra Hofferth, "Caring for Children at the Poverty Line," *Children and Youth Services Review* 17 (1995).

66. William Raspberry, "Superfluous Father Syndrome," *Washington Post,* March 9, 1994.

67. Hanna Rosin, "Separation Anxiety: The Movement to Save Marriage," *New Republic,* May 6, 1996, p. 17.

Chapter 4

The Future of Marriage

1. "Marriage in America: A Report to the Nation," Council on Families in America, New York, N.Y., March 1995, pp. 10–11, 13.

2. David Popenoe, "Modern Marriage: Revising the Cultural Script," in David Popenoe, Jean Bethke Elshtain, and David Blankenhorn, eds., *Promises to Keep: Decline and Renewal of Marriage in America* (Lanham, Md.: Rowman and Littlefield, 1996), p. 254; "Marriage in America," p. 4; David Popenoe, *Life Without Father: Compelling New Evidence That Fatherhood and Marriage Are Indispensable for the Good of Children and Society* (New York: The Free Press, 1996), p. 222; David Blankenhorn, *Fatherless America: Confronting Our Most Urgent Social Problem* (New York: Basic Books, 1995), p. 229; Charles Murray, "Keep It in the Family," *Times of London,* November 14, 1993; Maggie Gallagher, *The Abolition of Marriage: How We Destroy Lasting Love* (Washington, D.C.: Regnery Publishing, 1996), pp. 250–257; Barbara Dafoe Whitehead, "Dan Quayle Was Right," *Atlantic Monthly* 271 (April 1993), p. 49.

3. "Marriage in America," p. 4. The "deinstitutionalizing" phrase comes from Blankenhorn, *Fatherless America,* p. 224.

4. William Goode, *World Changes in Divorce Patterns* (New Haven, Conn.: Yale University Press, 1993), p. 330.

5. On the leveling off of family change, see Peter Kilborn, "Shifts in Families Reach a Plateau," *New York Times,* November 27, 1996. Other information in this and the following three paragraphs, unless otherwise noted, come from Steven Rawlings and Arlene Saluter, *Household and Family Characteristics: March 1994,* Current Population Reports Series P20–483 (Washington, D.C.: Bureau of the Census, U.S. Department of Commerce, September 1995), pp. xviii–ix; Michael Haines, "Long-term Marriage Patterns in the United States from Colonial Times to the Present," *History of the Family* 1 (1996); Arthur Norton and Louisa Miller, *Marriage, Divorce, and Remarriage in the 1990s,* Current Population Reports Series P23–180 (Washington, D.C.:

Bureau of the Census, October 1992); Richard Gelles, *Contemporary Families: A Sociological View* (Thousand Oaks, Calif.: Sage, 1995), pp. 116–120, 176; Shirley Zimmerman, "Family Trends: What Implications for Family Policy?" *Family Relations* 41 (1992), p. 424; Margaret Usdansky, "Single Motherhood: Stereotypes vs. Statistics," *New York Times*, February 11, 1996, p. 4; *New York Times*, August 30, 1994, p. A9; *New York Times*, March 10, 1996, p. A11, and March 17, 1996, p. A8; U.S. Bureau of the Census, *Statistical Abstracts of the United States* (Washington, D.C., 1992); McLanahan and Casper, "Growing Diversity and Inequality in the American Family," in Reynolds Farley, ed., *State of the Union: America in the 1990s*, vol. 1 (New York: Russell Sage, 1995).

6. Larry Bumpass, "Patterns, Causes, and Consequences of Out-of-Wedlock Childbearing: What Can Government Do?" *Focus*, 17 (University of Wisconsin–Madison Institute for Research on Poverty, 1995), p. 42; Larry Bumpass and R. Kelly Raley, "Redefining Single-Parent Families: Cohabitation and Changing Family Reality," *Demography* 32 (1995), p. 98. See also note 33.

7. *Olympian*, February 26, 1996, p. D6.

8. Susan Watkins, Jane Menken, and John Bongaarts, "Demographic Foundations of Family Change," *American Sociological Review* 52 (1987), pp. 346–358.

9. Barbara Wilson and Sally Clarke, "Remarriages: A Demographic Profile," *Journal of Family Issues* 13 (1992).

10. Gelles, *Contemporary Families*, pp. 344–345; Alan Booth, David Johnson, Lynn White, and John Edwards, "Women, Outside Employment, and Marital Instability," *American Journal of Sociology* 90 (1989), pp. 567–583.

11. Saul Hoffman and Greg Duncan, "The Effect of Incomes, Wages, and AFDC Benefits on Marital Disruption," *Journal of Human Resources* 30 (1993), pp. 1–41.

12. Barbara Ehrenreich, "On the Family," *Z Magazine*, November 1995, p. 10; Ailsa Burns and Cath Scott, *Mother-Headed Families and Why They Have Increased* (Hillsdale, N.J.: Lawrence Erlbaum, 1994), p. 183.

13. Terry Arendell, "Women and the Economics of Divorce in the Contemporary United States," *Signs* 13 (1987), p. 125.

14. Norton and Miller, *Marriage, Divorce, and Remarriage in the 1990s*, pp. 6–7; Gelles, *Contemporary Families*, pp. 344, 398; Lynn White, "Determinants of Divorce: A Review of Research in the Eighties," *Journal of Marriage and the Family* 52 (1990), pp. 904–912.

15. Valerie Oppenheimer and Vivian Lew, "American Marriage Formation in the Eighties: How Important Was Women's Economic Independence?" in K. O. Mason and A. Jensen, eds., *Gender and Family Change in Industrialized Countries* (Oxford: Oxford University Press, 1994); Aimee Dechter and Pamela Smock, "The Fading Breadwinner Role and the Economic Implications for Young Couples," Institute for Research on Poverty, Discussion Paper 1051–94, December 1994, p. 2; Marian Wright Edelman, *Families in Peril: An Agenda for Social Change* (Cambridge, Mass.: Harvard University Press, 1987), p. 55; Lawrence Lynn and Michael McGeary, eds., *Inner-City Poverty in the United States* (Washington, D.C.: National Academy Press, 1990), pp. 163–167; University of Michigan researcher Greg Duncan, Testimony before the House Select Committee on Children, Youth and Families, February 19, 1992; *New*

York Times, September 4, 1992, p. A1; Daniel Lichter, Diane McLaughlin, George Kephart, and David Landry, "Race and the Retreat from Marriage: A Shortage of Marriageable Men?" *American Sociological Review* 57 (1992), p. 797; Kristin Luker, "Dubious Conceptions—The Controversy Over Teen Pregnancy," *American Prospect,* Spring 1991.

16. Dirk Johnson, "Attacking No-Fault Notion, Conservatives Try to Put Blame Back in Divorce," *New York Times,* February 12, 1996, p. A8.

17. Maggie Gallagher, "Why Make Divorce Easy?" *New York Times,* February 20, 1996; "Welfare Reform and Tax Incentives Can Reverse the Anti-Marriage Tilt," *Insight,* April 15, 1996, p. 24; Suzanne Fields, "The Fault-Lines of Today's Divorce Politics," *Washington Times,* April 22, 1996. See also Maggie Gallagher, *The Abolition of Marriage: How We Destroy Lasting Love* (Washington, D.C.: Regnery Publishing, 1996).

18. Stephen Sugarman and Herma Hill Kay, eds., *Divorce Reform at the Crossroads* (New Haven, Conn.: Yale University Press, 1990); Cynthia Stearns, "Divorce and the Displaced Homemaker: A Discourse on Playing with Dolls, Partnership Buyouts and Dissociation Under No-Fault," *University of Chicago Law Review* 60 (1993), pp. 128–139; Ann Luquer Estin, "Maintenance, Alimony, and the Rehabilitation of Family Care," *North Carolina Law Review* 71 (1993). For my understanding of recent legal trends, I am greatly indebted to conversations with Olympia Attorney Christina Meserve.

19. Maggie Gallagher, "Recreating Marriage," in Popenoe, Elshtain, and Blankenhorn, eds., *Promises to Keep,* p. 237; Debra Friedman, *Towards a Structure of Indifference: The Social Origins of Maternal Custody* (New York: Aldine de Gruyter, 1995), p. 134; Bumpass is quoted in Johnson, "Attacking No-Fault Notion," *New York Times,* February 12, 1996.

20. Roderick Phillips, *Untying the Knot: A Short History of Divorce* (Cambridge: Cambridge University Press, 1991), p. 232. The one exception to this occurs in countries where men, but not women, have the right to divorce. High divorce rates in these countries tend to be associated with low status for women; in other situations, high divorce rates are associated with women's higher status and greater amount of economic and personal autonomy. See Burns and Scott, *Mother-Headed Families and Why They Have Increased,* p. 182.

21. Andrew Cherlin, *Marriage, Divorce, Remarriage* (Cambridge, Mass.: Harvard University Press, 1981), p. 49; Johnson, "Attacking No-Fault Notion," *New York Times,* February 12, 1996; William Goode, *World Changes in Divorce Patterns* (New Haven, Conn.: Yale University Press, 1993), p. 318; Shirley Zimmerman, "The Welfare State and Family Breakup: The Mythical Connection," *Family Relations* 40 (1991), p. 141.

22. Larry Bumpass, "What's Happening to the Family? Interactions Between Demographic and Institutional Change," *Demography* 27 (1990), p. 485.

23. Mike Males, "Poverty, Rape, Adult/Teen Sex: Why Pregnancy Prevention Programs Don't Work," *Phi Delta Kappan,* January 1994, p. 409; Ellen Goodman, "Return to Statutory Rape Laws," *Olympian,* Feb. 22, 1995, p. A9; Mike Males, *The Scapegoat Generation: America's War on Adolescents* (Monroe, Me.: Common Courage Press, 1996), pp. 17–18; Debra Boyer and David Fine, "Sexual Abuse as a Factor in

Adolescent Pregnancy and Child Maltreatment," *Family Planning Perspectives* 24 (1992).

24. *Vital and Health Statistics: Births to Unmarried Mothers,* series 21, no. 53 (Hyattsville, Md.: National Center for Health Statistics, Department of Health and Human Services, 1995), table 1, p. 27.

25. Sara McLanahan and Lynne Casper, "Growing Diversity and Inequality in the American Family," in Reynolds Farley, ed., *State of the Union: America in the 1990s,* vol. 2 (New York: Russell Sage, 1995), pp. 10–11; Stephanie Ventura, *Vital and Health Statistics: Births to Unmarried Mothers: United States, 1980–92,* series 21, Data on Natality, Marriage, and Divorce, no. 53 (Hyattsville, Md.: Department of Health and Human Services), no. PH5 95–1931, table 1, p. 27.

26. "More 'Murphy Brown' Moms," *Olympian,* July 14, 1993; *New York Times,* July 14, 1993, p. A1; Rachel Fuchs, *Poor and Pregnant in Paris: Strategies for Survival in the Nineteenth Century* (New Brunswick, N.J.: Rutgers University Press, 1992); Elizabeth Kuznesof, "Household Composition and Headship as Related to Changes in Mode of Production: Sao Paulo 1715 to 1836," *Society for Comparative Study of Society and History* 41 (1980), p. 100.

27. Usdansky, "Single Motherhood."

28. Katherine Edin, *Welfare Myths: Fact or Fiction? Exploring the Truth About Welfare* (New York: Center on Social Welfare Policy and Law, 1996); Joel Handler, "'Ending Welfare As We Know It': Another Exercise in Symbolic Politics," University of Wisconsin–Madison Institute for Research on Poverty, Discussion Paper 1053–95, January 1995, pp. 7–9.

29. Charles Murray, "Keep It in the Family," *London Times,* November 14, 1993.

30. Judith Bruce, Cynthia Lloyd, and Ann Leonard, with Patrice Engle and Niev Duffy, *Families in Focus: New Perspectives on Mothers, Fathers, and Children* (New York: The Population Council, 1995), p. 19; Tamar Lewin, "Decay of Families Is Global," *New York Times,* May 30, 1995, p. A5; Leon Eisenberg, "Is the Family Obsolete?" *Key Reporter* 60 (1995), pp. 1–5; Usdansky, "Single Motherhood"; Bumpass, "Patterns, Causes, and Consequences of Out-of-Wedlock Childbearing," p. 42.

31. John Billy and David Moore, "A Multilevel Analysis of Marital and Non-marital Fertility in the U.S.," *Social Forces* 70 (1992), pp. 977–1011; Elaine McCrate, "Expectation of Adult Wages and Teenage Childbearing," *International Review of Applied Economics* 6 (1992); Lawrence Lynn and Michael McGeary, eds., *Inner-City Poverty in the United States* (Washington, D.C.: National Academy Press, 1990), pp. 163–167. The best recent book on the causes and possible responses to teen pregnancy is Kristin Luker, *Dubious Conceptions: The Politics of Teenage Pregnancy* (Cambridge, Mass.: Harvard University Press, 1996).

32. Robert Moffitt, "Welfare Reform: An Economist's Perspective," *Yale Policy Review* 11 (1993); Sharon Parrott and Robert Greenstein, "Welfare, Out-of-Wedlock Childbearing, and Poverty: What Is the Connection?" (Washington, D.C.: Center on Budget and Policy Priorities, 1995), pp. 15–17.

33. Rebecca Blank, "What Are the Trends in Non-marital Births?" in R. Kent Weaver and William T. Dickens, eds., *Looking Before We Leap: Social Science and Welfare Reform* (Washington, D.C.: Brookings Institution, 1995); Mark Rank, *Living on the Edge: The Realities of Welfare in America* (New York: Columbia University Press, 1994).

34. Gregory Acs, "Do Welfare Benefits Promote Out-of-Wedlock Childbearing?" in Isabel Sawhill, ed., *Welfare Reform: An Analysis of the Issues* (Washington, D.C.: The Urban Institute, 1995); Usdansky, "Single Motherhood"; McLanahan and Casper, "Growing Diversity and Inequality in the American Family," pp. 10–11; Sara McLanahan and Irwin Garfinkel, "Welfare Is No Incentive," *New York Times*, July 29, 1994, p. A13; "Work and Child Care Choices," *Urban Institute Policy and Research Report*, Summer 1994, p. 17.

35. *New York Times*, August 30, 1994, p. A14.

36. Elaine McCrate, "Expectations of Adult Wages and Teenage Childbearing," *International Review of Applied Economics* 6 (1992); Ruth Conniff, "The Culture of Cruelty," *The Progressive*, September 1992, p. 16; Barbara Vobejda, "Gauging Welfare's Role in Motherhood: Sociologists Question Whether 'Family Caps' Are a Legitimate Solution," *Washington Post*, June 2, 1994; Spencer Rich, "Generous Welfare May Not Quash Upward Mobility," *Washington Post National Weekly Edition*, August 30–September 5, 1993, p. 28; "Statement on Key Welfare Reform Issues: The Empirical Evidence," Poverty and Nutrition Policy (Medford, Mass.: Tufts University Center on Hunger, 1995), pp. 7, 11, 15, 19; Barbara Crosselde, "U.N. Survey Finds World Rich-Poor Gap Widening," *New York Times*, July 15, 1996, p. A3; Mike Males, "In Defense of Teenage Mothers," *The Progressive*, August 1994, p. 22; Lynn and McGeary, eds., *Inner-City Poverty in the United States*, pp. 163–167; University of Michigan researcher Greg Duncan, Testimony before the House Select Committee on Children, Youth and Families, February 19, 1992; *New York Times*, September 4, 1992, p. A1. On America's higher degree of religious moralism and sexual conservatism, compared to countries with lower rates of teen pregnancy, see James Morone, "The Corrosive Politics of Virtue," *American Prospect* 26 (May–June 1996), pp. 31–32.

37. For sources on the following figures, consult the nonpartisan Congressional Budget Office. See also David Super et al., *The New Welfare Law* (Washington D.C.: Center on Budget and Policy Priorities, 1996); Alison Mitchell, "Two Clinton Aides Resign to Protest New Welfare Law," *New York Times*, September 12, 1996, pp. A1, A14; Robert Pear, "State Welfare Chiefs Ask for More U.S. Guidance," *New York Times*, September 10, 1996.

38. Clifford Levy, "Welfare and the Working Poor," *New York Times*, November 17, 1996.

39. John Edwards, "New Conceptions: Biosocial Innovations and the Family," *Journal of Marriage and the Family* 53 (1991), pp. 349–360; Andrea Bonnicksen, *In Vitro Fertilization: Building Policy from Laboratories to Legislatures* (New York: Columbia University Press, 1989).

40. *Olympian*, July 4, 1992, p. A5, October 29, 1990, p. A8, and October 1, 1989, p. A10; *New York Times*, January 8, 1996, pp. A1, A7; *New York Times*, January 10, 1996, pp. A1, B7; Lori Andrews, *Between Strangers: Surrogate Mothers, Expectant Fathers, and Brave New Babies* (New York: Harper and Row, 1989); Elaine Hoffman Baruch, Amadeo D'Adamo, and Joni Seager, *Embryos, Ethics, and Women's Rights* (Binghamton, New York: The Haworth Press, 1989); John Robertson, *Children of Choice: Freedom and the New Reproductive Technologies* (Princeton, N.J.: Princeton University Press, 1994); Derek Morrison, "A Surrogacy Issue: Who Is the Other Mother?" *International Journal of Law and the Family* 8 (1994); Jill Smolowe, "The Test-Tube Cus-

tody Fight," *Time*, March 18, 1996, p. 80; Janet Dolgin, "Just a Gene: Judicial Assumptions About Parenthood," *UCLA Law Review* 40 (1993); Ruth Macklin, *Surrogates and Other Mothers: The Debates Over Assisted Reproduction* (Philadelphia: Temple University Press, 1994).

41. Susan Chira, "Of a Certain Age, and in a Family Way," *New York Times*, January 2, 1994; Jan Hoffman, "Egg Donations Meet a Need and Raise Ethical Questions," *New York Times*, January 8, 1996; Elisabeth Rosenthal, "From Lives Begun in a Lab, Brave New Joy," *New York Times*, January 10, 1996; Bonnickson, *In Vitro Fertilization*.

42. Ruth Shalit, "Family Mongers," *New Republic*, August 16, 1993, p. 13; Popenoe, *Life Without Father*, p. 194; David Popenoe, "American Family Decline, 1960–1990," *Journal of Marriage and the Family* 55 (1993), p. 539; Blankenhorn, *Fatherless America*, pp. 220–233; and quoted in *Newsweek*, February 6, 1995, p. 43; "Marriage in America: A Report to the Nation," Council on Families in America, March 1995, p. 4.

43. Whitehead, "Dan Quayle Was Right," p. 49; Carole Sugarman, "Jack Sprat Should Eat Some Fat," *Washington Post National Weekly Edition*, May 2–8, 1994; *Olympian*, February 5, 1996, p. A8; Janet Giele, "Decline of the Family: Conservative, Liberal, and Feminist Views," in Popenoe, Elshtain, and Blankenhorn, *Promises to Keep*, p. 104.

44. Dan Quayle and Diane Medved, *The American Family: Discovering the Values That Make Us Strong* (New York: HarperCollins, 1996), pp. 2, 87, 114.

45. Katharine Seelye, "The Complications and Ideals," *New York Times*, November 24, 1994.

46. Katha Pollitt, "Bothered and Bewildered," *New York Times*, July 22, 1993.

Chapter 5

Putting Divorce in Perspective

1. David Blankenhorn, "Can We Talk? The Marriage Strategy," *Mirabella*, March 1995, p. 91.

2. Howard Wineberg and James McCarthy, "Separation and Reconciliation in American Marriages," *Journal of Divorce and Remarriage* 20 (1993).

3. Barbara Dafoe Whitehead, "Dan Quayle Was Right," *Atlantic Monthly*, April 1993, p. 55.

4. Paul R. Amato, "Life-Span Adjustment of Children to Their Parents' Divorce," *The Future of Children* 4, no. 1 (Spring 1994), p. 147; E. Mavis Hetherington, "An Overview of the Virginia Longitudinal Study of Divorce and Remarriage with a Focus on Early Adolescence," *Journal of Family Psychology* 7, no. 1 (June 1, 1993), p. 53.

5. Judith Wallerstein and Sandra Blakeless, *Second Chances: Men, Women and Children a Decade After Divorce* (New York: Ticknor & Fields, 1989); Frank Furstenberg, Jr., and Andrew Cherlin, *Divided Families: What Happens to Children When Parents Part* (Cambridge, Mass.: Harvard University Press, 1991), p. 68; Andrew Cherlin and Frank Furstenberg, "Divorce Doesn't Always Hurt the Kids," *Washington Post*, March 19, 1989 (emphasis added). Wallerstein and Kelly suggested that there was a

"sleeper effect" for young women, where problems caused by divorce were not evident until years later. But a ten-year Australian study found "no convincing evidence" for such an effect. Rosemary Dunlop and Ailsa Burns, "The Sleeper Effect—Myth or Reality?" *Journal of Marriage and the Family* 58 (May 1995), p. 375. It is possible that the young women who reported such effects to Wallerstein were engaging in an after-the-fact attempt to explain why they were having troubles.

6. Paul Amato, "Children's Adjustment to Divorce," *Journal of Marriage and the Family* 55 (1993); Paul Amato and Bruce Keith, "Parental Divorce and the Well-Being of Children: A Meta-Analysis," *Psychological Bulletin* 110 (1991); Arlene Skolnick and Stacey Rosencrantz, "The New Crusade for the Old Family," *American Prospect,* Summer 1994, p. 62; Rex Forehand, Bryan Neighbors, Danielle Devine, and Lisa Armistead, "Interparental Conflict and Parental Divorce: The Individual, Relative, and Interactive Effects on Adolescents Across Four Years," *Family Relations* 43 (1994), p. 387; Bonnie Thornton Dill, Maxine Baca Zinn, and Sandra Patton, "Feminism, Race, and the Politics of Family Values," *Report from the Institute for Philosophy and Public Policy* 13 (1993), p. 17; Alan C. Acock and David H. Demo, *Family Diversity and Well-Being* (Thousand Oaks, Calif.: Sage, 1994), p. 213; P. Lindsay Chase-Lansdale, Andrew Cherlin, and Kathleen Kiernan, "The Long-Term Effects of Parental Divorce on the Mental Health of Young Adults: A Developmental Perspective," *Child Development* 66 (1995).

7. Sara S. McLanahan, "The Two Faces of Divorce: Women's and Children's Interests," *Macro-Micro Linkages in Sociology* (Newbury Park, Calif.: Sage, 1991), p. 202. She notes that these "estimates assume that all of the negative impact of family disruption is due to the disruption itself as opposed to preexisting characteristics of the parents."

8. Kathryn Robinson, "The Divorce Debate: Which Side Are You On?" *Family Therapy Networker* (May/June 1994), p. 20.

9. D. M. Capaldi and G. R. Patterson, "Relation of Parental Transitions to Boys' Adjustment Problems: I. A Linear Hypothesis. II. Mothers at Risk for Transitions and Unskilled Parenting," *Developmental Psychology* 27, no. 3 (1991), p. 489; William S. Aquilino, "The Life Course of Children Born to Unmarried Mothers: Childhood Living Arrangements and Young Adult Outcomes," *Journal of Marriage and the Family* 58 (May 1996), p. 306.

10. David Grissmer, Sheila Nataraj Kirby, Mark Berends, and Stephanie Williamson, *Student Achievement and the Changing American Family* (Santa Monica, Calif.: Rand Institute on Education and Training, 1994), p. 66; Doris R. Entwisle and Karl L. Alexander, "A Parent's Economic Shadow: Family Structure Versus Family Resources as Influences on Early School Achievement," *Journal of Marriage and the Family* 57 (May 1995), p. 399.

11. Sara McLanahan and Gary Sandefur, *Growing Up with a Single Parent: What Hurts, What Helps?* (Cambridge, Mass.: Harvard University Press, 1995), pp. 2–3; Elizabeth Kolbert, "Television Gets a Closer Look as a Factor in Real Violence," *New York Times,* December 14, 1994; Rachel Wildavsky, "What's Behind Success in School?" *Reader's Digest,* October 1994, p. 52.

12. Sameera Teja and Arnold L. Stolberg, "Peer Support, Divorce, and Children's Adjustment," *Journal of Divorce and Remarriage* 20, no. 3/4 (1993); Robert

Haveman, Barbara Wolfe, and James Spaulding, "The Relation of Educational Attainment to Childhood Events and Circumstances, *Institute for Research on Poverty Discussion Paper No. 908–90,* Madison, Wisconsin, 1990, p. 28; David Demo and Alan Acock, "The Impact of Divorce on Children," in Alan Booth, ed., *Contemporary Families: Looking Forward, Looking Back* (Minneapolis: National Council on Family Relations, 1991), p. 185; Maxine Baca Zinn and Stanley D. Eitzen, *Diversity in American Families* (New York: Harper and Row, 1987), p. 317; "Frequent Moving Harmful, Study Says," *Olympian,* July 24, 1996, p. A3; Jay Teachman, Kathleen Paasch, and Karen Carver, "Social Capital and Dropping Out of School Early," *Journal of Marriage and the Family* 58 (1996), p. 782.

13. Adele Eskeles Gottfried and Allen W. Gottfried, eds., *Redefining Families: Implications for Children's Development* (New York: Plenum, 1994), p. 224.

14. Furstenberg and Cherlin, *Divided Families,* p. 70; Amato and Keith, "Parental Divorce and the Well-Being of Children," p. 40; Andrew Cherlin, "Longitudinal Studies of Effects of Divorce on Children in Great Britain and the United States," *Science,* June 7, 1991, pp. 1386–1389; Joan Kelly, "Longer-Term Adjustment in Children of Divorce," *Journal of Family Psychology* 2 (1988); Larry Lettich, "When Baby Makes Three," *Family Therapy Networker* (January/February 1993), p. 66; Forehand et al., "Interparental Conflict and Parental Divorce," p. 387; Stacy R. Markland and Eileen S. Nelson, "The Relationship Between Familial Conflict and the Identity of Young Adults," *Journal of Divorce and Remarriage* 20, no. 3/4 (1993), p. 204.

15. Hetherington quoted in Robinson, "The Divorce Debate," pp. 27–28.

16. Furstenberg and Cherlin, *Divided Families,* p. 64; Paul R. Amato and Alan Booth, "A Prospective Study of Divorce and Parent–Child Relationships," *Journal of Marriage and the Family* 58 (May 1996), pp. 356–357; Robert E. Emery and Michele Tuer, "Parenting and the Marital Relationship," in Tom Luster and Lynn Okagaki, eds., *Parenting: An Ecological Perspective* (Hillsdale, N.J.: Lawrence Erlbaum, 1993), p. 135.

17. Richard Weissbourd, "Divided Families, Whole Children," *American Prospect* (Summer 1994), p. 69.

18. E. Mavis Hetherington, "Coping with Family Transitions: Winners, Losers, and Survivors," in *Annual Progress in Child Psychiatry and Child Development* (New York: Brunner/Mazel, 1990), pp. 237–239.

19. Hetherington, "Coping with Family Transitions," p. 221.

20. Marilyn Coleman and Lawrence H. Ganong, "Family Reconfiguring Following Divorce," in Steve Duck and Julia T. Wood, eds., *Confronting Relationship Challenges,* vol. 5 (Thousand Oaks, Calif.: Sage, 1995), pp. 81–85. See also: Acock and Demo, *Family Diversity and Well-Being,* p. 224; Paul R. Amato, Laura Spencer Loomis, and Alan Booth, "Parental Divorce, Marital Conflict, and Offspring Well-being During Early Adulthood," *Social Forces* 73, no. 3 (March 1995), p. 895; Nan Marie Astone and Sara S. McLanahan, "Family Structure, Parental Practice and High School Completion," *American Sociological Review* 56 (June 1991), p. 318; Forehand et al., "Interparental Conflict and Parental Divorce," p. 392.

21. Furstenberg and Cherlin, *Divided Families,* p. 71. Ronald L. Simons and Associates, *Understanding Differences Between Divorced and Intact Families: Stress, Interaction, and Child Outcome* (Thousand Oaks, Calif.: Sage, 1996), pp. 208, 210, 222. For

an argument that it is almost entirely family processes rather than divorce per se that cause poor outcomes, see Teresa M. Cooney and Jane Kurz, "Mental Health Outcomes Following Recent Parental Divorce: The Case of Young Adult Offspring," *Journal of Family Issues: The Changing Circumstances of Children's Lives* 17, no. 4 (July 1996), p. 510.

22. Furstenberg and Cherlin, *Divided Families*, p. 21.

23. Janet Johnston, "Family Transitions and Children's Functioning," in Philip Cowan et al., eds., *Family, Self, and Society: Toward a New Agenda for Family Research* (Hillsdale, N.J.: Lawrence Erlbaum, 1993); Amato, "Life-Span Adjustment of Children to Their Parents' Divorce," p. 175; James Bray and Sandra Berger, "Noncustodial Father and Paternal Grandparent Relationships in Stepfamilies," *Family Relations* 39 (1990), p. 419.

24. Weissbourd, "Divided Families, Whole Children," p. 68.

25. Philip A. Cowan, Carolyn Pape Cowan, and Patricia Kerig, "Mothers, Fathers, Sons, and Daughters: Gender Differences in Family Formation and Parenting Style," in Cowan et al., eds., *Family, Self, and Society*, p. 186; Sharon Wilsnack, Albert Klasson, and Brett Schurr, "Predicting Onset and Pernicity of Women's Problem Drinking: A Five-Year Longitudinal Analysis," *American Journal of Public Health* 81 (1991), pp. 305–318.

26. Jennifer Clark and Bonnie Barber, "Adolescents in Postdivorce and Always-Married Families: Self-Esteem and Perceptions of Fathers' Interest," *Journal of Marriage and the Family* 56 (1994), p. 609.

27. Susan Gano-Phillips and Frank D. Fincham, "Family Conflict, Divorce, and Children's Adjustment," in Mary Anne Fitzpatrick and Anita L. Vangelisti, eds., *Explaining Family Interactions* (Thousand Oaks, Calif.: Sage, 1995), p. 207.

28. Emery and Tuer, "Parenting and the Marital Relationship," pp. 138–139.

29. Constance Ahrons, *The Good Divorce: Keeping Your Family Together When Your Marriage Comes Apart* (New York: Harper Perennial, 1994), p. 6; Amato, "Life-Span Adjustment of Children to Their Parents' Divorce," p. 167.

30. Joyce A. Arditti and Michaelena Kelly, "Fathers' Perspectives of Their Co-Parental Relationships Postdivorce: Implications for Family Practice and Legal Reform," *Family Relations* 43 (January 1994), p. 65; Furstenberg and Cherlin, *Divided Families*, pp. 26–27; Kevin P. Kurkowski, Donald A. Gordon, and Jack Arbuthnot, "Children Caught in the Middle: A Brief Educational Intervention for Divorced Parents," *Journal of Divorce and Remarriage* 20, no. 3/4 (1993), p. 149; Constance Ahrons and R. B. Miller, "The Effect of Postdivorce Relationship on Paternal Involvement: A Longitudinal Analysis," *American Journal of Orthopsychiatry* 63 (1993).

31. Ahrons, *The Good Divorce*, p. 82; Emery and Tuer, "Parenting and the Marital Relationship," p. 145. See also Melinda Blau, *Families Apart: Ten Keys to Successful Co-parenting* (New York: G. P. Putnam's Sons, 1993).

32. James H. Bray and Charlene E. Depner, "Perspectives on Nonresidential Parenting," in Charles E. Depner and James H. Bray, eds., *Nonresidential Parenting: New Vistas in Family Living* (Newbury Park, Calif.: Sage, 1993), pp. 6–7.

33. Paul R. Amato, "Father–Child Relations, Mother–Child Relations, and Offspring Psychological Well-Being in Early Adulthood," *Journal of Marriage and the Family* 56 (November 1994), p. 1039; Susan Chollar, "Happy Families: Who Says They

All Have to Be Alike?" *American Health* (July/August 1993); Simons and Associates, *Understanding Differences Between Divorced and Intact Families*, p. 224; Bonnie L. Barber, "Support and Advice from Married and Divorced Fathers: Linkages and Adolescent Adjustment," *Family Relations* 43 (1994), p. 433.

34. William Goode, *World Changes in Divorce Patterns* (New Haven, Conn.: Yale University Press, 1993), pp. 330, 345; Robert Emory, "Divorce Mediation: Negotiating Agreements and Renegotiating Relationships," *Family Relations* 44 (1995); Cheryl Buehler and Jean Gerard, "Divorce Law in the United States: A Focus on Child Custody," *Family Relations* 44 (1995).

35. "Letters to the Editor," *New York Times*, December 31, 1995.

36. Andrew Cherlin, "Remarriage as an Incomplete Institution," *American Journal of Sociology* 84 (1978); Mark A. Fine, "A Social Science Perspective on Stepfamily Law: Suggestions for Legal Reform," *Family Relations* 38 (1989); Andrew Schwebel, Mark Fine, and Maureena Renner, "A Study of Perceptions of the Stepparent Role," *Journal of Family Issues* 12 (1991); Mark A. Fine and David R. Fine, "Recent Changes in Laws Affecting Stepfamilies: Suggestions for Legal Reform," *Family Relations* 41 (1992); Andrew Cherlin and Frank Furstenberg, "Stepfamilies in the United States: A Reconsideration," *American Review of Sociology* 20 (1994), p. 378.

37. Virginia Rutter, "Lessons from Stepfamilies," *Psychology Today* (May/June 1994), pp. 66–67; Lynn White, "Growing Up with Single Parents and Stepparents: Long-Term Effects on Family Solidarity," *Journal of Marriage and the Family* 56 (1994), p. 946.

Chapter 6

How Holding on to Tradition Sets Families Back

1. Betty Carter and Joan Peters, *Love, Honor and Negotiate: Making Your Marriage Work* (New York: Pocket Books, 1996), pp. 55–64.

2. Pamela Adelmann, *Why Don't Men Do More Housework? A Job Characteristics Exploration of Gender and Housework Satisfaction*, Center for Urban Affairs and Policy Research, Working Paper–95–31, 1995, pp. 4, 18; Glenna Spitze, "Women's Employment and Family Relations: A Review," *Journal of Marriage and the Family* 50 (1988); Yoav Lavee, Shlomo Sharlin, and Ruth Katz, "The Effect of Parenting Stress on Marital Quality," *Journal of Family Issues* 17 (1996), pp. 131–132; Scott South and Glenna Spitze, "Housework in Marital and Nonmarital Households," *American Sociological Review* 59 (1994); Tamar Lewin, "Traditional Family Favored by Boys, Not Girls, Poll Shows," *New York Times*, July 11, 1994, p. A1.

3. On the connection of traditional values to many pathologies, see: Gayle Wash and Carmen Knudson-Martin, "Gender Identity and Family Relationships: Perspectives from Incestuous Fathers," *Contemporary Family Therapy* 16 (1994); Wini Breines and Linda Gordon, "The New Scholarship on Family Violence," *Signs* 8 (1983); Sarah Begus and Pamela Armstrong, "Daddy's Right: Incestuous Assaults," in Irene Diamond, ed., *Families, Politics, and Public Policy* (New York: Longman, 1983); Deborah Luepnitz, *The Family Interpreted: Feminist Theory in Clinical Practice* (New York: Basic Books, 1988), p. 225; Linda Gordon, *Heroes of Their Own Lives: The Politics*

and History of Family Violence, Boston 1880–1960 (New York: Viking, 1988), p. 230; Judith Herman with Lisa Hirschman, *Father–Daughter Incest* (Cambridge, Mass.: Harvard University Press, 1981), p. 110; James Maddock, "Healthy Family Sexuality: Positive Principles for Educators and Clinicians," *Family Relations* 38 (1989); Henry C. Kempe, "Incest and Other Forms of Sexual Abuse," in Henry C. Kempe and Ray E. Helfer, eds., *The Battered Child* (Chicago: University of Chicago Press, 1980), p. 205; John Demos, *Past, Present, and Personal: The Family and the Life Course in American History* (New York: Oxford University Press, 1986), p. 84; Murray Straus, "State-to-State Differences in Social Inequality and Social Bonds in Relation to Assaults on Wives," *Journal of Comparative Family Studies* 15 (1994), p. 18.

4. Arlene Skolnick, "Changes of Heart: Family Dynamics in Historical Perspective," in Philip Cowan et al., eds., *Family, Self, and Society: Toward a New Agenda for Family Research* (Hillsdale, N.J.: Lawrence Erlbaum, 1993), pp. 52–56.

5. While slaves and Native Americans were obviously excluded from this system, free African Americans had some possibility of following a similar path. Many were highly skilled artisans, and only in the second half of the nineteenth century were they driven out of the skilled trades and small businesses they had established.

6. This process is described in detail in Stephanie Coontz, *The Social Origins of Private Life: A History of American Families, 1600–1900* (London: Verso, 1988), esp. chapter 5. The way these economic changes forced middle-class families to reorganize their gender roles and personal behaviors is described by Mary Ryan, *Cradle of the Middle Class: The Family in Oneida Country, New York, 1790–1865* (New York: Cambridge University Press, 1981).

7. Paul Johnson, *A Shopkeeper's Millennium: Society and Revivals in Rochester, New York, 1815–1837* (New York: Hill & Wang, 1978); Mark Lender and James Martin, *Drinking in America: A History* (New York: Free Press, 1987); W. J. Rourabagh, *The Alcoholic Republic: An American Tradition* (New York: Oxford University Press, 1979).

8. Johnson, *A Shopkeeper's Millennium*; Irving Spergel, *The Youth Gang Problem* (New York: Oxford University Press, 1995), p. 7.

9. Coontz, *The Social Origins of Private Life*, pp. 219, 234; Nancy Cott, *The Bonds of Womanhood: 'Woman's Sphere' in New England, 1780–1835* (New Haven, Conn.: Yale University Press, 1977); Carroll Smith Rosenberg, "Davy Crockett as Trickster: Pornography, Liminality, and Symbolic Inversion in Victorian America," and "Beauty, the Beast, and the Militant Woman: A Case Study in Sex Roles and Social Stress in Jacksonian America," in Rosenberg, ed., *Disorderly Conduct: Visions of Gender in Victorian America* (New York: Oxford University Press, 1985).

10. Noel Ignatiev, *How the Irish Became White* (New York: Routledge, 1995), pp. 109, 131; David Roediger, *The Wages of Whiteness: Race and the Making of the American Working Class* (London: Verso, 1991).

11. Coontz, *The Social Origins of Private Life*, chapter 6, and John D'Emilio and Estelle Freedman, *Intimate Matters: A History of Sexuality in America* (New York: Harper and Row, 1988).

12. John Gillis, "Making Time for Family: The Invention of Family Time(s) and the Reinvention of Family History," *Journal of Family History* 21 (1996); John Gillis, *A World of Their Own Making: Myth, Ritual, and the Quest for Family Values* (New York: Basic Books, 1996).

13. Gillis, "Making Time for Family," p. 17; Evan Imber-Black and Janine Roberts, *Rituals for Our Times: Celebrating, Healing, and Changing Our Lives and Our Relationships* (New York: HarperCollins, 1992).

14. Elaine McCrate, "Accounting for the Slowdown in the Divorce Rate in the 1980s: A Bargaining Perspective," *Review of Social Economics* 50 (1992); Richard Gelles, *Contemporary Families: A Sociological View* (Thousand Oaks, Calif.: Sage, 1995), p. 344; Joe Pittman and David Blanchard, "The Effects of Work History and Timing of Marriage on the Division of Household Labor: A Life-Course Perspective," *Journal of Marriage and the Family* 58 (1996), p. 88.

15. Kathleen Gerson, *No Man's Land: Men's Changing Commitments to Family and Work* (New York: Basic Books, 1993), p. 164; Carolyn Grbich, "Male Primary Caregivers and Domestic Labour," *Journal of Family Studies* 1 (1995).

16. Andrew Greeley, "The Declining Morale of Women," *Sociology and Social Research* 73 (1989), p. 55; John Mirowsky and Catherine E. Ross, *The Social Causes of Psychological Distress* (New York: Aldine de Gruyter, 1989), p. 139.

17. Philip Cowan, Carolyn Pape Cowan, and Patricia Kerig, "Mothers, Fathers, Sons, and Daughters: Gender Differences in Family Formation and Parenting Style," in Philip Cowan et al., eds., *Family, Self, and Society*, p. 173.

18. Marilyn Ihinger-Tallman, Kay Paysley, and Cheryl Buehler, "Developing a Middle-Range Theory of Father Involvement Postdivorce," in William Marsiglio, ed., *Fatherhood: Contemporary Theory, Research, and Social Policy* (Thousand Oaks, Calif.: Sage, 1995); Linda Stephens, "Will Johnny See Daddy This Week? An Empirical Test of Three Theoretical Perspectives of Postdivorce Contact," *Journal of Family Issues* 17 (1996), p. 471; Terry Arendell, *Fathers and Divorce* (Thousand Oaks, Calif.: Sage, 1995). For more studies on how to make divorce work better for both parents and children, see Melinda Blau, *Families Apart: Ten Keys to Successful Co-parenting* (New York: G. P. Putnam's Sons, 1993); and Constance Ahrons, *The Good Divorce: Keeping Your Family Together When Your Marriage Comes Apart* (New York: HarperCollins, 1994).

19. Paul Amato, "Life-Span Adjustment of Children to Their Parents' Divorce," *Future of Children* 4 (1994), p. 149; David Demo and Alan Acock, "The Impact of Divorce on Children," in Alan Booth, ed., *Contemporary Families: Looking Forward, Looking Back* (Minneapolis: National Council on Family Relations, 1991), p. 170; Mary Elizabeth Curtner-Smith and Carol E. MacKinnon-Lewis, "Family Process Effects on Adolescent Males' Susceptibility to Antisocial Peer Pressure," *Family Relations* 43 (October 1994), p. 466; Rex Forehand, "Parental Divorce and Adolescent Maladjustment: Scientific Inquiry vs. Public Information," *Behaviour Research and Therapy* 30 (1992), pp. 319–327; Rex Forehand, Bryan Neighbors, Danielle Devine, and Lisa Armistead, "Interparental Conflict and Parental Divorce: The Individual, Relative, and Interactive Effects on Adolescents Across Four Years," *Family Relations* 43 (1994), p. 387; "Children of Divorce," *Olympian,* August 19, 1996, p. A3.

20. Terry Arendell, "After Divorce: Investigations into Father Absence," *Gender and Society* 6 (1992); Frank Furstenberg, Jr., and Andrew Cherlin, *Divided Families: What Happens to Children When Parents Part* (Cambridge, Mass.: Harvard University Press, 1991).

21. Carol Stack, "Cultural Perspectives on Child Welfare," *New York University Review of Law and Social Change* 12 (1983–1984); Sally Bould, "Familial Caretak-

ing: A Middle-Range Definition of Family," *Journal of Family Issues* 14 (1993), pp. 140–149.

22. Margaret Crosbie-Burnett and Edith A. Lewis, "Use of African-American Family Structures and Functioning to Address the Challenges of European-American Postdivorce Families," *Family Relations* 42 (1993), p. 244.

23. Larry Bumpass and R. Kelly Raley, "Redefining Single-Parent Families: Cohabitation and Changing Family Reality," *Demography* 32 (1995), p. 102.

24. John Scanzoni et al., *The Sexual Bond: Rethinking Families and Close Relationships* (Newbury Park, Calif.: Sage, 1989); John Edwards, "New Conceptions: Biosocial Innovations and the Family," *Journal of Marriage and the Family* 53 (1991), p. 357; Katha Pollitt, "Gay Marriage? Don't Say I Didn't Warn You," *The Nation,* April 29, 1996, p. 9; Janet Dolgin, "The Family in Transition: From Griswold to Eisenstadt and Beyond," *Georgetown Law Review* 82 (1994), p. 1571; Nancy Dowd, "Work and Family: Restructuring the Workplace," *Arizona Law Review* 32 (1990).

25. Nancy Folbre, *Who Pays for the Kids? Gender and the Structures of Constraint* (New York: Routledge, 1994), p. 254; Howard Dubowitz, Maureen Black, Raymond Starr, Jr., and Susan Zuravin, "A Conceptual Definition of Child Neglect," *Criminal Justice and Behavior* 20 (1993), p. 23.

26. Stack, "Cultural Perspectives on Child Welfare"; Alan Howard, Robert Heighton, Jr., Cathie Joran, and Ronald Gallimore, "Traditional and Modern Adoption Patterns in Hawaii," in Vern Carroll, ed., *Adoption in Eastern Oceania* (Honolulu: University of Hawaii Press, 1970).

27. Barbara Myerhoff, *Number Our Days: Culture and Community Among Elderly Jews in an American Ghetto* (New York: Meridian, 1994), p. 27; Crosbie-Burnett and Lewis, "African-American Family Structures"; Stack, "Cultural Perspectives on Child Welfare," pp. 542–543; Bould, "Familial Caretaking," p. 142.

28. Eleanor Leacock, "Montagnais Women and the Program for Jesuit Colonization," in Mona Etienne and Eleanor Leacock, eds., *Women and Colonization: Anthropological Perspectives* (New York: Praeger, 1980), p. 31.

29. Francesca Cancian, *Love in America: Gender and Self-Development* (New York: Cambridge University Press, 1987).

30. Rayna Rapp and Ellen Ross, "The Twenties' Backlash: Compulsory Heterosexuality, the Consumer Family, and the Waning of Feminism," in Amy Swerdlow and Hanna Lessinger, eds., *Class, Race, and Sex: The Dynamics of Control* (Boston: G. K. Hall and Co., 1983), p. 94. The 1993 quote comes from Elaine Tyler May, *Barren in the Promised Land: Childless Americans and the Pursuit of Happiness* (New York: Basic Books, 1995), p. 205.

31. Gerson, *No Man's Land,* p. 285.

Chapter 7

Looking for Someone to Blame

1. Robert J. Samuelson, "Great Expectations," *Newsweek,* January 8, 1996, p. 24; Simon Head, "The New Ruthless Economy," *New York Review of Books,* February 29, 1996, p. 47; Robert J. Samuelson, *The Good Life and Its Discontents: The American Dream in the Age of Entitlement, 1945–1995* (New York: Times Books, 1996).

2. Steven Pearlstein, "Warming But Still Cool: The Nation's Expanding Economy Has Steam Left—and Few Signs of Danger," *Washington Post National Weekly Edition*, December 12–18, 1994, p. 6; Alvin Toffler and Heidi Toffler, *Creating a New Civilization: The Politics of the Third Wave* (Atlanta: Turner Publishing, 1995).

3. Edward N. Luttwak, "Our Anxious Economy: Turbo-capitalism Has a Downside That Seems to Escape Many of the 'Experts,'" *Washington Post National Weekly Edition*, April 8–14, 1996, p. 21; Bill Gates, *The Road Ahead* (New York: Viking, 1995); Bill Gates, "Perspectives," in David Sanger and Steve Lohr, "The Downsizing of America," *New York Times*, March 9, 1996, p. 10.

4. Samuelson, "Great Expectations," p. 32; William Safire, "Thrift Is Back!" *New York Times*, April 15, 1996, p. A15; Michael Elliott, *The Day Before Yesterday: Reconsidering America's Past, Rediscovering the Present* (New York: Simon and Schuster, 1996).

5. George Will, "Success of a Nation Leads to Boredom," *Olympian*, March 1, 1996, p. A13.

6. Louis Uchitelle and N. R. Kleinfield, "On the Battlefields of Business, Millions of Casualties: the Downsizing of America," *New York Times*, March 3, 1996, p. 14Y; Daniel Burstein and David Kline, *Road Warriors: Dreams and Nightmares Along the Information Highway* (New York: Dutton, 1995).

7. Lester Thurow, "Companies Merge; Families Break Up," *New York Times*, September 3, 1995, p. 11.

8. Robert Kuttner, "The Incredible Shrinking American Paycheck: The One Thing That Hits Home for Most Voters Is Getting Short Shrift from Politicians," *Washington Post National Weekly Edition*, November 6–12, 1995, p. 23; Sheldon Danziger and Peter Gottschalk, *America Unequal* (Cambridge, Mass.: Harvard University Press, 1995), pp. 4–5, 10.

9. Danziger and Gottschalk, *America Unequal*, p. 2.

10. Robert Kuttner, "The Fruits of Our Labor," *Washington Post National Weekly Edition*, September 11–17, 1995, p. 5; Lorrine Thompson, "No End in Sight," *Olympian*, February 19, 1995, p. C3.

11. *Economic Report of the President Together with the Annual Report of the Council of Economic Advisors* (Washington, D.C.: U.S. Government Printing Office, 1994), p. 320; David Gordon, *Fat and Mean: The Corporate Squeeze of Working America and the Myth of Managerial "Downsizing"* (New York: Martin Kessler Books/The Free Press, 1996).

12. Andrew Sum, Neal Fogg, and Robert Taggert, "The Economics of Despair," *American Prospect* 27 (1996), pp. 83–84.

13. Uchitelle and Kleinfield, "On the Battlefields of Business, Millions of Casualties," p. 1.

14. Lance Morrow, "The Temping of America," *Time*, March 29, 1993, pp. 40–41; Janice Castro, "Disposable Workers," *Time*, March 29, 1993, pp. 43–47.

15. Lester Thurow, "Why Their World Might Crumble," *New York Times*, November 19, 1995, p. 78.

16. Robert Kuttner, "Capital Economics: Tipping the Income Scale," *Washington Post National Weekly Edition*, July 1–7, 1996, p. 5; Edward N. Wolff, "How the Pie Is Sliced: America's Growing Concentration of Wealth," *American Prospect* 22 (1995),

p. 58; Edward N. Wolfe, *Top Heavy: A Study of the Increasing Inequality of Wealth in America* (New York: The Twentieth Century Fund, 1996); Lawrence Mishel and Jared Bernstein, for the Economic Policy Institute, *The State of Working America, 1994–95* (Armonk, N.Y.: M. E. Sharpe, 1994), p. 244; National Center on Hunger, Poverty, and Nutrition Policy, *Statement on Key Welfare Reform Issues: The Empirical Evidence* (Medford, Mass.: Tufts University, 1995), p. 15.

17. Danziger and Gottschalk, *America Unequal,* p. 12; Greg Duncan, Timothy Smeeding, and Willard Rodgers, "W(h)ither the Middle Class? A Dynamic View" and Rebecca Blank, "Why Were Poverty Rates So High in the 1980s?" in Dimitri Papadimitriou and Edward Wolff, eds., *Poverty and Prosperity in the USA in the Late Twentieth Century* (New York: St. Martin's Press, 1993).

18. Steven Holmes, "Income Disparity Between Poorest and Richest Rises: Trend in U.S. Confirmed: New Report by Census Bureau Shows Gap Is at Its Widest Since World War II," *New York Times,* June 20, 1996, p. A1; *Olympian,* August 28, 1992, p. A3, and October 30, 1992, p. B7; Kevin Phillips, *Boiling Point: Democrats, Republicans and the Decline of Middle-Class Prosperity* (New York: Random House, 1993); Wolff, "How the Pie Is Sliced," p. 60; Keith Bradsher, "Gap in Wealth in U.S. Called Widest in West," *New York Times,* April 17, 1995, pp. A1, C4; On the "U-turn," see Lynn Karoly, "The Trend in Inequality Among Families, Individuals, and Workers in the United States: A Twenty-Five Year Perspective," in Sheldon Danziger and Peter Gottschalk, eds., *Uneven Tides: Rising Inequality in America* (New York: Russell Sage, 1993), p. 37; and "U.S. Social-Health Index Dips, Scientists Report," *New York Times,* October 15, 1995, p. 12. On the reaction of anger and loss of trust, see Kathryn Marie Dudley, *The End of the Line: Lost Jobs, New Lives in Postindustrial America* (Chicago: University of Chicago Press, 1994).

19. Thurow, "Why Their World Might Crumble," p. 78.

20. Edward Luttwak, "Will Success Spoil America? Why the Pols Don't Get Our Real Crisis of Values," *Washington Post,* November 27, 1994.

21. Ann Crouter and Beth Manke, "The Changing American Workplace: Implications for Individuals and Families," *Family Relations* 43 (1994), p. 119; Maxine Baca Zinn and D. Stanley Eitzen, *Diversity in Families* (New York: HarperCollins, 1989), p. 338; Richard Gelles, *Contemporary Families: A Sociological View* (Thousand Oaks, Calif.: Sage, 1995), p. 397; Sheila Zimmerman, "Family Trends: What Implications for Family Policy?" *Family Relations* 41 (1992), p. 425.

22. Robert Putnam, "The Strange Disappearance of Civic America," *American Prospect* (Winter 1996); Michael Shudson, "What If Civic Life Didn't Die?" *American Prospect* (March–April, 1996); Paul Taylor, "It Wasn't Supposed to Be Like This," *Washington Post National Weekly Edition,* February 19–25, 1996, p. 9.

23. Alan Macfarlane, *Witchcraft in Tudor and Stuart England* (New York: Harper and Row, 1970).

24. David Grissmer, Sheila Nataraj Kirby, Mark Berends, and Stephanie Williamson, *Student Achievement and the Changing American Family* (Santa Monica, Calif.: Rand Institute on Education and Training, 1994), p. 22.

25. Randy Albeda and Nancy Folbre, *The War Against the Poor: A Defense Manual* (New York: The New Press, 1996), p. 107; Jason De Parle, "Sharp Increase Along the Border of Poverty," *New York Times,* March 31, 1994.

26. Richard Morin, "Fed Up with Welfare," *Washington Post National Weekly Edition*, April 29–May 5, 1996, p. 37; James Fallows, *Breaking the News: How the Media Undermine American Democracy* (New York: Pantheon, 1996).

27. Robert Frank and Philip Cook, *The Winner-Take-All Society: How More and More Americans Compete for Ever Fewer and Bigger Prizes, Encouraging Economic Waste, Income Inequality, and an Impoverished Cultural Life* (New York: Free Press, 1995).

28. Robert Pear, "Poor in U.S. Grew Faster Than Population Last Year," *New York Times*, October 5, 1993, p. A10; Robert Naylor, "U.S. Moving Toward Two-Tiered Labor Market," *Hawaii Tribune-Herald*, June 17, 1994, p. 11.

29. Gordon Lafer, "The Politics of Job Training: Urban Poverty and the False Promise of JTPA," *Politics and Society* 22 (1994); Katherine Newman and Chauncy Lennon, "The Job Ghetto," *American Prospect* 22 (1995), pp. 66–67; Lawrence Mishel and John Schmitt, "Cutting Wages by Cutting Welfare," *Economic Policy Institute Briefing Paper*, September 1995.

30. *Welfare Reform: A Twentieth Century Fund Guide to the Issues* (New York: The Twentieth Century Fund, 1995), p. 13.

31. James Donahue, "The Corporate Welfare Kings," *Washington Post National Weekly Edition*, March 21–27, 1994, p. 24; James Donahue, *Aid for Dependent Corporations* (Washington, D.C.: Essential Information, 1994); Karen Tumulty, "Why Subsidies Survive," *Time*, March 25, 1996, p. 46; Laura Ginsburg, ed., *Public Employees: Facts at a Glance* (Washington, D.C.: AFL-CIO, 1995), p. 11. These estimates were confirmed by phone calls to the Office of Management and the Budget and the Joint Committee on Taxation.

32. Peter Gottschalk and Timothy Smeeding, *Cross-National Comparisons of Levels and Trends in Inequality*, Luxembourg Income Study, Working Paper 126, July 1995; Lee Rainwater and Timothy M. Smeeding, *Doing Poorly: The Real Income of American Children in a Comparative Perspective*, Luxembourg Income Study, Working Paper No. 128, August 1995; Anthony Atkinson, Lee Rainwater, and Timothy Smeeding, *Income Distribution in Advanced Economies: Evidence from the Luxembourg Income Study*, Luxembourg Income Study, Working Paper No. 130, October 1995; Aaron Bernstein, "Why the Gap Isn't So Giant in Europe and Japan," *Business Week*, August 14, 1994, pp. 82–83.

33. Todd Schafer, "Public Investment: Budgeting the Old-Fashioned Way," in Todd Schafer and Jeff Faux, eds., for the Economic Policy Institute, *Reclaiming Prosperity: A Blueprint for Progressive Economic Reform* (Armonk, N.Y.: M. E. Sharpe, 1996).

34. Ramon McLeod, "White Women, Young Minorities Make Pay Gains," *San Francisco Chronicle*, September 6, 1993; Frank Swoboda, "The Shifting American Work Force," *Washington Post National Weekly Edition*, August 8–14, 1994, p. 37; Thomas Edsall, "The U.S. Male, Caught in a Cultural Shift," *Washington Post National Weekly Edition*, May 8–14, 1995, p. 25.

35. Maureen Steinbruner and James Medoff, *Jobs and the Gender Gap: The Impact of Structural Change on Worker Pay, 1984–1993* (Washington, D.C.: Center for National Policy, May 1994).

36. Steven Pearlstein and DeNeen Brown, "More Than the Invisible Hand of the Market Is at Work Here," *Washington Post National Weekly Edition*, June 13–19,

1994; D. Stanley Eitzen and Maxine Baca Zinn, *The Reshaping of America: Social Consequences of the Changing Economy* (Englewood Cliffs, N.J.: Prentice-Hall, 1989), pp. 174–175. William Julius Wilson, "When Work Disappears," *New York Times Magazine*, August 18, 1996; For more on stereotypes about black families, see chapter 10 of Coontz, *The Way We Never Were.*

37. Mike Males, *The Scapegoat Generation: America's War on Adolescents* (Monroe, Me.: Common Courage Press), pp. 161, 175; Ron Harris, "Blacks Feel Brunt of Drug War," *Los Angeles Times*, April 22, 1990; Sam Meddis, "Is the Drug War Racist? Disparities Suggest the Answer Is Yes," *USA Today*, July 23–25, 1993.

38. Holly Sklar, *Chaos or Community? Seeking Solutions, Not Scapegoats, for Bad Economics* (Boston: South End Press, 1995), p. 8; Ronald Yates, "Adding Up Arguments on CEO Pay," *Chicago Tribune*, March 3, 1996; Allan Sloan, "The Hit Men," *Newsweek*, February 26, 1996; Louis Uchitelle, "1995 Was Good for Companies, and Better for a Lot of C.E.O.'s," *New York Times*, March 29, 1996.

39. Bennett Harrison, *Lean and Mean: The Changing Landscape of Corporate Power in the Age of Flexibility* (New York: Basic Books, 1995); E. J. Dionne, Jr., "Pinkos for Pat?" *Washington Post National Weekly Edition*, March 4–10, 1996, p. 28; Keith Bradsher, "Skilled Workers Watch Their Jobs Migrate Overseas," *New York Times*, August 29, 1995; Alan Downs, "The Wages of Downsizing," *Mother Jones* (July/August 1996), pp. 28–29.

40. David Howell, "The Skills Myth," *American Prospect* (Summer 1994), pp. 84, 87–90; Aaron Bernstein, "Inequality," *Business Week*, August 15, 1994, p. 81; Barry Bluestone, "The Inequality Express," *American Prospect* (Winter 1995), pp. 84–85.

41. Steven Pearlstein, "No More Mr. Nice Guy: Corporate America Has Done an About-Face in How It Pays and Treats Employees," *Washington Post National Weekly Edition*, December 18–24, 1995, p. 10; Kuttner, "Capital Economics," p. 5; Steven Pearlstein, "The Winners Are Taking All: In the New Economy, More and More of Us Qualify as 'Losers,'" *Washington Post National Weekly Edition*, December 11–17, 1995, p. 6; Richard Barnet, "Lords of the Global Economy," *The Nation*, December 19, 1994, p. 754.

42. Paul Taylor, "It Wasn't Supposed to Be Like This: In Levittown, Families Share a National Loss of Trust in Government—and Each Other," *Washington Post National Weekly Edition*, February 19–25, 1996, p. 8.

43. Frank and Cook, *The Winner-Take-All Society;* Michael J. Sandel, *Democracy's Discontent: America in Search of a Public Philosophy* (Cambridge: Belknap Press, 1966); Edward Herman, *Triumph of the Market: Essays on Economics, Politics, and the Media* (Boston: South End Press, 1995).

44. Mead, quoted in George Will, "Stable Families Key to Stable Children," *Olympian*, September 27, 1991; David Blankenhorn, *Fatherless America: Confronting Our Most Urgent Social Problem* (New York: Basic Books, 1995), p. 2; Progressive Policy Institute, *Mandate for Change* (Washington, D.C.: PPI, 1992), p. 157.

45. Coontz, *The Way We Never Were*, pp. 258–270; *Washington Post*, January 17, 1992, p. 14; Gary Gowen, Laura Desimore, and Jennifer McKay, "Poverty and the Single Mother Family: A Macroeconomic Perspective," *Marriage and Family Review* 20 (1995).

46. Sklar, *Chaos or Community?* p. 91.

47. "Key Study on Divorce Debunked," *Olympian*, May 17, 1996; *New York Times*, May 9, 1996, p. A9; Daniel Meyer and Judi Bartfeld, "Compliance with Child Support Orders in Divorce Cases," *Journal of Marriage and the Family* 58 (1996), p. 201.

48. *New York Times*, January 15, 1993, p. A6; Don Burroughs, "Love and Money," *U.S. News & World Report*, October 19, 1992, p. 58; John Billy and David Moore, "A Multilevel Analysis of Marital and Nonmarital Fertility in the U.S.," *Social Forces* 70 (1992), pp. 977–1011; Sara McLanahan and Irwin Garfinkel, "Welfare Is No Incentive," *New York Times*, July 29, 1994, p. A13; *New York Times*, January 15, 1993, p. A6; Elaine McCrate, "Expectations of Adult Wages and Teenage Childbearing," *International Review of Applied Economics* 6 (1992); Ellen Coughlin, "Policy Researchers Shift the Terms of the Debate on Women's Issues," *Chronicle of Higher Education*, May 31, 1989; Marian Wright Edelman, *Families in Peril: An Agenda for Social Change* (Cambridge, Mass.: Harvard University Press, 1987), p. 55; Lawrence Lynn and Michael McGeary, eds., *Inner-City Poverty in the United States* (Washington, D.C.: National Academy Press, 1990), pp. 163–167; Jonathan Crane, "The Epidemic Theory of Ghetto and Neighborhood Effects on Dropping Out and Teenaged Childbearing," *American Journal of Sociology* 96 (1991), pp. 1226–1259; Sara McLanahan and Lynne Casper, "Growing Diversity and Inequality in the American Family," in Reynolds Farley, ed., *State of the Union*, vol. 2 (New York: Russell Sage, 1995), pp. 10–11; Mike Males, "Poverty, Rape, Adult/Teen Sex: Why 'Pregnancy Prevention' Programs Don't Work," *Phi Delta Kappan* (January 1994), p. 409; Mike Males, "In Defense of Teenaged Mothers," *The Progressive* (August 1994), p. 23.

49. Males, *The Scapegoat Generation*, pp. 11, 61.

50. Ramon McLeod, "Why More Families Are Without a Father," *San Francisco Chronicle*, April 24, 1995.

51. Bernstein, "Inequality"; Sam Roberts, *Who We Are: A Portrait of America Based on the Latest U.S. Census* (New York: Times Books, 1995), p. 168; Judith Chafel, ed., *Child Poverty and Public Policy* (Washington, D.C.: Urban Institute Press, 1993), pp. 96–97; *Money Income of Households, Families, and Persons in the United States: 1992*, U.S. Bureau of the Census, Current Population Reports, Consumer Income, Series P–60, no. 184 (Washington, D.C.: U.S. Government Printing Office, September 1993); *Kids Count* (Baltimore: The Annie E. Casey Foundation, 1995), pp. 5–6.

52. Donald Hernandez, *America's Children: Resources from Family, Government and the Economy* (New York: Russell Sage, 1993), pp. 325, 311–312; Michael Katz, *The Undeserving Poor: From the War on Poverty to the War on Welfare* (New York: Pantheon Books, 1989), p. 213; Christopher Jencks, *Rethinking Social Policy: Race, Poverty, and the Underclass* (Cambridge, Mass.: Harvard University Press, 1994); Greg Duncan and Willard Rodgers, "Longitudinal Aspects of Childhood Poverty," *Journal of Marriage and the Family* 50 (November 1988), p. 1012; "Black Families Headed by Single Mothers," *Social Work* 33 (July–August 1988), p. 310; "Still Far from the Dream: Recent Developments in Black Income, Employment and Poverty," (Washington, D.C.: Center on Budget and Policy Priorities, October 1988), p. 12; Mary Jo Bane, "Household Composition and Poverty," in Sheldon Danziger and Daniel Weinberg, eds., *Fighting Poverty: What Works and What Doesn't* (Cambridge, Mass.: Harvard University Press, 1986), pp. 214–216; *Chicago Tribune*, March 2, 1991, p. 9; Pear, "Poverty in

U.S. Grew Faster Than Population Last Year," p. A10; Hayward Horton, Melvin Thomas, and Cedric Herring, "Rural–Urban Differences in Black Family Structure: An Analysis of the 1990 Census," *Journal of Family Issues* 16 (1995), pp. 298–313; Grissmer et al., *Student Achievement*.

53. "Statement on Key Welfare Reform Issues," p. 20, and foreword (no page number); Daniel T. Lichter and David J. Eggebeen, "The Effect of Parental Employment on Child Poverty," *Journal of Marriage and the Family* 56 (August 1994), p. 637; Steven Holmes, "Children of Working Poor Up Sharply, Study Says," *New York Times,* June 4, 1996, p. C19.

54. Hernandez, *America's Children,* pp. 290, 325, 311–312.

Chapter 8

How Ignoring Historical and Societal Change Puts Kids at Risk

1. Nancy Folbre, *Who Pays for the Kids? Gender and the Structures of Constraint* (New York: Routledge, 1994), pp. 112–119; James Coleman, "The Rational Reconstruction of Society," *American Sociological Review* 58 (1993), p. 12.

2. John Coatsworth, "Presidential Address," *American Historical Review* 101 (1996), p. 9; P. Lindsay Chase-Lansdale and Maris A. Vinovskis, "Whose Responsibility? An Historical Analysis of the Changing Roles of Mothers, Fathers, and Society," in P. Lindsay Chase-Lansdale and J. Brooks-Gunn, eds., *Escape from Poverty: What Makes a Difference for Children?* (New York: Cambridge University Press, 1995); Linda Gordon, *Heroes of Their Own Lives: The Politics and History of Family Violence, Boston 1880–1960* (New York: Viking, 1988), p. 42.

3. Michael Katz, *Improving Poor People: The Welfare State, the "Underclass," and Urban Schools as History* (Princeton, N.J.: Princeton University Press, 1995); Gordon, *Heroes of Their Own Lives,* p. 42; Brian Gratton and Frances Rotundo, "Industrialization, the Family Economy, and the Economic Status of the American Elderly," *Social Science History* 15 (1991), p. 356; Walter Trattner, *From Poor Law to Welfare State: A History of Social Welfare in America* (New York: Free Press, 1984); Seth Koven and Sonya Michel, eds., *Mothers of a New World: Maternalist Politics and the Origins of Welfare States* (New York: Routledge, 1993); Gwendolyn Mink, *The Wages of Motherhood: Inequality in the Welfare State, 1917–1942* (Ithaca, N.Y.: Cornell University Press, 1995); Julius B. Richmond, "The Hull House Era: Vintage Years for Children," *American Journal of Orthopsychiatry* 65 (1995).

4. Judith Bruce, Cynthia Lloyd, and Ann Leonard, with Patrice Engle and Niev Duffy, *Families in Focus: New Perspectives on Mothers, Fathers, and Children* (New York: The Population Council, 1995), p. 14; Geoffrey Holtz, *Welcome to the Jungle: The Why Behind "Generation X"* (New York: St. Martin's Press, 1995), p. 50; Mike Males, *The Scapegoat Generation: America's War on Adolescents* (Monroe, Me.: Common Courage Press, 1996), p. 10; Sylvia Hewlett, *When the Bough Breaks: The Costs of Neglecting Our Children* (New York: Basic Books, 1991), p. 211; Lynn Curtis, *The State of Families* (Milwaukee, Wisc.: Family Service America, 1995), p. 25; *Welfare Myths: Fact or Fiction? Exploring the Truth About Welfare* (New York: Center on Social Welfare Policy and Law, 1996), p. 36; Steven Rendall, Jim Naurekas, and Jeff

Cohen, *The Way Things Aren't: Rush Limbaugh's Reign of Error* (New York: The New Press, 1995), p. 25.

5. Hewlett, *When the Bough Breaks*, p. 211; Iris Marion Young, "Reply to Jean Elshtain and Margaret Steinfels," *Dissent* (Spring 1994), p. 272; Joan Smith, "Transforming Households: Working-Class Women and Economic Crisis," *Social Problems* 34 (1987), p. 436.

6. *Olympian*, December 13, 1989, p. A8; Betsy Wagner and Stephen Hedges, "Education in Decay," *U.S. News & World Report*, September 12, 1994, p. 79; Joseph Altonji and Thomas Dunn, "Using Siblings to Estimate the Effect of School Quality on Wages," *Center for Urban Affairs and Policy Research Working Paper 96–10* (Evanston, Ill.: Northwestern University, 1996); Shazia Rufiullah Miller and James Rosenbaum, "The Missing Link: Social Infrastructure and Employers' Use of Information," *Center for Urban Affairs and Policy Research Working Paper 96–15* (Evanston, Ill.: Northwestern University, 1996).

7. Jonathon Kozol, *Savage Inequalities: Children in America's Schools* (New York: Crown, 1991), p. 237; "Hard Data," *Washington Post National Weekly Edition*, September 28–October 4, 1992, p. 37.

8. David Whitman, "The Forgotten Half," *U.S. News & World Report*, June 26, 1989; Randy Abelda, Nancy Folbre, and the Center for Popular Economies, *The War Against the Poor: A Defense Manual* (New York: The New Press, 1996), p. 68; Peter Applebome, "U.S. Gets 'Average' Grade in Math and Science Studies," *New York Times*, November 21, 1996.

9. Jason De Parle, "Slamming the Door," *New York Times*, October 20, 1996, p. 52.

10. Folbre, *Who Pays for the Kids?* pp. 112–119, 208–210.

11. Bruce et al., *Families in Focus*, p. 14; Folbre, *Who Pays for the Kids?;* Holly Sklar, *Chaos or Community? Seeking Solutions, Not Scapegoats for Bad Economics* (Boston: South End Press, 1995), p. 145.

12. Folbre, *Who Pays for the Kids?*; Pamela Smock, "Gender and the Short-Run Economic Consequences of Marital Disruption," *Social Forces* 73 (1994), p. 259; Joan Acker, "Class, Gender, and the Relations of Distribution," *Signs* 13 (1988), p. 496.

13. For an insightful analysis of the class, cultural, and sexual tensions behind the Spur Posse story, see Joan Didion, "Trouble in Lakewood," *The New Yorker*, July 26, 1993.

14. Vonnie McCloyd, "The Impact of Economic Hardship on Black Families and Children: Psychological Distress, Parenting, and Socioemotional Development," *Child Development* 61 (1990), pp. 324–325; Richard Gelles, "Through a Sociological Lens: Social Structure and Family Violence," in Richard Gelles and Donileen Loseke, eds., *Current Controversies on Family Violence* (Newbury Park, Calif.: Sage, 1993), p. 33; Ralph Catalano et al., "Using ECA Data to Examine the Effect of Job Layoffs on Violent Behavior," *Hospital and Community Psychiatry* 44 (1993), pp. 874, 878; Rand D. Conger, Xiaojia Ge, Glen H. Elder, Jr., Frederick O. Lorenz, and Ronald L. Simons, "Economic Stress, Coercive Family Process, and Developmental Problems of Adolescents," *Child Development* 65 (1994).

15. Robert Solow, *Wasting America's Future* (Boston: Beacon Press, 1994), pp. 30–32; Gene H. Brody, Zolinda Stoneman, and Douglas Flor, "Linking Family

Process and Academic Competence Among Rural African American Youths," *Journal of Marriage and the Family* 57 (1995), p. 567; Ralph Catalano, "The Health Effects of Economic Insecurity," *American Journal of Public Health* 81 (1991), p. 1149; Conger et al., "Economic Stress, Coercive Family Process"; McLoyd, "Impact of Economic Hardship," pp. 330–331; P. Lindsay Chase-Lansdale and Jeanne Brooks-Gunn, "Introduction," in Chase-Lansdale and Brooks-Gunn, eds., *Escape from Poverty*, p. 3; Gerald Patterson, John Reid, and Thomas Dishion, *Antisocial Boys* (Eugene, Ore.: Castalia, 1992); Craig Mason, Ana Mari Cauce, Nancy Gonzales, Yumi Hiraga, and Kwai Grove, "An Ecological Model of Externalizing Behaviors in African-American Adolescents: No Family Is an Island," *Journal of Research on Adolescence* 4, no. 4 (1994), p. 651; Rand D. Conger and Glen H. Elder, Jr., in collaboration with Frederick O. Lorenz, Ronald L. Simons, and Les B. Whitbeck, *Families in Troubled Times: Adapting to Change in Rural America* (New York: Aldine de Gruyter, 1994), pp. 219–220.

16. McLoyd, "Impact of Economic Hardship," p. 324; Vonnie McLoyd and Constance Flanagan, eds., *Economic Stress: Effects on Family Life and Child Development* (San Francisco: Jossey-Bass, 1991).

17. Conger and Elder et al., *Families in Troubled Times*, p. 261; Constance Flanagan, "Families and Schools in Hard Times," and Rainier Silberstein, Sabine Walper, and Helfried Albrecht, "Family Income Loss and Economic Hardship: Antecedents of Adolescents' Problem Behavior," in McLoyd and Flanagan, eds., *Economic Stress*.

18. Flanagan, "Families and Schools in Hard Times," p. 19; McLoyd, "Impact of Economic Hardship," p. 319; Jeffrey K. Liker and Glen H. Elder, Jr., "Economic Hardship and Marital Relations in the 1930s," *American Sociological Review* 48 (June 1983), p. 356.

19. McLoyd, "Impact of Economic Hardship," pp. 330, 336; Ann Crouter and Beth Manke, "The Changing American Workplace: Implications for Individuals and Families," *Family Relations* 43 (1994), p. 119; Liker and Elder, "Economic Hardship and Marital Relations in the 1930s," p. 343; Conger and Elder et al., *Families in Troubled Times*, pp. 219–221.

20. Conger and Elder et al., *Families in Troubled Times*, p. 259.

21. Rector quoted in *Washington Post National Weekly Edition*, September 11–17, 1995, p. 8.

22. Perri Klass, "Tackling Problems We Thought We Solved," *New York Times Magazine*, December 13, 1992, p. 62; Robert A. Hahn, Elaine Eaker, Nancy D. Barker, Steven M. Teutsch, Waldemar Sosniak, and Nancy Krieger, "Poverty and Death in the United States—1973 and 1991," *Epidemiology* 6 (1995), p. 490. My thanks to Carole Oshinsky of the New York-based National Center for Children in Poverty for supplying additional references and fact sheets.

23. "Tough Lead-Paint Rule Issued," *Olympian*, March 7, 1996, p. A4; Geoffrey Cowley, "Children in Peril," *Newsweek Special Issue*, Summer 1991, p. 20; James Sargent, Mary Jean Brown, Jean Freeman, Adrian Bailey, David Goodman, and Daniel H. Freeman, Jr., "Childhood Lead Poisoning in Massachusetts Communities: Its Association with Sociodemographic and Housing Characteristics," *American Journal of Public Health* 85 (1995), p. 531; Jane Brody, "Aggressiveness and Delinquency in Boys Is Linked to Lead in Bones," *New York Times*, February 7, 1996, p. B6.

24. Harold Hodgkinson, "Reform Versus Reality," *Phi Delta Kappan*, Septem-

ber 1991, p. 14; Herbert Needleman, "Childhood Exposure to Lead: A Common Cause of School Failure," *Phi Delta Kappan,* September 1992, p. 36; Brody, "Aggressiveness Linked to Lead."

25. Rector quoted in Albeda and Folbre, *The War Against the Poor,* p. 34. See also Solow, *Wasting America's Future,* p. 15; J. Larry Brown and Ernesto Pollitt, "Malnutrition, Poverty and Intellectual Development," *Scientific American,* February 1996, p. 38; Rendall, Naurekas, and Cohen, *The Way Things Aren't,* p. 22; Jane E. Miller and Sanders Korenman, "Poverty and Children's Nutritional Status in the United States," *American Journal of Epidemiology* 140 (1994), p. 233. Estimates of the prevalence of hunger are currently being revised, with researchers beginning to talk about "food insecurity" rather than hunger and malnutrition alone. The Food Security Study, directed by Dr. John T. Cook, should be available in 1997. For further information, contact the Center on Hunger, Poverty and Nutrition Policy, Tufts University, Medford, Massachusetts 02155. The George Will quote appeared in Will, "Soft Voice in a Deadly Crisis," *Washington Post,* June 19, 1994.

26. Solow, *Wasting America's Future,* pp. 29–36, 88; Mason et al., "An Ecological Model of Externalizing Behaviors in African-American Adolescents"; Robert Sampson and John Laub, "Urban Poverty and the Family Context of Delinquency: A New Look at Structure and Process in a Classic Study," *Child Development* 65 (1994); Males, *The Scapegoat Generation,* p. 109.

27. Katherine Brown Rosier and William A. Corsaro, "Competent Parents, Complex Lives: Managing Parenthood in Poverty," *Journal of Contemporary Ethnography* 22 (1993); Patricia Garrett, Nicholas Ng'andu, and John Ferron, "Poverty Experiences of Young Children and the Quality of Their Home Environments," *Child Development* 65 (1994); Bonnie Leadbeater and Sandra Bishop, "Predictors of Behavior Problems in Preschool Children of Inner-City Afro-American and Puerto Rican Adolescent Mothers," *Child Development* 65 (1994).

28. Michael Katz, ed., *The "Underclass" Debate: Views from History* (Princeton, N.J.: Princeton University Press, 1993); Douglas Massey and Nancy Denton, *American Apartheid: Segregation and the Making of the Underclass* (Cambridge, Mass.: Harvard University Press, 1993).

29. Katz, *The "Underclass" Debate*; James Gabarino and Kathleen Kostelny, "Neighborhood and Community Influences on Parenting," in Tom Luster and Lynn Okagaki, eds., *Parenting: An Ecological Perspective* (Hillsdale, N.J.: Lawrence Erlbaum, 1993), p. 205.

30. Jane McLeod and Michael Shanahan, "Poverty, Parenting, and Children's Mental Health," *American Sociological Review* 58 (1993), p. 351; Spencer Rich, "Study: Poverty in First 5 Years Lowers Kids' IQs," *Morning News Tribune,* March 28, 1993; Greg J. Duncan et al., "Economic Deprivation and Early-Childhood Development," *Child Development* 65 (1994), pp. 296–318; McLoyd "Impact of Economic Hardship," p. 318; Gabarino and Kostelny, "Neighborhood and Community Influences on Parenting," p. 205.

31. Solow, *Wasting America's Future,* pp. 82, 90; Greg J. Duncan, Jeanne Brooks-Gunn, and Pamela Kato Klebanov, "Economic Deprivation and Early Childhood Development," *Child Development* 65 (1994), p. 296; Pamela Kato Klebanov, Jeanne Brooks-Gunn, and Greg J. Duncan, "Does Neighborhood and Family Poverty Affect

Mothers' Parenting, Mental Health, and Social Support?" *Journal of Marriage and the Family* 56 (May 1994), p. 441; Sanders Korenman, Jane Miller, and John Sjaastad, "Long-Term Poverty and Child Development in the United States: Results from the NLSY" (National Longitudinal Study of Youth), *Children and Youth Services Review* 17 (1995); Carolyn Smith and Marvin Krohn, "Delinquency and Family Life Among Male Adolescents," *Journal of Youth and Adolescence* 24 (1995).

32. Albeda and Folbre, *War Against the Poor*, p. 27; James Garbarino, "The Meaning of Poverty in the World of Children," *American Behavioral Scientist* 35 (1992), p. 228; Solow, *Wasting America's Future*, p. 82.

33. Barbara Dafoe Whitehead, "Dan Quayle Was Right," *Atlantic Monthly*, April 1993, p. 77.

34. Solow, *Wasting America's Future*, pp. 82–91; Irving Spergel et al., *Gang Suppression and Intervention: Problem and Response* (Washington, D.C.: U.S. Department of Justice, 1994), p. 4; Martin Sanchez Jankowski, *Islands in the Street: Gangs and American Urban Society* (Berkeley: University of California, 1991), p. 39. For an insight into the socioeconomic and cultural context of gangs, see the disturbing memoir of gang life by Luis Rodriguez, *Always Running: La Vida Loca: Gang Days in L.A.* (New York: Simon and Schuster, 1993). Rodriguez came from a two-parent family that tried continually to escape the poverty of L.A.'s barrios and to provide an education for their kids. What turned Rodriguez around was not his family life but the sense of pride and social solidarity he began to feel when he was exposed to the Chicano power movement.

35. Marvin Free, Jr., "Clarifying the Relationship Between the Broken Home and Juvenile Delinquency: A Critique of the Current Literature," *Deviant Behavior: An Interdisciplinary Journal* 12 (1991), p. 130.

36. Melvin Oliver and Thomas Shapiro, *Black Wealth/White Wealth: A New Perspective on Racial Inequality* (New York: Routledge, 1995), p. 119; Korenman, Miller, and Sjaastad, "Long-Term Poverty," pp. 147–148; Greg Duncan, Wei-Jun Yeung, and Jeanne Brooks-Gunn, *Does Childhood Poverty Affect the Life Chances of Children?* Working Paper 96–2, Center for Urban Affairs and Policy Research, Northwestern University, April 24, 1996; Solow, *Wasting America's Future*, p. 91; Jeanne Brooks-Gunn, "Strategies for Altering the Outcomes of Poor Children and Their Families," in Chase-Lansdale and Brooks-Gunn, eds., *Escape from Poverty*, pp. 88–89.

37. Free, "Clarifying the Relationship Between the Broken Home and Juvenile Delinquency," pp. 144, 158.

38. Free, "Clarifying the Relationship Between the Broken Home and Juvenile Delinquency," p. 158; Sklar, *Chaos or Community?* pp. 128–129.

39. Sklar, *Chaos or Community?* p. 128; William Chambliss, "Policing the Ghetto Underclass: The Politics of Law and Law Enforcement," *Social Problems* 41 (1994).

40. Karole Kumpfer, *Strengthening America's Families: Promising Parenting Strategies for Delinquency Prevention* (Washington, D.C.: Office of Juvenile Justice and Delinquency Prevention, 1993), p. 9; Solow, *Wasting America's Future*, pp. 53–55; Robert Angel and Jacqueline Angel, *Painful Inheritance: Health and the New Generation of Fatherless Families* (Madison: University of Wisconsin Press, 1993), pp. 22, xix; Patricia Hashima and Paul Amato, "Poverty, Social Support, and Parental Behavior," *Child Development* 65 (1994), p. 400.

41. Sam Roberts, *Who We Are: A Portrait of America Based on the Latest U.S. Census* (New York: Times Books, 1995), p. 181; Reynolds Farley and Walter Allen, *The Color Line and the Quality of Life in America* (New York: Russell Sage, 1987); Maxine Baca Zinn, "Minority Families in Crisis: The Public Discussion" (Memphis, Tenn.: Center for Research on Women, 1985); "Still Far from the Dream: Recent Developments in Black Income, Employment and Poverty," Washington, D.C.: Center on Budget and Policy Priorities, October 1988; Phillip Bowman, "The Adolescent-to-Adult Transition: Discouragement Among Jobless Black Youth," in McLoyd and Flanagan, eds., *Economic Stress.*

42. George Will, "Powell's Candidacy in Question," *Olympian*, April 16, 1995, p. A9; John Mirowsky and Catherine E. Ross, *Social Causes of Psychological Distress* (New York: Aldine de Gruyter, 1989), p. 17.

43. To see the odds such children and their families face, even when they try their best, watch the documentary *Hoop Dreams*, or read Alex Kotlowitz, *There Are No Children Here: The Story of Two Boys Growing Up in the Other America* (New York: Doubleday, 1991).

44. For more on Marshall's work, see his book, *Street Soldier: One Man's Struggle to Save a Generation—One Life at a Time* (New York: Delacorte, 1996).

45. Jerome Skolnick, "What Not to Do About Crime," *Criminology* 33 (1995), p. 2; Geiss quoted in Mike Males and Faye Docuyanan, "Crack-down on Kids," *The Progressive*, February 1996, p. 24.

Chapter 9

Working with What We've Got

1. Laurence Steinberg, Nina Mounts, Susie Lamborn, and Sanford Dornbusch, "Authoritative Parenting Across Varied Ecological Niches," *Journal of Research on Adolescence* 1 (1991), p. 19. The classic work on parenting styles was done by Diana Baumrind. See, for example, "Child Care Practices Anteceding Three Patterns of Preschool Behavior," *Genetic Psychology Monographs* 75 (1967); "Current Patterns of Parental Authority," *Developmental Psychology Monographs* 4 (1971); "Parental Disciplinary Patterns and Social Competence in Children," *Youth and Society* 9 (1978).

2. Mary Elizabeth Curtner-Smith and Carol E. MacKinnon-Lewis, "Family Process Effects on Adolescent Males' Susceptibility to Antisocial Peer Pressure," *Family Relations* 43 (October 1994), pp. 462, 466; James Patrick Connell, Margaret Beale Spencer, and J. Lawrence Aber, "Educational Risk and Resilience in African-American Youth: Context, Self, Action, and Outcomes in School," *Child Development* 54 (1994), p. 504; Richard A. Mendel, *Prevention or Pork? A Hard-Headed Look at Youth-Oriented Anti-Crime Programs* (Washington, D.C.: American Youth Public Forum, 1995), pp. 4–5.

3. See Stephanie Coontz, *The Way We Never Were*, chapters 9 and 11. See also "Men Benefit More from Marriage," *Olympian*, October 12, 1993, p. D6; Betty Holcomb, "Why Is Everybody Picking on Working Moms?" *Working Mother*, January 1992, p. 49.

4. Arlie Hochschild with Anne Machung, *The Second Shift: Working Parents*

and the Revolution at Home (New York: Viking, 1989), pp. 211–212; Anita Shreve, *Remaking Motherhood: How Working Mothers Are Shaping Our Children's Future* (New York: Viking, 1987); Harriet Mischel and Robert Fuhr, "Maternal Employment: Its Psychological Effects on Children and Their Families," in Sanford Dornbusch and Myra Strober, eds., *Feminism, Children, and the New Families* (New York: Guilford, 1988).

5. Martha Moorehouse, "Work and Family Dynamics," in Philip Cowan, Carolyn Pape Cowan, and Patricia Kerig, eds., *Family, Self, and Society: Toward a New Agenda for Family Research* (Hillsdale, N.J.: Lawrence Erlbaum, 1993), p. 271.

6. James A. Levine with Edward W. Pitt, *New Expectations: Community Strategies for Responsible Fatherhood* (New York: Families and Work Institute, 1995), p. 35.

7. Doris R. Entwisle and Karl L. Alexander, "Family Type and Children's Growth in Reading and Math Over the Primary Grades," *Journal of Marriage and the Family* 58 (May 1996), p. 341 (emphasis added).

8. David K. Flaks, Ilda Fischer, Frank Masterpasqua, and Gregory Joseph, "Lesbians Choosing Motherhood: A Comparative Study of Lesbian and Heterosexual Parents and Their Children," *Developmental Psychology* 31 (1995), p. 105.

9. Julie Schwartz Gottman, "Children of Gay and Lesbian Parents," in Frederick W. Bozett and Marvin B. Sussman, eds., *Homosexuality and Family Relations* (New York: The Haworth Press, 1990).

10. John Laird and Robert-Jay Green, eds., *Lesbians and Gays in Couples and Families: A Handbook for Therapists* (San Francisco: Jossey-Bass, 1996); Adele Eskeles Gottfried and Allen W. Gottfried, eds., *Redefining Families: Implications for Children's Development* (New York: Plenum, 1994), p. 225; Flaks et al., "Lesbians Choosing Motherhood," pp. 105–113; Daniel Goleman, "Gay Parents Called No Disadvantage," *New York Times*, December 2, 1992, p. B7; Bianca Cody Murphy, "Difference and Diversity: Gay and Lesbian Couples" (New York: The Haworth Press, 1994); Charlotte Patterson, "Children of the Lesbian Baby Boom: Parents' Division of Labor and Children's Adjustment," *Developmental Psychology* 31 (1995).

11. Gottfried and Gottfried, eds., *Redefining Families*, p. 225; Flaks et al., "Lesbians Choosing Motherhood," p. 105; Esther Rothblum, ed., "Mental Health of Lesbians and Gay Men" (Special Issue), *Journal of Consulting and Clinical Psychology* 63 (1994); Patterson, "Children of the Lesbian Baby Boom," p. 115; Jan Hare and Leslie Richards, "Children Raised by Lesbian Couples: Does Context of Birth Affect Father and Partner Involvement?" *Family Relations* 42 (1993), p. 254.

12. J. Michael Bailey, David Bobrow, Marilyn Wolfe, and Sarah Mikach, "Sexual Orientation of Adult Sons of Gay Fathers," *Developmental Psychology* 31, no. 1 (1995), p. 124; Gottman, "Children of Gay and Lesbian Parents"; Laird and Green, *Lesbians and Gays in Couples and Families*. The Spur Posse father was quoted in the *New York Times*, March 29, 1993, p. A9.

13. Diana Baumrind, "Commentary on Sexual Orientation," *Developmental Psychology* 31 (1995), p. 125; Gottman, "Children of Gay and Lesbian Parents," p. 191; personal interview with Dr. Gottman.

14. Gottman, "Children of Gay and Lesbian Parents," p. 191; Gottfried and Gottfried, *Redefining Families*, p. 25; Arlene Skolnick, "The Family Revisited: Themes in Recent Social Science Research," *Journal of Interdisciplinary History* 4 (1975), p. 710; Jean

MacFarlane, "Perspectives on Personality Consistency and Change from the Guidance Study," *Vita Humana* 7 (1964), p. 123.

15. Carol Stack, *All Our Kin: Strategies for Survival in a Black Community* (New York: Harper and Row, 1974); Barbara Bilge and Gladis Kaufman, "Children of Divorce and One-Parent Families: Cross-Cultural Perspectives," *Family Relations* 32 (January 1983), p. 69.

16. Ronald L. Simons and Associates, *Understanding Differences Between Divorced and Intact Families: Stress, Interaction, and Child Outcome* (Thousand Oaks, Calif.: Sage, 1996), p. 16; Theodora Lurie, "Fathers and Families: Forging Ties That Bind," *USA Today Magazine*, May 19, 1993; Sandra Danziger and Norma Radin, "Absent Does Not Equal Uninvolved: Predictors of Fathering in Teen Mother Families," *Journal of Marriage and the Family* 52 (1990); James Levine, Dennis Murphy, and Sherrill Wilson, *Getting Men Involved: Strategies for Early Childhood Programs* (New York: Scholastic, 1993).

17. Simons and Associates, *Understanding Differences Between Divorced and Intact Families*, p. 224; Mary Tabor, "Comprehensive Study Finds Parents and Peers Are Most Crucial Influences on Students," *New York Times*, August 7, 1996, p. A12.

18. Sara S. McLanahan, Nan Marie Astone, and Nadine F. Marks, "The Role of Mother-Only Families in Reproducing Poverty," in A. Huston, ed., *Children and Poverty* (New York: Cambridge University Press, 1991), p. 58; Nan Marie Astone and Sara S. McLanahan, "Family Structure, Parental Practice and High School Completion," *American Sociological Review* 56 (June 1991), p. 318; Alan Acock and David Demo, *Family Diversity and Well-Being* (Thousand Oaks, Calif.: Sage, 1994), pp. 124–125; E. Mavis Hetherington, "Coping with Family Transitions: Winners, Losers, and Survivors," *Annual Progress in Child Psychiatry and Child Development* (New York: Brunner/Mazel, 1990), p. 228; Leslie N. Richards and Cynthia J. Schmlege, "Problems and Strengths of Single-Parent Families: Implications for Practice and Policy," *Family Relations* 42 (1993), p. 278; Sanford Dornbusch and Kathryn Gray, "Single-Parent Families," in Dornbusch and Strober, *Feminism, Children, and the New Families* (New York: Guilford, 1988), pp. 286–287, 292; Nancy Morrison, "Successful Single-Parent Families," *Journal of Divorce and Remarriage* 22 (1995).

19. Mukti Jan Campion, *Who's Fit to Be a Parent?* (New York: Routledge, 1995), p. 216.

20. David Demo and Alan Acock, "The Impact of Divorce on Children," in Alan Booth, ed., *Contemporary Families: Looking Forward, Looking Back* (Minneapolis: National Council on Family Relations, 1991), p. 170; B. Berg and R. Kelly, "The Measured Self-Esteem of Children from Broken, Rejected and Accepted Families," *Journal of Divorce* 2 (1979); Barbara Cashion, "Female-Headed Families: Effects on Children and Clinical Implications," *Journal of Marital and Family Therapy* 8, no. 2 (April 1982), p. 77; Lawrence H. Ganong, Marilyn Coleman, and Dennis Mapes, "A Meta-analytic Review of Family Structure Stereotypes," *Journal of Marriage and the Family* 52 (May 1990), p. 293; Blechman, "Children with One Parent," *Journal of Marriage and the Family* 44 (1982), pp. 186, 189; Joseph Guttmann, Nehemia Geva, and Sally Gefen, "Teachers' and School Children's Stereotypic Perception of 'the Child of Divorce,'" *American Educational Research Journal* 25 (1988); Sanford Dornbusch and Kathryn Gray, "Single-Parent Families," in Dornbusch and Strober,

Feminism, Children, and the New Families, pp. 286, 288; Krantz, "Children and Divorce," p. 255; Valerie Polakow, *Lives on the Edge: Single Mothers and Their Children in the Other America* (Chicago: University of Chicago Press, 1993); Doris R. Entwisle and Karl L. Alexander, "A Parent's Economic Shadow: Family Structure Versus Family Resources as Influences on Early School Achievement," *Journal of Marriage and the Family* 57 (May 1995), p. 399. Stigmatization, or anxiety about it, can also affect "objective" test scores. Dr. Claude Steele of Stanford University found that when blacks and whites are given a test and told it is to measure their abilities, most black students score below most whites. When a similar mix of students is told it's just a lab test, with no practical purpose, the difference between black and white scores is insignificant (Norman Lockman, "Bell Curve Sure to Draw Fire," *Olympian,* November 24, 1994).

21. Bette J. Dickerson, *African American Single Mothers: Understanding Their Lives and Families* (Thousand Oaks, Calif.: Sage, 1995); Sara McLanahan, "The Consequences of Single Motherhood," *American Prospect,* Summer 1994, p. 49; Frank Furstenberg, Jr., and Andrew Cherlin, *Divided Families: What Happens to Children When Parents Part* (Cambridge, Mass.: Harvard University Press, 1991), pp. 99, 103, 105; Janis Kupersmidt, Pamela Griesler, Melissa DeRossier, Charlotte Patterson, and Paul Davis, "Childhood Aggression and Peer Relations in the Context of Family and Neighborhood Factors," *Child Development* 66 (1995), pp. 369–370.

22. Diana Baumrind, "An Exploratory Study of Socialization Effects on Black Children: Some Black–White Comparisons," *Child Development* 43 (1972); John Lewis McAdoo, "A Black Perspective on the Father's Role in Child Development," *Marriage and Family Review* 9 (1986); George Knight, Lynn Virdin, and Mark Roosa, "Socialization and Family Correlate of Mental Health Outcomes Among Hispanic and Anglo Children: Consideration of Cross-Ethnic Scalar Equivalence," *Child Development* 65 (1994), pp. 220–221; Carl Husemoller Nightingale, *On the Edge: A History of Poor Black Children and Their American Dreams* (New York: Basic Books, 1993); Judith Blake, "Number of Siblings and Personality," *Family Planning Perspectives* 23 (1991), p. 272; Judith Blake, *Family Size and Achievement* (Los Angeles: University of California, 1989); D. B. Downey, "When Bigger Is Not Better: Family Size, Parental Resources, and Children's Educational Performance," *American Sociological Review* 60 (1995); Kathleen Harris and S. Philip Morgan, "Fathers, Sons, and Daughters: Differential Paternal Involvement in Parenting," *Journal of Marriage and the Family* 53 (1991).

23. E. Mavis Hetherington and W. Glenn Clingempeel, *Coping with Marital Transitions: A Family Systems Perspective* (Chicago: Monographs of the Society for Research in Child Development, Serial No. 227, vol. 57, 1992), pp. 3–4; Gottfried and Gottfried, *Redefining Families,* p. 106; Barbara J. Risman and Kyung Park, "Just the Two of Us: Parent–Child Relationships in Single-Parent Homes," *Journal of Marriage and the Family* 50 (November 1988), p. 1059; Leslie N. Richards and Cynthia J. Schmlege, "Problems and Strengths of Single-Parent Families: Implications for Practice and Policy," *Family Relations* 42 (1993), p. 282; Mary Elizabeth Curtner-Smith and Carol E. MacKinnon-Lewis, "Family Process Effects on Adolescent Males' Susceptibility to Antisocial Peer Pressure," *Family Relations* 43 (October 1994), p. 466; Christy Buchanan, Eleanor Maccoby, and Sanford Dornbusch, "Adolescents and Their Fam-

ilies After Divorce: Three Residential Arrangements Compared," *Journal of Research on Adolescence* 2 (1992), pp. 285–286.

24. For more on these dynamics, see Shoshana Alexander, *In Praise of Single Parents: Mothers and Fathers Embracing the Challenge* (Boston: Houghton Mifflin, 1994), esp. the chapter entitled, "When Our Children Are Our Friends: Love and Limits." On the need for parents to maintain discipline and monitoring after divorce, see Simons, *Understanding Differences Between Divorced and Intact Families,* p. 224.

25. Robert E. Emery and Michele Tuer, "Parenting and the Marital Relationship," *Parenting: An Ecological Perspective* (Hillsdale, N.J.: Lawrence Erlbaum, 1993), p. 128; Cowan et al., "Transitions to Parenthood: His, Hers, and Theirs," *Journal of Family Issues* 6 (1986); Philip A. Cowan and Carolyn Pape Cowan, "Changes in Marriage During the Transition to Parenthood: Must We Blame the Baby?" in G. Y. Michaels and W. A. Goldberg, eds., *The Transition to Parenthood: Current Theory and Research* (Cambridge: Cambridge University Press, 1988). Most of my evidence for the idea that financially secure single mothers may have an easier time in the first few months comes from stories I have been told at workshops around the country, and may therefore not be representative. Some written support for this impression is provided by Margaret Louise Fox, *Unmarried Adult Mothers: A Study of the Parenthood Transition from Late Pregnancy to Two Months Postpartum* (Boston University School of Education, Ann Arbor, Mich.: University Microfilms International, 1979).

26. Mel Hovell, Carol Sipan, Elaine Blumberg, Cathie Atkins, C. Richard Hofstetter, and Susan Kreitner, "Family Influences on Latino and Anglo Adolescents' Sexual Behavior," *Journal of Marriage and the Family* 56 (November 1994), p. 973.

27. Bonnie Strickland, "Research on Sexual Orientation and Human Development: A Commentary," *Developmental Psychology* 31 (1995), p. 139.

28. Barbara Dafoe Whitehead, "Dan Quayle Was Right," *Atlantic Monthly,* April 1993, p. 71; "School Dropout Rates for Families," *USA Today,* March 15, 1993; "Stepfamilies Aren't Bad for Most Kids," *USA Today,* August 17, 1992; Frank Mott, "The Impact of Father Absence from the Home on Subsequent Cognitive Development of Younger Children," Paper delivered at the American Sociological Association, August 1992; Furstenberg and Cherlin, *Divided Families,* p. 89; Andrew J. Cherlin and Frank F. Furstenberg, Jr., "Stepfamilies in the United States: A Reconsideration," *Annual Reviews in Sociology* 20 (1994), p. 372.

29. Kay Pasley and Marilyn Ihinger-Tallman, "Stress and the Remarried Family," *Family Perspectives* 12 (1982), p. 187.

30. James Bray and Sandra Berger, "Developmental Issues in Stepfamilies Research Project: Family Relationships and Parent–Child Interactions," *Journal of Family Psychology* 7, no. 1 (1993), p. 86; Hetherington and Clingempeel, *Coping with Marital Transitions,* pp. 205–206; William S. Aquilino, "The Life Course of Children Born to Unmarried Mothers: Childhood Living Arrangements and Young Adult Outcomes," *Journal of Marriage and the Family* 58 (May 1996), p. 307.

31. E. Mavis Hetherington, "An Overview of the Virginia Longitudinal Study of Divorce and Remarriage with a Focus on Early Adolescence," *Journal of Family Psychology* 7 (1993); Kay Pasley and Marilyn Ihinger-Tallman, *Remarriage and Stepparent-*

ing: Current Research and Theory (New York: Guilford, 1987), pp. 105–109; Bray and Berger, "Developmental Issues in Stepfamilies Research Project," p. 89.

32. Alan Booth and Judy Dunn, eds., *Stepfamilies: Who Benefits? Who Does Not?* (Hillsdale, N.J.: Lawrence Erlbaum, 1994); Virginia Rutter, "Lessons from Stepfamilies," *Psychology Today* (May/June 1994), p. 32.

33. Lawrence H. Ganong and Marilyn Coleman, *Remarried Family Relationships* (Thousand Oaks, Calif.: Sage, 1994), p. 122; Pasley and Ihinger-Tallman, *Remarriage and Stepparenting*, p. 108; Hetherington and Clingempeel, *Coping with Marital Transitions*, pp. 200–205.

34. Monica McGoldrick and Betty Carter, "Forming a Remarried Family," in McGoldrick and Carter, eds., *The Changing Family Life Cycle: A Framework for Family Therapy*, 3rd ed. (Boston: Allyn and Bacon, in press).

35. John Visher and Emily Visher, *Therapy with Stepfamilies* (New York: Brunner/Mazel, 1996); McGoldrick and Carter, "Forming a Remarried Family."

36. Demo and Acock, "Impact of Divorce on Children," pp. 201–202; Ganong and Coleman, *Remarried Family Relationships*, pp. 123–137; James Bray and David Harvey, "Adolescents in Stepfamilies: Developmental Family Interventions," *Psychotherapy* 32 (1995), p. 125; Visher and Visher, *Therapy with Stepfamilies*; McGoldrick and Carter, "Forming a Remarried Family."

37. Lynn White, "Growing Up with Single Parents and Stepparents: Long-Term Effects on Family Solidarity," *Journal of Marriage and the Family* 56, no. 4 (November 1994); Rutter, "Lessons from Stepfamilies," p. 66; Furstenberg and Cherlin, *Divided Families*, p. 78; McGoldrick and Carter, "Forming a Remarried Family"; John Visher and Emily Visher, *Old Loyalties, New Ties: Therapeutic Strategies with Stepfamilies* (New York: Brunner/Mazel, 1988).

38. E. Mavis Hetherington, "Presidential Address: Families, Lies, and Videotapes," *Journal of Research on Adolescence* 1, no. 4 (1991), pp. 341, 344.

39. Ganong and Coleman, *Remarried Family Relationships*; James Bray and Sandra Berger, "Noncustodial Father and Paternal Grandparent Relationships in Stepfamilies," *Family Relations* 39 (1990).

40. Mark Fine and Lawrence Kurdek, "The Adjustment of Adolescents in Stepfather and Stepmother Families," *Journal of Marriage and the Family* 54 (1992); Bray and Harvey, "Adolescents in Stepfamilies"; Margaret Crosbie-Burnett and Jean Giles-Sims, "Adolescent Adjustment and Stepparenting Styles," *Family Relations* 43 (October 1994); Hetherington and Clingempeel, *Coping with Marital Transitions*, pp. 10, 200–205; Visher and Visher, *Old Loyalties, New Ties*.

41. McGoldrick and Carter, "Forming a Remarried Family"; Visher and Visher, *Therapy with Stepfamilies*; Nancy Burrell, "Community Patterns in Stepfamilies: Redefining Family Roles, Themes, and Conflict Styles," in Mary Anne Fitzpatrick and Anita Vangelisti, eds., *Explaining Family Interactions* (Thousand Oaks, Calif.: Sage, 1995); Carolyn Henry and Sandra Lovelace, "Family Resources and Adolescent Family Life Satisfaction in Remarried Family Households," *Journal of Family Issues* 16 (1995); Marilyn Coleman and Lawrence H. Ganong, "Family Reconfiguring Following Divorce," in Steve Duck and Julia Wood, eds., *Confronting Relationship Challenges*, vol. 5 (Thousand Oaks, Calif.: Sage, 1995).

42. Rutter, "Lessons from Stepfamilies," pp. 60–62; Phyllis Bronstein, Miriam

Frankel Stoll, JoAnn Clauson, Craig L. Abrams, and Maria Briones, "Fathering After Separation or Divorce: Factors Predicting Children's Adjustment," *Family Relations* 43 (October 1994), p. 478.

43. E. Mavis Hetherington, Kathleen Camara, and David L. Featherman, "Achievement and Intellectual Functioning of Children in One-Parent Households," in Janet Spence, ed., *Achievement and Achievement Motives: Psychological and Sociological Approaches* (San Francisco: W. H. Freeman, 1983), p. 264.

44. The teachers' observations have been confirmed by researchers. See Beth Manke, Brenda Seery, Ann Crouter, and Susan McHale, "The Three Corners of Domestic Labor: Mothers', Fathers', and Children's Weekday and Weekend Housework," *Journal of Marriage and the Family* 56 (1994), p. 666.

45. Donald Hansen, "Family-School Articulations: The Effects of Interaction Rule Mismatch," *American Educational Research Journal* 23 (1986), p. 643; James Coleman, "The Corporation Versus the Family," *Innovation* 4 (1988), p. 540; Hetherington, Camara, and Featherman, "Achievement and Intellectual Functioning," p. 270; Hetherington, "Overview of the Virginia Longitudinal Study," p. 55; Norman Garmezy, "Resiliency and Vulnerability to Adverse Developmental Outcomes Associated with Poverty," *American Behaviorial Scientist* 34 (1991), p. 427.

46. Ronald Mincy, ed., *Nurturing Young Black Males: Challenges to Agencies, Programs, and Social Policy* (Lanham, Md.: Urban Institute Press, 1994).

47. Garmezy, "Resiliency and Vulnerability," pp. 419–421; Emmy Werner and Ruth Smith, *Kauai's Children Come of Age* (Honolulu: University of Hawaii, 1977); Emmy Werner and Ruth Smith, *Vulnerable But Invincible: A Longitudinal Study of Resilient Children* (New York: McGraw-Hill, 1982); Emmy Werner, "Children of the Garden Isle," *Scientific American* 273, April 1989; Isabel Wilkerson, "Doing Whatever It Takes to Save a Child," *New York Times,* December 30, 1994; Mary Pharis and Victoria Levin, "'A Person to Talk to Who Really Cared': High-Risk Mothers' Evaluation of Services in an Intensive Research Program," *Child Welfare* 3 (1991); Lisbeth Schorr, *Within Our Reach: Breaking the Cycle of Disadvantage* (New York, Anchor, 1988); James Garbarino, "Can We Measure Success in Preventing Child Abuse? Issues in Policy, Programming and Research," *Child Abuse and Neglect* 10 (1986); Edward Zigler, Nancy Rubin, and Joan Kaufman, "Do Abused Children Become Abusive Parents?" *Parents,* May 1988; Bonnie Benard, "Fostering Resiliency in Kids: Protective Factors in the Family, School, and Community," Portland: Northwest Regional Educational Laboratory, August 1991, pp. 9–14.

48. Ron Haskins, "Losing Ground or Moving Ahead? Welfare Reform and Children," in P. Lindsay Chase-Lansdale and Jeanne Brooks-Gunn, eds., *Escape from Poverty: What Makes a Difference for Children?* (New York: Cambridge University Press, 1995), p. 257.

49. Lillian Rubin, *The Transcendent Child: Tales of Triumph Over the Past* (New York: Basic Books, 1996); Gary Walker and Marc Freedman, "Social Change One on One," *American Prospect* 27 (July–August 1996), pp. 77–78.

50. Levine, *New Expectations,* p. 120; James Comer, "Educating Poor Minority Children," *Scientific American* 259 (1988); Lynn A. Curtis, *The State of Families: Family, Employment and Reconstruction: Policy Based on What Works* (Milwaukee: Families International/Family Service America, 1995), pp. 53–54.

51. Levine, *New Expectations*, p. 121; Tamar Lewin, "Creating Fathers Out of Men with Children," *New York Times*, June 18, 1995, pp. A1, A10; Jonathon Rabinovitz, "A Hartford Program to Put Fathers Back in the Family," *New York Times*, June 16, 1996, pp. A1, A12; Jonathan Alter, "What Works," *Newsweek*, May 29, 1995, p. 21.

52. Marsha Mueller and Michael Q. Patton, "Working with Poor Families—Lessons Learned from Practice," *Marriage and Family Review* 21 (1995); Lisbeth Schorr, *Successful Programs and the Bureaucratic Dilemma: Current Deliberations* (New York: National Center for Children in Poverty, 1991); Lisbeth Schorr, "Daring to Learn from Our Successes," *Aspen Institute Quarterly* 5 (1993); Anthony Lewis, "The Two Societies," *Liberal Opinion Week*, March 15, 1993, p. 12; Nicholas Lemann, "The Myth of Community Development," *New York Times Magazine*, January 9, 1994, p. 54; Danziger and Danziger, "Child Poverty and Public Policy," pp. 75–76; Patrick Tolan and Nancy Guerra, *What Works in Reducing Adolescent Violence: An Empirical Review of the Field* (Boulder, Colo.: Center for the Study and Prevention of Violence, 1994).

53. Schorr, "Daring to Learn from Our Successes," pp. 90–92.

54. Sandra Danziger and Sheldon Danziger, "Child Poverty, Public Policies, and Welfare Reform," *Children and Youth Services Review* 17 (1995), p. 771; Curtis, *The State of Families*; Jesse Jackson, "The Cities: Time to Stop the Posturing," *Liberal Opinion Week*, May 25, 1992, p. 21; Milton S. Eisenhower Foundation, *Investing in Children and Youth: Reconstructing Our Cities* (Washington, D.C.: Milton S. Eisenhower Foundation, 1993).

55. Sylvia Hewlett, *When the Bough Breaks: The Cost of Neglecting Our Children* (New York: Basic Books, 1991), pp. 262–263, 269–270; Matthew Miller, "Clinton's Budget, Gingrich's Budget," *New York Times*, September 13, 1995, p. A17; Andrew Cockburn, "Swords into Stock Shares," *New York Times*, October 3, 1995, p. A19; Curtis, *The State of Families*, p. 125.

56. Sam Roberts, *Who We Are: A Portrait of America Based on the Latest U.S. Census* (New York: Times Books, 1995), p. 212; Marc Linder, "Eisenhower-Era Marxist-Confiscatory Taxation: Requiem for the Rhetoric of Rate Reduction for the Rich," *Tulane Law Review* 70 (1996), p. 1033; CDF Reports, January 1996, p. 4; Mark Zepezauer and Arthur Naiman, *Take the Rich Off Welfare* (Tucson: Odonian Press, 1996), p. 6.

57. Richard Morin, "Suffer the Little Children?" *Washington Post National Weekly Edition*, September 25–October 1, 1995, p. 37; Steve Rendall, Jim Naurekas, and Jeff Cohen, *The Way Things Aren't: Rush Limbaugh's Reign of Error* (New York: The New Press, 1995), p. 67; "Young Adults At-Risk: Public Perceptions About a Growing National Problem and What Should Be Done," Yankelovic Partners, Los Angeles, July 1995, pp. 40–42; Bob Herbert, "The Real Welfare Cheats," *New York Times*, April 26, 1996, p. A15.

58. "Report on U.S. Social Health Says It's Slightly on the Mend," *New York Times*, October 24, 1994; Dennis Kelly, "Preschool Has Lasting Effects," *USA Today*, April 22, 1993; Charles Leroux and Cindy Schreuder, "Preschool Worth the Cost," *Chicago Tribune*, November 1, 1994; Wilkerson, "Doing Whatever It Takes to Save a Child"; Hewlett, *When the Bough Breaks*, pp. 247–248; Peter Passell, "'Bell Curve' Crit-

ics Say Early IQ Isn't Destiny," *New York Times,* November 9, 1994; Frances Campbell and Craig Ramey, "Effects of Early Intervention on Intellectual and Academic Achievement: A Follow-up Study of Children from Low-Income Families," *Child Development* 65 (1994); Richard Whitmire, "Child Experts Defend Value of Head Start," *Olympian,* February 2, 1996, p. A8.

59. Camille Sweeney, "Portrait of the American Child, 1995," *New York Times Magazine,* October 8, 1995, p. 52; Mike Males, "'Top School Problems' Are Myths," *Phi Delta Kappan,* September 1992, p. 55; *Great Transitions: Preparing Adolescents for a New Century: Executive Summary* (New York: Carnegie Council on Adolescent Development), p. 4.

60. Jennifer James, *Thinking in the Future Tense: Leadership Skills for a New Age* (New York: Simon and Schuster, 1996).

Index

Abuse, domestic: and single-parenthood, 150; social causes of, 110; and two-parent family, 140; and unemployment, 129

Acker, Joan, 145

Acock, Alan, 100

Adolescents: alienation of, 154; birth rates of, 40, 90–91, 138–39; causes of pregnancy in, 85; parental conflict with, 12–18, 165; reaction to remarriage, 167, 168, 170; self-esteem loss for girls, 22; and single-parent families, 164, 165–66; social support programs for, 176; and violence statistics, 28

Adulthood, postponing of, 13–14

African Americans: definition of family for, 120; exclusion from 1950s prosperity, 44; extended families among, 160, 162–63; and family disruption, 164; and poverty, 139, 148; and risk factors for violence, 152, 153; as scapegoats for social problems, 133–34; and unwed motherhood, 90

After-school care, problems of, 68–69

Aggression. *See* Violence

Agrarian society, industrial transformation of, 13, 110–14

Ahrons, Constance, 106

Aid to Families with Dependent Children. *See* Welfare

Alan Guttmacher Institute, 139

Alimony, need for, 83

Allen, Robert, 43

Amato, Paul, 99, 100

American Enterprise Institute, 6, 30, 88

Antisocial behavior: and family form, 151–56; and industrial transformation, 112–13; manipulation of statistics on, 28–29; and parenting styles, 158; and unemployment, 145–46

Arendell, Terry, 117

Aristotle, 26

Attachment, infant, and working mothers, 67

August, Eugene, 22

Authoritarian parenting, 157–58

Authoritative parenting, 158